MW00641721

The Pizza Guide to Digital Marketing

A DELICIOUS FIRST BYTE OF THE BIGGEST BUSINESS GAME CHANGERS OF YOUR LIFETIME

Written by Digital Marketing Strategic Advisor, creator of the WALT$ System, who builds for and guides the most valuable brands in the world.

The only proven Digital Marketing Strategy that will last until 2030 and beyond.

"I believe every company needs to be literate in Digital Marketing to succeed, nowadays."

—Christian Farioli

CDO, Digital Marketing Lecturer & Strategic Advisor

PASSIONPRENEUR
P U B L I S H I N G

Publishing information
Publishing, design, and production facilitated by Passionpreneur Publishing
www.PassionpreneurPublishing.com

Melbourne, Victoria Australia

TESTIMONIALS

Ahmed Moharram
Digital Marketing Manager—Huawei

Christian is a very knowledgeable person with a wide span of experiences covering the Digital space as well as Marketing. Very few professionals in digital marketing business can really deliver value and I believe Christian is definitely one of them.

Chris Dabu
Brand and Digital Marketing—Jumeirah Group / Jumeirah Hotels & Resorts

I could not have asked for a better SEO Instructor/Lecturer during my Digital Marketing Diploma course.

Thank you, Christian, for extending your knowledge and wisdom to the group.

Amith Horra
Senior Marketing—DP World

I recently attended through DM3 Institute a digital marketing course highlighting the introduction into Digital Marketing and SEO with Christian Farioli as the lecturer. His knowledge and presentations into the Digital Marketing world were extremely impressive and were easy to grasp because of his vast knowledge in the subjects. His enthusiastic approach in explaining all elements for digital marketing made it easier to comprehend whilst adding a humanistic approach to his course and group interaction.

I look forward to attending and working more closely with Christian in the future for all of my digital marketing requirements.

Helen Spei
Head of Marketing & Corporate Communication—Majid Al Futtaim Retail—Carrefour UAE

I had the pleasure to attend Christian's lectures in SEO and Analytics in a DMI course in Dubai. Christian is an influential and inspiring speaker, a passionate professional with a strong business background in digital marketing. There is a lot to learn from him and his long experience and even more to be inspired by.

Arlene Luther (Hooper)
Digital Communications Manager—Pfizer KAM CoE

Christian is a Digital Marketing Specialist that is a thought leader in the industry. His lectures were fun, interesting and very engaging. With his guidance, I will always remember to keep my Digital Marketing Plans relevant and constantly think about tracking, tweaking and measuring success against KPIs set.

Mazhar Salam
Head of Brands—China Mobile Pakistan (Zong)

Witty and Italian. Made the two-day workshop on digital marketing strategy a great learning experience.

Brutally honest about what actually works in digital and what looks/sounds good in boardrooms.

Mohammad Banat
Technology Manager—Paris Gallery LLC

Christian is simply a brilliant expert in his field. I had the chance to attend one of his lectures and he was great, passionate and entertaining in a way you want to stay longer to learn more and more. He has a great way for reaching to your mind and making you understand complicated things easily.

Nasser Alshenaifi
Marketing Communications & Public Relations—Saudi Aramco

It was an honour meeting Mr. Christian Farioli, and benefiting from his experience in Display & Video Advertising, Analytics, Digital Strategy; I'm really glad I had the chance of meeting him at this time with my passion to change my career to the digital marketing field.

Philippe Khouri
Commercial Director Publishing & Digital—Abu Dhabi Media

Christian is, first of all, a great speaker with an in-depth knowledge of digital marketing (SEO and analytics). He explains the most complex subject in such a way everyone with little digital knowledge can capture. After attending his session, I was able to understand and manipulate a great number of tools that will directly impact my daily business.

Ahmad Moustafa
Head of Digital Marketing—Ajman University

Christian is a gifted instructor because he is highly knowledgeable in his field of Digital Marketing. He is always encouraging and positive. He gives nice examples (specially the Italian pizza). He is the best instructor I have ever had. If you want to improve your SEO skills quickly, hire Christian.

Mohamed AlQassab
Head of Digital Channels—Gulf International Bank

Christian is a brilliant lecturer and experienced consultant. He has vast knowledge in digital marketing and has a unique ability to deliver a state of the art pre-packaged set of techniques in an entertaining way. I highly recommend him. PS. keep making those Pizzas ;)

Raghda Al Tamimi
Business Operations—Abu Dhabi Global Market

Christian was very informative and inspiring. I have learned tips and hints about the industry that I use almost every day. Will definitely be looking out for future training courses given by him!

Ali Zeeshan Khan
Fueling Sales and Marketing Alignment—Informa

I can recommend Christian as a person with great expertise and deep experience of modern business solutions.

His background and leadership makes Christian view solutions instead of problems. A motivated, insightful, customer focused and detail oriented professional. Makes the impossible possible.

Loy Machedo
The World's #1 Personal Branding Strategist

Christian is a very friendly, very genuine and a very sincere person to do business with. Through my interactions, I have found him to be liked by everyone irrespective of which every nationality, culture or race people were from—that I believe makes him a Global Ambassador. Coupled with his ability to deliver great results, I feel he is a great asset to keep in touch with.

I highly recommend Christian Farioli.

Karim El Marmari
Head of Digital Marketing—Sharjah Commerce and Tourism Development Authority

Mr. Christian gave one of the most interesting lectures I have attended being a DM3 Institute candidate seeking to complete the Professional Diploma in Digital Marketing here in Dubai. I can say that, without a doubt, I learned so much from Mr. Christian and it was by far the most fun I've had in a lecture for a very long time. I will definitely be interested in attending his next seminars, lectures or speeches as the information, experience and knowledge he passes on are extremely valuable.

Jawaid Chaudhry
Manager Marketing Services / Digital Marketing / Social Media / Business Development—BTC Networks

I have attended many seminars and trainings, and I always wonder "what makes a great teacher?" Teaching is one of the most complicated jobs. It demands broad knowledge of subject matter, enthusiasm, a caring attitude and a desire to make a difference in the lives of students. All these qualities are in Christian and I have this honour to be his student.

Karim Bou Said
Digital Transformation, Customer Experience, eCommerce, Oracle Cloud, AI, IoT, Blockchain, CRM, Analytics, BI, Mobile

Christian is a gifted teacher and expert digital marketer. Many people have knowledge but very few know how to deliver this knowledge effectively to others with great passion and humour. Christian is one of those few. Love the pizza marketing analogy! Classes were fun, interesting and I left wanting more. Complex subjects were made easy and simple to understand for anyone from any background. I highly recommend learning digital marketing with Christian.

Nathalie Garino
General Manager Sales & Marketing at INFINITI of ARABIAN AUTOMOBILES CO.LLC

Thank you Christian, your training was amazingly insightful. Walked away with a new look on SEO. Thank you for such refreshing teaching.

Michela Simone
Events and Marketing Director at Vogue Arabia

Christian Farioli is a creative digital marketing genius. Every time our paths crossed I go home with lots of new learning in my pockets. Not the usual stuff you can read about but serious marketing intelligence insights that translate into business wisdom.

Contents

Digital Marketing
Made in Italy

This book is dedicated to every person eager to become digital savvy. You entered the marketing world as a miracle! Great! Give me five!

Maybe you come from sales, marketing, or from IT. Or maybe from business development, or entrepreneurship. During your life and career, you will have been exposed to many marketing ideas, good, bad, and dangerous.

So what is going to happen now?

You are going to read my book and gain the ability, strength, and discipline to "digitally market" your ideas. This is a neologism—a specific neologism—called Fariologism! What does it mean? It means:

You are the author
of your digital marketing future
and you have the power
to live the career of your dreams.

This book represents many years of experience, beginning in 2003 to be precise.

I am talking about experience gained through beautiful and bad moments, successes and direction changes, achievements and troubles. When I look back, I think with gratitude toward many people who deeply influenced my marketing life. I cannot mention everyone; there are too many! However, I do want to name those whom I remember in special moments of happiness.

My lovely wife **Gianna Gabriel,** always next to me in any important decision; also mother of our two little and smart Alessandro and Amedeo

My parents, **Piero Farioli** and **Rosanna Maino,** for the teachings and the support they have always given me, allowing me an excellent education, a great lifestyle, and many dream vacations. The most important thing for which I will always be grateful for is their acceptance of my every decision, especially the most important and difficult choice for an only child: living abroad.

I then thank all my professors and teachers, beginning from:

Mother Maria Annunziata: Tireless and always positive, she taught me the principles of ethics when the word "ethics" was still rarely used.

All professors of ITIS C. Facchinetti, the institute where I trained technically and learned the concept and the practice of problem solving.

All professors of the Politecnico di Milano, a faculty who trained more managers than engineers; in particular, **Piero**

Fraternali, who left me, through the techniques of software engineering, with many useful methods that I apply in difficult decisions.

All the professors of the **Dublin Business School**, where I finally understood the essence of marketing and multinational companies.

My **colleagues at Oracle** in Dublin and Madrid, and particularly **Vincenzo Bassi,** one of the best salesmen at whose side I had the pleasure of spending a year; **Conor Shaw**, the most charismatic leader I have ever known; and **Luiz Vianna**, my managerial mentor and friend.

My friends in Busto Arsizio, a little city near Milan, including **Alessandro Agostini** and **Riccardo Pozzi,** who will always be close to me even if thousands of kilometres away. The teachers of personal growth courses I have undertaken, in chronological order: **Roberto Re, Anthony Robbins, Giorgio Toscani ,John Pozun, Robert Cialdini, Bob Urichuck, Ernesto Verdugo, Tony Buzan, Gianluca Lo Stimolo** and **Dave Crane**.

My friends in Valencia, San Diego, Dublin, London, Madrid, and Dubai, who I often meet with pleasure in other countries, and **Amedeo Ferri Ricchi**, a true finance genius and an ever-inspirational character for my career.

I also thank the inner strength that guides me, from creating ideas to attracting people and circumstances to making those ideas a reality. Writing this book was one of my goals, and after a lot of hard work, it has now been made possible.

This book is dedicated to **all those students (more than 5,000 so far)** that I have had the pleasure of training and sharing digital marketing knowledge.

Finally, there is another person, a person you must know very well.

This person is you.

You: a CEO, GM, MD, CMO, CDO, or Marketing Executive. You are the most important in the world. Without you, there would have been no reason to write this book.

Thank you.

I wish you a great digital future!

Christian Farioli

DIGITAL MARKETING

What Is Digital Marketing?

Here we are. Let us start!

If you are here reading my book, I am sure **you want to know what Digital Marketing** is, why you should use it, and what benefits it can provide to your business. You may feel like you really need to understand what Digital Marketing is, because it is not currently clear to you. Many people and companies are talking about it because it is cool, but they really do not know what Digital Marketing is, so you often get confused, right? Well, **keep calm and read my book**; everything will become clear. Okay?

Digital Marketing *is like pizza!*

What? Are you joking?! **Yes, I am joking**, but I always use pizza to explain things in my classrooms, so if you participate in some of my training about Digital Marketing, you will see pizza over and over and over again.

I am going to tell you the secret of my family. Since I am Italian, that secret is: how to make the best pizza in the world! My grandfather handed the recipe to my father, and my father told me, "Please don't give the secret to anyone." Hence, I am going to be the first one breaking the family tradition, and you are going to be the first non-Italian to know the secret. There are some secret ingredients nobody knows: flour, salt, yeast, tomato, mozzarella, olive oil, and water. Unbelievable, right? Why are you laughing? This is my family secret!

Pizza and Google: *Many similarities*

I chose pizza because I find a lot of similarities between pizza and Google. What?

Well, look at it this way. Pizza is made with **simple ingredients** (apparently). I am sure that even in Africa or Vietnam, you could find those ingredients in every grocery store. **It is very cheap to produce, with some of the ingredients being free** (e.g., water, salt)**, and it is impossible to make it 100% perfect.** No matter how many times you go to the same pizzeria, you order ten pizzas and **every pizza looks a little different**.

Google, in the same way, is a set of very different tools. You use one of those tools on a daily basis, Google Search. However, when we look at Google, there are a lot more tools than that. Like pizza, it is **very cheap**. In fact, most Google **tools are free**, so it is even cheaper than pizza. It is also impossible to make it perfect.

So, pizza and Google are very similar for these reasons:

- very simple ingredients
- very cheap to produce (almost free)
- impossible to make 100% perfect!
- always changing

For example, consider search engine optimisation and analytics. **Every few months, something changes**. The same thing that worked before does not work anymore. Even if you do the same things, something has changed: exactly like pizza. This is why I tell you that digital marketing is a little bit more than just learning a skill. Digital marketing is now a vast subject. **Once you find out what makes you passionate, you have to immerse yourself into it for a long time, because it is something that is going to continuously change**. You cannot just learn everything and think that, in ten years, it is still going to be the same. No way! Because of that, it makes sense to dig in.

So what is Digital Marketing?

Let us see what Digital Marketing is. Are you ready? Here you will find three definitions: the first comes from Google, the second from an important institute, but the best is the last one.

1. *"Digital marketing is the process of building and maintaining customer relationships through online activities to facilitate the exchange of ideas, products and services that satisfy the goals of both parties."* *(Google)*

How do I know that? I do not. I just Googled it and this is what showed up. But, as you are here reading my book, let us check out a better definition.

2. *"Digital marketing is the use of digital channels to promote or market products and services to consumers and business."* *(Digital Marketing Institute)*

That was said by the Digital Marketing Institute and it is true, but I am going to give you an even better definition.

3. *"Digital marketing is getting customers using only the computer and the Internet." (Christian Farioli)*

Now you understand why it is the best one, right?

My definition reflects the fact that digital marketing is exactly like pizza: simple, cheap, and always changing. In the future, it will look different, but my definition will always be true. In the next section, I will go deeper, and you will learn many very interesting things that will change your business and help you get new customers.

---

1 *"Non esiste!" is a typical Italian slang expression you can't live without, which means, "It doesn't make sense."*

Here's Why You Are Confused about Digital Marketing

My definition of Digital Marketing is getting customers using only the computer and the internet. "Okay, this is too simple," you may say. "In my company, we have lots of different platforms and they often change direction because they follow the new trends to keep up with the times." To explain why my simple definition is useful to you, I am going to tell you my story and you will see the reason for my opinion.

In the beginning . . .

Before I learned about the word and concept of Digital Marketing, I was thinking as an IT engineer. I was used to solve problems, so I wondered, "With this computer, that can execute millions and billions of operations per second, at our disposal, why are we limiting ourselves to humans to make a sale? Humans need to manually pick up the phone to call the customer, but the same contact can be made more efficiently using computers and the internet. If I put something online, customers find me, and I save a lot of time. Instead of calling a million human beings, I find the people who want to buy my product."

Today, this is called Digital Marketing.

What is the **role of marketing***?*

It is important to understand the actual challenge: Google, Facebook, or other platforms, whatever they are. But keep in mind, one day they are going to be others. One day, some of them are going to disappear. If you are clever enough, you are going to use new tools to help generate sales, often not to close the sales for yourself, but to help generate the sales.

In my opinion, the role of marketing in general (digital or otherwise) is not to sell. There are sales people, and they get their commission.

> *"The role of marketing is to make the phone ring."*

Yes, it is my job to get "walking clients." When a client walks into my shop, as a marketing person, I have done my job. When the phone rings and somebody inquires about the product or service, I have done my job. Now, closing a sale is the job of the salesperson.

Companies*, and the big cool topic of the moment*

"Okay," you may say, "you can make my phone ring, but how can I do it? There are so many platforms. How do we know which one is the best for us? I am so confused!"

Here is my opinion, one you may not like. I know this because I have been working for a big digital company for five years, and they need their long-term goals to convey some cool message to convince companies to put massive investments into massive projects.

Every few years, there is a big, cool topic of the moment. Usually, these last three to five years. A few years ago, it was grid computing, then the Business Intelligence, then the Cloud, then Big Data and Internet of Things. These are cool, theoretical concepts that have a practical use, but because **not even 1% of a company can make sense of these things, everyone gets caught in a dream that they do not understand.**

So, when you think, "We need it," I come in with my big corporate, setup a two-year project that is going to cost you $300 million, and you like it. You think you will sign the contract and . . . boom! Next one! Every few years, there is a new big topic. BUT is this what you want? Is this really what you need?

Digital Marketing, *not just a fancy trend*

Now, Digital Marketing is also a nice trend. Some of the things I am doing now are exactly the same as what I used to do thirteen years ago. Now, I just repackage them with the fancy "Digital Marketing" tag, and people love it! Thirteen years ago, it did not have a fancy name and people said, **"No, I don't need it!"** Even Facebook is now called Social Media, and the reaction is, **"Yes, I need it, I like it, and I love it!"**

Another good example is the Cloud. So many companies go for the Cloud service, etc. but nobody really understands what it is. Most normal human beings, those who sign the contract for several million dollars, they have no clue. Therefore, fancy trends always exist in the market, like Big Data today. Big Data is the reediting of Business Intelligence, and it has existed for the last 10 to 15 years. Now we call it Big Data, and ah! People love it! Well, I don't trust these things too much.

Forget the names and focus on your company's goal!

You now understand why you are so confused and why, in your company, Digital Marketing is so far from reality, and some people say it does not work, or (on the opposite side) they believe in miracles!

Nobody should care about what we call things. In marketing, we care when we get more clients, with or without internet, app, or mobile. If you get more clients through the internet, as a Digital Marketing person, you have done your job.

Independently, if you use Big Data, the Cloud, or whatever, tomorrow they are going to call it something else. I do not care what they call it. The bottom line is to get people coming to your business through any possible media and for any possible reason.

Remember: The purpose of marketing is to get customers to your business. Digital Marketing allows you to get them using just your computer and internet!

Digital Marketing Means Grabbing the Numbers

Numbers are an essential part of Digital Marketing. Why? Because you have to know how the world is changing, and what people are doing in your marketplace.

> *"If you find out who the customers are,*
> *you put the money there.*
> *And the game is done [2]!"*

Now, Google *"Gary's social media count"*[3] and click on the first result. You will see live numbers concerning online consumers' behaviour on Social Media, Mobile, Games, Heritage and more. You will be surprised.

---

2 "Il gioco è fatto!" an Italian expression that means, "That's it!"
3 https://www.personalizemedia.com/garys-social-media-count/

These are the numbers you should look at

These numbers can move more clients in one minute than any other TV or outdoor media combined. When you understand these numbers, there is nothing that can beat you. Whatever these numbers are—one million, whatever—these are the numbers on the most popular platforms of today.

Some of these will be replaced by others in a few years. Some of them will be purchased by a different company. Some of them will disappear completely. But the point is:

"Look at what the numbers are
and then go for it."

Or, look at what the numbers are in your marketplace. If your pizzeria is based in Dubai, you do not care about somebody searching for a pizzeria in Miami; you want people in Dubai, so you check out what the numbers are in Dubai and go after them. This is the idea behind digital marketing. Whatever channel is carrying a lot of people, you want to be there, and not just in one of them but as many as possible.

Grabbing these numbers is Digital Marketing

How do you grab them? Every day. There is no guidebook on it. Marketing has been a little science, for the last few decades, and that is how it is studied at universities. However, you cannot study Digital Marketing as a science at university. It does not even exist at the tertiary level. It is so new that it simply does not exist.

To teach a subject at a university, whether undergraduate or postgraduate, you need professors. Those professors need a PhD (a doctorate, an advanced university degree), but completing a PhD can take five or more years. If somebody starts researching Digital Marketing today, in five years, they could be a professor of Digital Marketing. However, in five years, that person's knowledge will be outdated, because everything will have changed.

This is why you cannot find university books about Digital Marketing. Instead, you will find independent trainers, training companies and training facilities like the Digital Marketing Institute.

> *"You have to grab these numbers every day,*
> *in order to know where people are.*
> *This is Digital Marketing."*

Online purchasing behaviour

So let us look at some stats about online purchasing behaviour in the United Arab Emirates and Middle East:

- Almost 50% of United Arab Emirates (UAE) internet users have made a purchase online in the past.
- 25% would be classed as regular (every month) purchasers.
- Electronics, software, airline tickets, and hotel bookings are by far the most popular purchase categories in the UAE and Middle Eastern countries.
- The vast majority of online spend in the region is spent with international
- web retailers (non GCC — Gulf Cooperation Council).
- More than 50% of online users in the UAE have made an offline purchase decision based on online research they carried out in advance (B2C and B2B purchases).
- Limitations with payment gateways have seriously hindered online retail sales in the UAE.

Now, the interesting thing about online purchasing behaviour in the Middle East is that almost 50% of UAE (United Arab Emirates) internet users have made a purchase online in the past.

So, when they say, "Yeah, but people here . . . the culture is different . . . it doesn't work," this is just a senior manager making an excuse. What they really mean is, "I know nothing about digital things but I will not admit it."

They prefer to say, "No, it doesn't work here, because the culture is different here," when what they really think is, "I don't know, I don't wanna know, I don't wanna learn, I don't wanna do." Well, regardless of whether the culture is different or not, that is not my business.

My business is to tell them the numbers: that 50% of UAE internet users have made a purchase online in the past. And that this also happens in the B2B market, okay? Yes, this works even if you produce valves for Oil & Gas. *This is the reality. Now it's up to you.*

The Incredible Gap between Companies and Consumers

I will repeat incessantly that **you have to go where your consumers are: this is the point of marketing**. So, what do you think companies are doing? Are they investing in advertising on the most popular media? Are they really grabbing the numbers? Now, I am going to give you some more numbers, and you are going to be really surprised.

Consumers' media consumption vs. advertising investments

You will laugh, but this is the reality!

- **Online: 40% consumption vs. 2% advertising investments.**
- TV: 25% consumption vs. 45% advertising investments.
- Newspapers: 6% consumption vs. 41% advertising investments.
- Magazines: 7% consumption vs. 7% advertising investments.
- Radio: 9% consumption vs. 5% advertising investments.
- Mobile: 14% consumption vs. 0% advertising investments.

If you noticed that the consumption percentage adds up to 101%, that is not my fault! Google published the data!

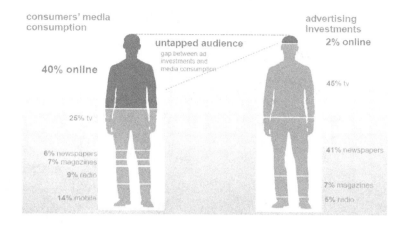

Most people consume more media online or on mobile than on TV and radio, or in newspapers and magazines, but companies are still investing very little into digital. They still invest mostly into TV and magazines because the mentality of the old-school of marketing people is, well, old-school!

Small companies are smarter, and they invest most of their budget online, but the biggest money spenders are still spending on TV. Of course, if I run a small company and I can afford only 5.000 Dirham a month, I cannot even approach TV. But the big companies, with the big budgets? They spend most of it on TV and newspapers.

TV Centric Age has passed!

We come from the age where they said, "Ah, whatever they say on TV is true." Why? "Because they don't lie to us. There are regulatory entities, checking and regulating what they say on TV. It has to be true. They cannot lie to us."

Now consumers are smart!

We are in the Internet Centric Age

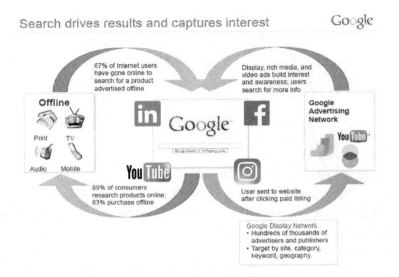

So, on TV, they can tell you, "Oh, this magic cream is so amazing that you put it on your face and you look 20 years younger!" But now, before purchasing, you Google it to check if it's true about the magic cream. You find a forum with people saying, "Don't buy the magic cream! It doesn't work!" What you do, now? You do not buy the magic cream, of course!

50% of people search on Google before purchasing; in some countries and for some products, the percentage is 85%. So, if you commit someone to buying your product right now, if they just pull out their smartphone and find bad reviews, you're in trouble. They're going to search on Google, YouTube, forums, reviews and so on.

*"If you don't care about your reputation online,
your perception online, your digital marketing,
you risk going bankrupt."*

In the USA, there's an App that came out many years ago, called **Google Goggles⁴**, an image recognition mobile app developed by Google. It is used for searches based on pictures taken by handheld devices. For example, taking a picture of a famous landmark searches for information about it, or taking a picture of a product's barcode searches for information on the product, and shows you the reviews.

So, you could see people in the supermarket playing with this App, reading reviews about products and changing their choice. "No, this tomato sauce is not good; I will buy this other one instead."

Where are you investing your money?

Now ask yourself: **Am I focused on the right place, where people are and spend their time? Is my company investing in the most consumed media? Am I using a proper, effective Digital Marketing strategy?**

If your answer is "No" or "Hmm" or "I need to check," you have a really good reason to continue reading this book.

---

4 https://play.google.com/store/apps/details?id=com.google.android.apps.unveil&hl=it

The Digital Marketing Framework

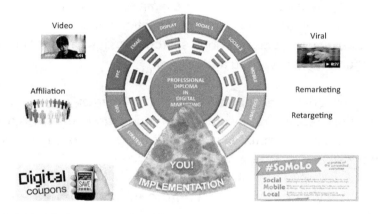

Now I present to you the Digital Marketing Framework, in order to give you an overview and help you understand what we will explore in the next steps about Digital Marketing. There are many channels; some of them are important, others less so. If you follow me, you will really understand how it works and you will be able to choose the correct method and strategy for your business and your goals.

So when we talk about digital marketing, we are talking about:

- Strategy
- Search Engine Optimisation (SEO)

- Pay Per Click (PPC)
- Email Marketing
- Digital Display Advertising
- Social Media Marketing
- Mobile Marketing
- Web Analytics
- Planning

All these are part of the Digital Marketing mix. However, there are more, because every day, some crazy American comes out with an idea that is better, faster, cheaper, or stronger. Before we check out the interesting and useful Digital Marketing Tools to use for your business strategy, I will give you an overview of the crazy tools that have come out in recent years. Here are some examples:

- Affiliation
- Video
- Viral
- Digital Coupons
- Remarketing and Retargeting
- #SoLoMo

Affiliation Marketing

Nearly a decade back, somebody introduced Affiliation. Never heard about Affiliation Marketing?

Well, Affiliation Marketing works this way: Let us say you are selling training for your Digital Marketing company. Here, you have a little space in the content somewhere that mentions "affiliates." The consumer sees that, registers and gets a special code. Then, in their social media, website, whatever they want, they publish a little banner or a link about your company and mention, "You know what? There is a great digital marketing training course coming out! You can check it out here." If people click their link, they go to your company website, they see the training and they say, "That's great," and they purchase it. Automatically, the original consumer gets a commission.

There are people that believe in doing only Affiliation Marketing. These are internet marketers: people making money online by selling other peoples' stuff. It is good and bad; good because you brand yourself, and bad because you do not know who is selling for you, and if that person uses unethical tactics, their actions can spoil your name. With affiliation marketing, you lose control.

Video Marketing

Everyone started talking about Video Marketing a few years ago. Now they say, "Video is nothing if it is not viral." But creating a viral video is not easy. You can do a lot of documentation, have a lot of ideas, do a lot of things, but there is nothing you can do to officially guarantee that a video is going to go viral.

Someone came out with digital coupons, because everyone has a mobile phone. Soon, everyone had a digital coupon. It was all about digital coupons! Every day, someone came out with a new idea.

Google introduced Remarketing a few years ago. Then Facebook copied and invented Retargeting.

Then someone came out with #SoMoLo: Social Mobile Local. This involved taking existing things, mixing them and creating something else. I showed you the ingredients for the pizza, right? If, instead of using all of them, you just use mozzarella, tomato and olive oil, you could make a "caprese salad." You used the same ingredients, but used them differently and made something else. This is what SoMoLo means. You take Social Marketing, Mobile Marketing and Local Marketing, you combine them together . . . and boom! SoMoLo! There are millions of ramifications to this, but we will come back to that later.

So, at the end of this, there is pizza! The slice of pizza represents your implementation. You must act; otherwise all of this is just a nice, fancy concept. If you do not put your head down to implement them, you will just have nice, fancy ideas. That is all. Is this what you want? I do not think so!

Consumers Reveal Who They Are

It is access to these activities that gives digital marketing its power

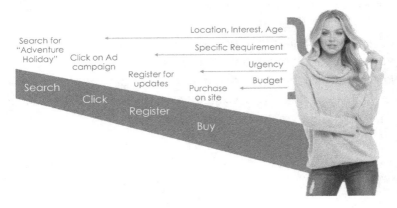

What is the big difference between physical and digital?

The big difference between physical and digital is that you may have some statistics on how many people are passing by every day on a street like Sheikh Zayed Road in Dubai, where you have put your advertising banner, but in digital **we know for a fact who our customers are**. We know about them in terms of, for example, location, interest, age, what they need, how fast or how urgently they need something, and more or less if they have a budget ready for it.

How we know that? Because the normal consumer follows the same path. First, they search for something, then they click on something, then they either register for updates, a newsletter, or like and follow, etc. And then, they decide to purchase or not.

This is the standard path every consumer goes through in the digital world.

"Start with the customer and work backwards"
Market Reality is a better indicator of customer needs than Market Research

Another concept that comes from traditional marketing is:

*"Start with the customer and work
backwards."*

As an IT engineer, I can tell you this, "We can plan and built the best product ever. So, if you want to build one of these, we study, we plan, and we build the most advanced product in history. We believe that, if it is the best, it will sell automatically!"

No! That is a big mistake, because engineers never make money. The people who make money are the marketers and salespeople. Why is that? Because they know what the customers are ready to buy, and what they are ready to pay for.

You have to know your customers!
Hence, the marketing approach is: first, research.

For example, do you need a pointer to use for you slideshow? Okay, which functions would you like? Would you like one with a screen or not? One button, two buttons, or three buttons? Would you like one with a laser or without?

Then, the marketer asks the most important question: If I give you all you want, how much money are you willing to pay? You say 80 dirhams. Here is the thing. If I build the best laser pointer ever, I would need to sell it for 500 dirhams to make a profit. But even if it is the best possible laser pointer, nobody is going to buy it! But if I build a product according to my marketing research, with a price tag that people are happy to pay, I am going to sell millions of laser pointers!

This is the marketing approach. In digital, it is even easier because we have a history with our clients, through our statistics and analytics. We can plan perfectly any product or service, or we can adjust the way we do things until we find the perfect match with customer needs.

Iterate Principles

Effective Digital Marketing is an Iterative Process

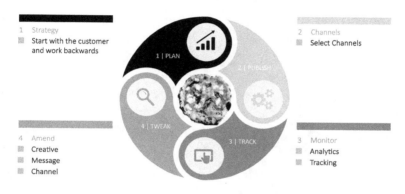

1 Strategy
- Start with the customer and work backwards

2 Channels
- Select Channels

4 Amend
- Creative
- Message
- Channel

3 Monitor
- Analytics
- Tracking

We start with the Strategy, then we choose the Channels (Facebook, Google, Twitter, whichever channel we choose), we Monitor the results, and then we Tweak.

Next, we come back with a new Plan, with a new Strategy, new Tracking and new Tweaks. We keep doing this, on and on and on. This is one of the big differences that we will see between Traditional Marketing and Digital Marketing. Traditional Marketing is a one-shot, but Digital Marketing is an iterating strategy that keeps going on forever.

The Quality Scale of Engagement

In Digital Marketing the dynamic is from Quantity to Quality. There is a quality scale in the interactions of an audience with an organization.

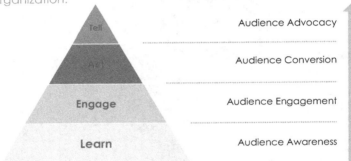

What does Quality Scale of Engagement mean?

At the bottom of the pyramid, there are the learners: people that want to understand more about our product and services. They are the vast majority. Not everyone is going to purchase from us, but they are going to engage with us: visit our website, read our content, use our app, read our Social Media, or engage with us by commenting on the content we post on our Social Media page, Twitter, or Instagram.

Only some of these people who engage are going to act, meaning that they are going to purchase. Plus, it does not end after our customer's purchase. Some of them will become our advocates, and that is what we should aim at: to get as many of our customers as possible to become advocates.

What does it mean to be an advocate?

I will give you an example. Do you have an iPhone? The iPhone is the worst phone ever produced, and the most expensive, and it is crap! Now, I can imagine your face if you have an iPhone. Well, do not worry, I am just joking. However, when you read that the iPhone is worst, and that it is crap, you are inclined to think, "Oh, I'm going to kill him! Tt is not true, just not true! I love my iPhone! I love it!"

What does this mean? It means that Apple is a clear benefactor of advocate behaviour in their consumers. Most Apple users (if not all Apple users) are Apple advocates.

"Being an advocate means that you are ready to fight for your brand."

So, when somebody tells you that the brand you use and love is crap, you will say, "It's not true, it's not true!"

This is because they are advocates. Now, it is not easy to get somebody to that level. This is branding, and Apple is a "love brand." Steve Jobs was the first person to realise that you can like a trend up to certain stage, but at some point, you need to put a human face in front of it. That is why, so many years ago, Steve Jobs put his face in front of the Apple brand. It appeared more and more in public, making it the opposite of any of the other big corporates like Microsoft, IBM, and Oracle.

Then, suddenly, the others realised that, "Oh, Apple is putting Steve Jobs in front of it, we need to do the same." So, even Bill Gates left his geek desk and came out in public to launch the new Windows and other products. Larry Ellison, chairman of Oracle, did the same, going to big conferences and showing his face. They realised this attracted more love from their customers. But it is also a risky strategy: if you put a face in front of your brand, when that face disappears, you lost part of it. When Steve Jobs died, people were sad because their beloved brand was dead.

But that is just one of the options for advocacy. The point is:

"Get your consumer to love you so much that they are happy to fight for you."

They advertise your brand; they promote your brand; they defend your brand. If somebody in a forum posts a comment saying your company is crap, the company itself cannot fight back. The company cannot write, "No, you are crap! You don't know anything! We're good and you are crap."

You cannot do it, but your followers—your advocates—can. They can fight for you, while you just stand back and watch your advocates fighting on your behalf. Of course, this will only happen once you attain that level of consumer advocacy.

Traditional Marketing vs. Digital Marketing

Traditional *Marketing*

Traditional marketing channels are characterised as:

- **Broadcast**: one-way communication, push
- **Message driven**: brand focused, features, benefits.
- **Didactic**: tells, explains, elaborates, instructs
- **Constrained**: by programming and print schedules, and geographic boundaries.
- **Calendar & Budget bound**: limits, and start and end points
- **Power**: retained by the media owner and the advertiser

Traditional marketing is based on broadcast, one-way communication. The company speaks and everyone listens.

It is **Message driven**, brand focused: It is always "We, we, we. Our product, our market, our brand, our company. We are, we are." It is about features and benefits. "Our product is the best. We are the best in this nation."

It is **Didactic**: it tells, it explains, it elaborates, it informs people how good the product is, how to use it, how well the product works.

It is **Constrained** by programming and print schedules, and geographic boundaries. Only the people in the GCC can read the GCC (Gulf Cooperation Council) magazine. It is also time constrained. If I want to put in a banner, they say, "No, the banner is booked for the next five months. There is no space available."

It is Calendar and Budget bound. You know that a banner costs a certain amount, you cannot say "give me only half of it" or "give me only 10% of it." That is not going to work.

The **Power** is obtained by the media owner and the advertiser. If Pepsi goes with a big contract, they can force the advertiser by saying, "Okay, so this year, I'm giving you a lot of money, so give me a guarantee that Coca-Cola is not going to be there." And if the advertiser—the media owner—says yes, that is it! Coca-Cola cannot put up a banner for the entire year, or any advertising on TV, or whatever the medium.

Digital *Marketing*

Digital Marketing has an approach based on openness, transparency, and engagement with the consumer:

- **Interactive**: many-to-many communication
- **Consumer driven**: in terms of their interests and preferences
- **Listening**: follows the consumers' needs
- **Un-constrained**: liberated from schedules & boundaries
- **Open ended**: iterative (launch, review, adjust, relaunch)
- **Power**: control and influence is with the consumer

It is **Interactive**. When we talk about digital marketing instead of traditional, then it is an interactive, many-to-many communication. This is why the Social Networks are handy.

It is **Consumer driven**, in terms of their interests and preferences. The consumer chooses and decides, not us.

It is about **Listening**. This is the difficult part. When we talk about digital transformation, the first thing is listening. "No, no, no . . . I need to tell my customer what they need to buy, because if not, they will say that my product is bad, and they will let negative comments."

First of all, if you know that your product is bad, you should listen and find a way to change the perception, and assess your customers' problems. Eventually, you will move the negative commenters away from the general public into a specific channel meant for customer support.

Big corporates have started opening a second Social Media page for customer care. This is a page where people can complain and are allowed to do that, but where people will be available to assist them. This acts as a department that is separated from the main entrance.

If a client enters the lobby of a hotel and starts complaining, the hotel employees will take the client to customer service or a separate place, to avoid a furor in the lobby where every other guest is entering. Now, we do the same in Digital Marketing by using a separate Social Media page for customer service.

Some companies have even started doing their customer service on WhatsApp. That makes it even more personalised, and definitely separated from the public audience.

Digital Marketing is **Un-constrained**, liberated from schedules and boundaries.

And lastly, it is **Open ended**. This is the crazy concept that digital marketing is **Iterative**: launch, review, adjust, relaunch, on and on and on and on. It is not, "the February promotion is going to be like this."

"Digital Marketing:
We start now, and we never end."

We adjust, but we keep going on. Sometimes, we coordinate with traditional marketing, which has the February promotion, but in digital, you keep continuing. Sometimes, you accelerate and use more budget; sometimes, you reduce a little bit, based on your sales fluctuation, but, either way, you just keep going on.

The **Power**, control and influence in Digital Marketing is with the consumers. The consumers decide what they want, when they want it and where you want to stop. And if you are clever enough to listen, you will have a bright future.

Digital technologies are transformative and disruptive, and characterised by a shift in power to the consumer. Now, everyone pretends that they know what their customer wants, but as we have seen in the media before, there is no precise way to guess this.

Campaign Planning *implications*

What are the implications for marketing departments and their campaign planning?

- **Structure**: start small and get better (iterative)
- **Budget**: start small and invest based on success
- **Calendar**: organic with no end point
- **Personnel**: new work so new skills required
- **Beyond Marketing**: we are all in marketing now

Let us check out the implications for Digital Marketing.

The **Structure**: Normally, we start small and get better. Even big companies start small. I can give you an example. A few years ago, I met a guy. He was the first person starting a digital division of a company and he started doing Social Media. Now, they have twenty people in the Digital Marketing Division. So, even this big company did not start with twenty people and a million dollars. At first, when they were still putting 20 million dollars into traditional media, events, road shows, and exhibitions; in digital, they started with one person doing Social Media.

So, for the **Budget**, start small and invest based on success.

The **Calendar** is organic with no end point. It has a schedule that may include something like this: "On Sunday, we are going to talk about this topic, on Monday about this, Tuesday, Wednesday, Thursday and Friday, Saturday, and then you start again from Sunday." It is not that Social Media stops after one week. No, it is without an endpoint. It is a new job, so new skills are required and, eventually, new employees. So, if you are in charge of a big organisation, you will need to eventually hire more people with marketing skills, or to train more of those.

It is **Beyond Marketing**. We are all in marketing, now. I have done a few campaigns where I used the biggest marketing workforce ever, which are the employees of the company. They do not need to know marketing, they do not need to work in marketing, but simply by doing easy little things, you can make a big difference.

For example,, when I launched a video for a commercial bank in Qatar, they released a professional video and they put it on YouTube. Because it was an emotional video, they expected a large number of people to view it, but after a month, it had only had 125 views. Just before the National Day in Qatar, we needed to boost that, so we had to find a way to make it worth their time. The bank employed more than 4000 people in total. So we just sent an email to all of them saying, "Guys, check it out our new, amazing, incredible video." They just clicked "OKAY" and closed the video after two seconds, so at least it got 4000 more views. Simple. You do more, you get more.

Now, I will tell you a funny story. I was part of the digital campaign for Dubai Airport. We were shooting some viral videos, and they needed a flash mob where they got a professional pool champion to do some pool tricks in the airport.

Here is the video: *https://www.youtube.com/watch?v=4xWj_GwVuHA*

They grabbed the media, saying, "He's just waiting in the airport and he goes to the pool table and starts doing some tricks." The video said that the pooler was very cool, and that you would not expect something like this to happen in the airport. That was great, but to make the video go viral, you need to boost it; you need to blast it everywhere.

I prepared for the full blasting plan. We launched it and, after less than one hour, the video was showing 999+ views. Sometimes, when the video goes up so fast, even YouTube servers cannot count it, so they show 999+. Two hours later, it started booming. Three to four hours later, they shut the video: YouTube thought the views were faked because it had never ever seen such fast growth before.

The video was good, it was cool, but it was not "wow." However, because we blasted it so much, to every human possible, even YouTube thought it was a fraud and shut it down. How did we do that? We just told people exactly what they needed to do. We sent the video, with a certain number of steps, to a list of fifteen thousand employees, all prepared to take action. This made the difference!

The idea is that you can use the biggest workforce in the marketing that you can ever possibly have: your employees. You need not to force them to do this every day or even every year, but if you have the approval from HR, from time to time HR can send one specific task that your employees need to do. If you manage it properly, it works really well.

Digital Marketing is Beyond Marketing

Digital Channels are now impacting all aspects of product lifecycle.

Market Research
Market Research V
Market Reality

Production
Apple

Transparency CSR
Customer Likes a
product on Facebook

Product Lifecycle

Product Design
Nike

Customer Support
Southwest

Beyond Marketing means that, in digital, we do not do only sales. Instead, we work on many different things, because digital channels are now impacting all aspects of a product's life cycle.

With digital, we do **Market Research**. Using Facebook, for example, we know exactly what our customer would like or not. If we examine our competitors, we know what our potential customer would like or not. If we only have 1000 followers and our competitor has 1 million followers, let us see what our competitor and what our potential clients want. Let us read what our competitor company reads, what they post, what they ask, how they engage. This way, we know exactly what our potential customers want.

We do **Product design**. Nike has asked many times on Facebook, "How do you want your next Nike to be?" Then you say pink, purple, with rubber, without rubber, longest stretch, etc. Based on that, Nike produces a new Nike shoe. Apple applies this religiously, going through every possible piece of feedback from clients.

Customer support. Northwest Airlines, and now KLM Airlines, have been awarded repeatedly as the best online customer supported airlines: the ones that reply the fastest. At one conference, it was announced that KLM got 18 million euros revenue in one month though Social Media. Yes, 18 million euros, coming from Social Media! Now, they have 250 employees working on Social Media; it is not one or two people the entire day. It makes sense: if you are making 18 million euros, you can pay for 250 people!

Corporate Social *Responsibility*

If your company is running corporate social responsibility programs, in this case, with digital, you blast. When you post a special promotion of the day, nobody cares. You think as a marketer, "It's amazing! 50% discount. This is incredible," and you blast your promotion every few minutes. However, all your competitors do the same blasting and the same promotions, because they see your page and they copy. If you are giving a 50% discount, they will give 60%. Because "we are even smarter!"

Nobody cares about this! But, if you post that you did something amazing, everyone is going to share that. Everyone shares a good cause. A good example is from Vatika, the largest company producing shampoo in India. They ran a campaign for cancer awareness, with a video showing a lady with advanced cancer. She was completely bald. Instead of promoting shampoo using someone with long and shiny hair, they used a lady without hair at all. That campaign was massive; over 20 times more than any other campaign they had ever launched before. Soon, people start loving the brand.

Here is the video: *https://www.youtube.com/watch?v=Qomo Nyfkqvg*

The Digital Marketing Method

The method I use involves what I call the three "I" principles:

- **Initiate**
- **Iterate**
- **Integrate**

Digital Marketing is exactly like the full development of a website; you think that the website in complete when it is launched, but, in fact, it is not. A website is a continuous, 360 degrees development. Even when you have finished, you keep seeing what is missing, and you keep adding.

We do exactly the same in Digital Marketing. It is about Initiate, Iterate and Integrate.

1   3i PRINCIPLES
- Initiate
- Iterate
- Integrate

2   FRAMEWORK
- Visual Scheme
- Digital Channels
- Strategic Choices
- Quality Scale

4   IMPLEMENTATION
- Customer Goals
- Business Goals
- Application

3   TOOLS
- Email
- Search
- Social
- Mobile

I often use this chart during my Digital Marketing Training Classes.

I show it many times because we start with the Principles, then move onto the Framework (planning the visual scheme, digital channels, which strategic choice do we make based on the targeted audience, quality scale, as some channels are better for some topics and not for others). Then we go to the Tools (including which tools we are going to use and how to use all of them) and lastly, Implementation, based on customer goals and business goals.

This helps us go through one direction. It is not about doing things because everyone else is doing them. We do not need Social Media because everyone else is doing it; we always need to have a goal in mind based, and build on consumer goals and business goals. When we help our consumers to achieve their own goals then . . . Boom! We are in.

We need to have our business goals planned in advance, and not just continue with Social Media because we want to increase the number of Likes. That is not a business goal. A business goal is always to sell more. What is important is to do it in an iterating way, so that, even if we are finished, we can plan a different strategy and keep iterating.

The Tools of Digital Marketing

We have seen the framework, the method and the pizza. Now we see the tools, one by one. We are going to look at the surface, so that you may have an overview to begin with. We will then go deeper into each tool, one by one, in the subsequent chapters.

These are the best tools you need have to master to become a proper Digital Marketing Officer:

- **Search Optimisation (SEO)**
- **Pay Per Click (PPC) or Search Marketing (SEM)**
- **Email Marketing**
- **Digital Display Advertising**
- **Social Media**
- **Mobile**
- **Analytics**

SEO: *Search Engine Optimisation*

What does SEO mean? It stands for Search Engine Optimisation. SEO is a very technical subject. Most of the people who work on SEO are geeks, but SEO is no longer a one-person job. Nowadays, SEO is a three-person job:

1. *a marketing job*
2. *a geek job*
3. *a content writing job.*

When you have these three people, and when all of them know exactly what to do, you can do SEO. You can also do it with just one person, and you can also do just a little bit of it. Or, instead of hiring three people, you can outsource and pay a lot less.

SEO is an on-going dynamic process with goals, actions, review and iteration

What is SEO? It is the art of making your website appear first in search. Why do I call it an art? Because it is no longer just a geeky thing you can follow step-by-step to guarantee first position.

The only people who can guarantee you this are Michael Page and Sergey Brin. Do you know who they are? They are the owners and founders of Google. They are the only people who know 100% of the formula of Google. Apart from them, nobody else can, but we can get really close to that.

SEO is based on the concept of positioning. The higher that your result appears, the more clicks it gets and so the more potential clients it gets.

Know where organic and paid search results display.

Email Marketing

I always joke about email marketing during my seminars. I tell my students that the system is so old and abused that it makes me laugh even just talking about it.

There are some very cool tools, despite that, and email is still the most economical way of Loyalty and keeping existing clients. However, it is absolutely not the way to get new clients.

In terms of useful email tools, personally I really believe in marketing automation like Hubspot, GetResponse, and other helpful tools you can find online. Each of these falls within the category of Loyalty, which you will find later in this book.

I do not dwell on email systems because here we are talking about future-proof concepts, not about software. I'm a Strategic Advisor, remember.

PPC: *Pay Per Click*

There is an area called Organic Search and one called Paid Search Area. If your website appears in the first one, you are doing SEO. If it appears in the second one, you are doing Pay Per Click, or SEM (Search Engine Marketing).

I call Pay Per Click the shortcut for SEO. For example, say you want to go to a restaurant. The restaurant is very busy, and there is a queue outside. So, how do you enter? You skip the queue, you hand some cash to the bouncer, and you enter.

We do similar things with Google. This is called Pay Per Click and it is totally legal. So, instead of working hard to get your SEO, you can pay Google to put you first. And you pay only for the clicks you get. This is why it's called PPC: Pay Per Click.

This is a clever business model for Google and for you, because you are guaranteed that when you pay, you are getting somebody on your website. Of course, whether they buy or not once they get there is a different thing. Still, at least you know you are getting somebody.

Digital Display Advertising

Digital Display Advertising is the closest thing to traditional advertising. Digital Display means banners. The banners you see on websites are Digital Display Advertising. Instead of placing a banner on the road, you are placing it on different websites.

Effective Mobile Marketing is an Iterative Process

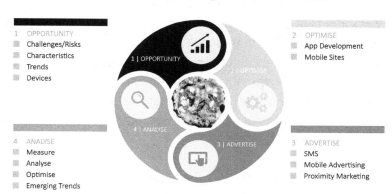

1 OPPORTUNITY
- Challenges/Risks
- Characteristics
- Trends
- Devices

2 OPTIMISE
- App Development
- Mobile Sites

4 ANALYSE
- Measure
- Analyse
- Optimise
- Emerging Trends

3 ADVERTISE
- SMS
- Mobile Advertising
- Proximity Marketing

Mobile Marketing

During my Digital Marketing training classes, I always ask people, "Which mobile do you have?" The majority of participants use Android or iPhone. Sometimes, one of them has a BlackBerry. A few years ago, it was half BlackBerry, half anything else. Now, if you have a BlackBerry and you go to the United States, everyone looks at you like, "What's this? Are you a dinosaur?!"

The second question I ask is, "What is the best mobile? Apple or Android? Who says Apple? Who says Android? Who says Windows Phone? So, what is the best mobile?" The students all answer with the phone they have. Then, I show the students a very, very big smartphone that, in, reality is a piece of digital signage I found at an exhibition in Dubai. It was made for a Dubai government announcement that every public and government service in Dubai would be available on mobile devices.

47

So, what is the best mobile? The answer is reflected in what my students always say. **The best mobile is the one that your customer has.** If you personally have a Windows Phone that you love and you want to optimise your product for your strategy on Windows Phone but the vast majority of your customers do not have a Windows Phone, you are wasting your money! Do things based on your customers' preferences, not based on your own ideas!

If some of your customers have an iPhone, you should invest a little bit in iPhone. If most of them have Android, you should invest much more in Android. And if nobody has a Windows Phone? Then you do not invest in Windows Phone. Simple.

In mobile, we are going to talk about challenges, risks, characteristics, strengths, devices, app development, and mobile sites. We are going to learn how to develop an app, and we are going to learn the concepts involved.

But first, a question: does it make sense to develop an app just because your competitor has an app? No, it does not make sense. If you make an app just for the sake of it and you do not plan the entire process properly, you get zero anything. You get zero customer, zero sale, zero retention. If that is the case, you should just do a mobile website. It is more than enough. With a mobile website, you can do 99% of the things that you can do with an app.

Therefore, you need to follow the complete process: optimise, advertise and then analyse the results.

The Convergence

Convergence refers to device functionality beginning to come together in one device:

- SMS
- Camera
- Music
- Phone
- Browser
- GPS
- Email
- Office Applications
- Social Media
- Gaming

Never before in history did we have a device that could send SMS, take photos, play music, browse the internet, give GPS directions, run Office applications, and be used for Social Media and gaming.

Everything in one device.

If you remember the first mobile phones from the distant past, they are funny to think about. They were very big, chunky and bulky. Then, they became smaller and smaller. Motorola created the smallest ever, the one people called "the pebble." And then, suddenly, they started to increase in size. Now, you get a 5.5-inch display, and bigger.

We passed on from the idea that "smaller is better." Now, "bigger is better" again, because it is not just a mobile phone anymore. It is everything else too. To make a phone call, I need a tiny little device, but to do anything else, I need a bigger device.

Evolution of Online Interaction

The evolution of the web places the user centre stage and increasingly in control.

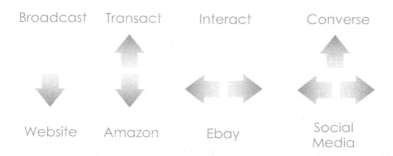

Broadcast   Transact   Interact   Converse

Website   Amazon   Ebay   Social Media

Let us look at how we evolve the interaction. We passed from websites to transactional websites, allowing people to purchase and transact with the business. eBay was first website that allowed interaction, and people could even review the buyer. That removed doubts like, "I don't trust this seller. Maybe he is going to steal my money, and maybe he is never going to ship the product."

With the reviews, you can see if it is trustworthy or not. And now, in the Social Media era, people can converse with companies.

Analytics

Analytics is an on-going dynamic process with goals, setup, management and review and iteration.

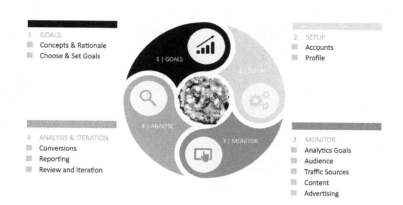

1   GOALS
- Concepts & Rationale
- Choose & Set Goals

2   SETUP
- Accounts
- Profile

4   ANALYSIS & ITERATION
- Conversions
- Reporting
- Review and Iteration

3   MONITOR
- Analytics Goals
- Audience
- Traffic Sources
- Content
- Advertising

For me, Analytics is the best topic! Even if you do not care much about Analytics, I hope that you will gain the minimum amount of information that you are going to need to survive in the digital future.

Because, whatever you do, if you are not able to measure it, do not do it. Somebody is going to ask you, and try to make you accountable for the ROI (Return on Investment), so if you cannot measure it, do not do it.

Sometimes, I work with companies that I instruct this way, "First of all, make sure that the tracking code is set 100% correct, in order to track exactly what we are looking for. Then, I can push as much traffic as you want to that campaign, but we are going to be able to measure it."

When you are investing money—for example, in a Pay Per Click campaign—you are paying a company, or a Social Media platform. You have a team, and they write, comment, and post, and you pay for the advertising, etc. You have to measure everything. The last section of this book covers how Analytics works, and how many good things you can get out of it.

It is good to see that some managing directors and CEOs are using Google Analytics to evaluate how their business is going. They do not know the complete picture and the in-depth details, but they know enough to understand. Every few days, they open it up and see what is going on. When something is wrong, they convey a message to their managers and staff.

Laws and Guidelines

Now, let us discuss the laws and guidelines surrounding Digital Marketing. You may be surprised, but at the moment, there is a lot to know. That is because the digital marketing is not well regulated.

This is good because it does not limit the creativity of marketers.

At present, only the laws regulating advertising in each country also regulate online advertising.

There is, however, one exception: Search Engine Optimisation. You know why? Because SEO is not considered advertising; it can be used for anything.

You do, however, need to be aware of the data protection and privacy laws in your country. In general, these are the common electronic privacy characteristics:

- Provide the option to opt-out at collection point
- Tell your subscriber why their information is being gathered
- Send emails only about similar products
- Always give the option to opt-out on every email
- Opt-in only valid for 12 months.

The Chief Digital
Officer - CDO

The Digital Manager *of the Future!*

Before going deeper into the different digital marketing tools, I want to talk to you about the Chief Digital Officer: the digital manager of the future. The CDO is a key figure that will become increasingly important and necessary in any company that wants to keep abreast of change and not miss the boat.

Our digitally dominated times hold out enormous challenges and enormous opportunities for businesses. Companies must be able to keep up with advances in technology and changing consumer habits. Today, every business strategy must be perfectly integrated with fast-moving digital strategies. All of this is forcing businesses to rethink every single aspect of their strategies.

The relationships between businesses and their customers have been reversed and, for some time now, we have been looking at a scenario where customers have a great deal of information about the products they want to buy and the businesses that sell them. As a result, the old equilibrium has been overturned, and power is now in the buyer's hands rather than the seller's.

Challenges *for businesses*

This scenario is very difficult for all businesses and their leaders to cope with. What is your experience? Do you agree with me?

The consumer experience is increasingly multichannel, and businesses must come to grips with a market where big data rules the roost. This has caught many businesses unprepared, forcing them to look for new procedures and new people who can deal with the wealth of information that can now be accessed thanks to digital media.

If they are not to perish, businesses must move quickly to adapt to the changes brought about by technology and the new buying habits it encourages in consumers, remembering that the latter need information that is always up-to-date. They expect to be able to make transactions wherever, whenever and however they want.

Businesses that have been able to implement their digital technologies effectively have reaped major benefits. By contrast, companies that have applied inappropriate or unproductive strategies have achieved negligible results. These have prevented them from making the changes needed to avoid going out of business.

The changes I am referring to concern all of a company's processes, whether external or internal. In fact, digital is not just a fad or a set of communication strategies; it is a new working model that impacts the entire corporate organisation.

An irreversible revolution!

The digital transformation has revolutionised the way of working and doing business. It is a revolution that has impacted many sectors, including those that are far from the world of technology. It has made them rapidly rethink their business models and corporate processes. And, by now, it is an irreversible revolution.

In this scenario, Human Resources departments must also transform themselves. They have to embrace the new digital tools and new competences, reorganise the way they work, and introduce new professional roles in the company.

Briefly, we have to deal with two needs:

- Promote and spread a new digital culture at all levels of the organisation.
- Use digital technology to redefine talent management processes.

As we have seen, the digital transformation means that all corporate areas must develop new skills and bring new professionals on board who are capable of guiding their teams through the change. They have to know how to make the most of the new opportunities. Social media manager, e-commerce manager, data scientist, and digital strategist are just a few of the new job descriptions that are increasingly in demand, although they are still poorly understood and insufficiently recognised.

Of all the digital jobs now on offer, the one that is currently hardest to fill in Italy is that of the Chief Digital Officer, or CDO. This is the person who is responsible for managing and coordinating all the other digital professionals.

We can thus say that this new corporate figure, the CDO, is both a clear sign of the extent of the digital transformation and a direct consequence of it. So, are you ready to hire a CDO, or to transform your career by launching yourself in this future-proof job?

CDO, *the New Chief Officer 2.0*

Now, what does the Chief Digital Officer do? The CDO coordinates and supervises all digital strategies, and guides the entire company through this change. Flanking the Marketing Director, the CDO can replace or work together with existing figures such as the Chief Information Officer.

In reality, this role has existed since 2005, when MTV, in the United States, hired Jason Hirschhorn as Chief Digital Officer, a world first.

Though the role is now well-established in the US, European countries are reacting more slowly. Certainly, even in Europe, the demand for CDOs is increasing significantly, especially in the United Kingdom, and Northern Europe. It is clear by now that the time has come for Italy to step its corporate culture up another notch as well. Though we are lagging behind other countries, several large Italian corporate groups have already added a CDO to their top management team.

In this moment in history, businesses have an urgent need for the Chief Digital Officer. Nevertheless, many companies are showing a certain reluctance to embark on a change that, by adding another C-level role, could generate internal tensions between the CIO, CMO, and other top-ranking figures.

Let us take a look at CDO's characteristics and then at their skill set.

The CDO as a Driver of Change

A Chief Digital Officer is tasked with bringing order to the confusion that the digital onslaught often causes in a company, by introducing strategic changes and new skills in all departments. The CDO's main goal is to guide the entire team towards the digital realm.

Concretely, the CDO is responsible for the company's entire digital strategy, with competencies that cut across sectors as diverse as marketing, communication, ICT, and personnel management. The CDO coordinates with all the corporate business units, and is a support for the other chief officers.

The CDO must not only have digital acumen, technical skills, operating experience, a strategic mentality, and management capabilities, but they must also be an expert general manager with great sensitivity and authority. This is because they must provide leadership in a variety of areas to guide the entire team towards a digital transformation. They must not be perceived as an intruder in the company, or as a potential danger to the other management positions. Instead, they must provide systematic support to the other executives, fostering maturity and awareness.

Though the CDO has a highly operative role, the CDO is a top manager who works at the CEO's right hand as a driver for the company's growth.

The CDO brings together the competencies of several existing corporate roles: the Chief Data Officer, the CMO, the CIO; accordingly, they must be able to analyse numbers, be familiar with market trends, and have skills in programming, marketing, social media, SEO, SEM, and mobile. But the CDO is not a superhero, or an all-round expert; that would be impossible.

Each CDO will have their own personal aptitude in one or two particular areas. Outside of those areas, they must know a little of everything in order to be able to oversee, check, and coordinate the work done by specialists in each sector.

As I mentioned earlier, while the CDO's main goal is to guide the entire team towards the digital future, the second goal is to do so quickly. That is, the CDO must make their role useless as soon as possible.

In fact, despite the continual evolution of digitalisation at all corporate levels, it cannot be taken for granted that this profession will last. It may serve a purely transitional purpose. However, there can be no doubt that the CDO's role will evolve over time, on the basis of the natural changes in business dynamics. It is possible that, once the CDO's task is accomplished, they will become CEO or, in any case, occupy a place on the company's board.

The Chief Digital Officer's Skill set

A CDO must have wide knowledge and extensive skills—though without being a specialist in everything—and must obviously have considerable experience in digital technology. In this case, the CDO may be a millennial with strategic experience, but is more likely to be a more seasoned figure from marketing or IT who, over the years, has gained a 360 degree knowledge of the digital world.

Here is a short list of the basic skills required to be a CDO:

- Web marketing
- Social media
- Lead generation
- Basic programming
- E-commerce
- Mobile
- Analytics
- SEO
- SEM
- Local marketing
- Strategic planning
- Personnel management
- Corporate branding and personal branding
- Sales
- Customer care
- Communication

From this standpoint, CIOs, CMOs, and CDOs have separate and distinct tasks, but must collaborate at all times. The CDO must know how to operate both inside the company, to bring all personnel closer to digital, and outside it, to guarantee a unique consumer experience.

In addition to leading the company towards technological innovation, the CDO's work obviously aims at increasing revenues through monetisation. As their role is wide-ranging and not fully defined, it is important that a CDO also have their own KPIs and that the resources available to them are clearly specified so that results can be monitored.

Even if the CDO's work leads to measurable results, it is possible that colleagues in the company will continue to view it with scepticism and distrust, at least in the early period. In the long run, though, meeting targets and exercising firm leadership will help the CDO win the entire team's trust.

Chief Digital Officer, the Winning Card for a Company's Future

The move towards digital will continue to gain pace in the coming years, as will the investments in time and resources that will be necessary.

Businesses that have invested and obtained results will be determined to boost the share of their budget earmarked for investments in digital strategies and resources, understanding that this is the winning card for their future.

In this section, I have attempted to highlight the need for a digital-oriented vision, and the advantages digital technologies and specialised personnel can have for businesses. I would like to emphasise that the only way to accomplish concrete results is to follow a well-planned and well-organised strategy. You must invest in human capital, personnel training, and advanced technology.

The businesses that are able to achieve this mix of vision, strategy, technology, skills, and capacity for execution are the ones certain to succeed.

Are you ready?

DIGITAL
DISPLAY
ADVERTISING

What is Digital Display?

Now, let us move onto the topic of Digital Display, which is the closest thing to traditional advertising. Two topics related to Digital Display are SEO and Analytics.

- Why Analytics? Because if you pay for Digital Advertising, you will want know the results.
- Why SEO? Because when you do Digital Display Advertising, you get more links and more traffic going to work to your website. So, at a certain stage, it helps to have some SEO. It is about what adds more advantage; do not think, "Oh, I do this, so I don't need SEO!" No, it does help, even if a little bit.

Effective Digital Display Marketing is an Iterative Process

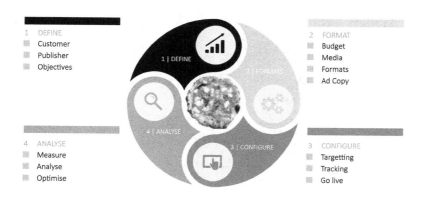

1 DEFINE
- Customer
- Publisher
- Objectives

2 FORMAT
- Budget
- Media
- Formats
- Ad Copy

4 ANALYSE
- Measure
- Analyse
- Optimise

3 CONFIGURE
- Targetting
- Tracking
- Go live

How *does Digital Display work?*

- We define the customer, publisher and objectives.
- We choose the format: budget, media, and the text ad copy.
- We configure targeting and tracking, and then we go live.
- Once live, we analyse, measure, and tweak the campaign, and so we continue. It is an ongoing thing.

Digital Display Marketing definitions

"Graphically rich online advertising presented in consistent size formats." (Source: Digital Marketing Institute)

"Banner Ads" (Source: Christian Farioli)

The Mechanics *of Digital Display*

Advertiser	Publisher	Website	Consumer	Advertiser
Create Ad	Publish Ad	Serve Ad	Click Ad	Track Ad
Choose Format	Distributes ad across websites based on targetting and budget	Serves ads thorugh website	Views, engages with and clicks ad	Measure Impressions
Design Ad		Ad Impression		CTR
Choose Publisher		Page Impression		Conversions

It is not a simple as, "Yeah, give me some money and I put a banner in my website." That was how Banner Ads worked a few years ago.

Digital Display works on five players and five steps, as shown above.

The advertiser creates the ad. So, if you want to advertise your company, you create the ad, and then what? Eventually, you can go to the Christian Farioli website and say, "Christian, put the banner on your website, and then I'll give you 5000 Dirham a month." Okay, good, thank you, bye.

Or, if you're really clever, what do you do? You give the banner to a publisher.

The publisher is somebody who distributes the ad across not just one or two, but thousands of websites. And then, when a possible consumer is looking at one of these websites, they see the ad and they decide to click it.

Once they click it, they go to your company website and the advertiser tracks the click. They can see that some-body clicked the banner on the Christian Farioli website and that they went to our website and purchased the product or service.

This is the mechanism, and you really need to understand it so you know what we mean when we refer to the publisher.

For example, one of the publishers is Google Display Network. There is also Yahoo Display Network. There are some display networks that are specific to mobile apps.

Marketing Benefits
of Digital Display Advertising

Depending on consumption channel users apply personal preferences and etiquette and expect marketers to do likewise.

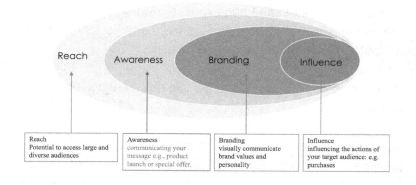

Reach	Awareness	Branding	Influence
Reach Potential to access large and diverse audiences	Awareness communicating your message e.g., product launch or special offer.	Branding visually communicate brand values and personality	Influence influencing the actions of your target audience: e.g. purchases

First of all, there is the **Reach**, because everyone is spending most of their day on a computer or on a mobile. Wherever you are, you are in front of a device, and I can put a banner in your face, so it is not just that you drive on a major road and you see the banner, like with traditional advertising. Even if you stay at home all day, I can still put a banner in your face!

Awareness. This means that you didn't know that I have a product and now you know because I shot it in your face 20 times a day.

I do **Branding** because, in the banner, I make my brand big and I influence your decision. So, the last advantage is **Influence**. When you go to the supermarket and you want to buy some chocolates, you see a Kit-Kat and you know that Kit-Kat is going to be tastier than the other options. You may not know why, but you are sure because you have seen it on television enough, or you have seen enough banners. It is the same story.

What are the Values *gained by the business through Digital Display?*

- **Control**: targeting and measurement capabilities lead to better ROI, less wastage and greater focus.
- **User response**: ability to generate clicks, interactions, conversions, and online and offline responses.
- **Integration (online)**: integrates with other aspects of the digital marketing mix, i.e. display drives Social Media.
- **Integration (offline)** with campaigns (TV, Radio, Print).

Control: Targeting and measurement capabilities lead to better ROI, less wastage and greater focus. We know exactly where people are looking at the banner, where they click, where they go, and where they buy. Maybe you notice that lots of people are clicking on a banner and coming to your website, but for some reason, none of them buys the product. By doing the research, you might find out that they come from a banner on a website where people are talking about the worst training company in the Middle East. Of course, you would want to remove your banner from that website!

User response: You can generate clicks, interaction, conversion, and online and offline responses.

Integration online: You integrate with other aspects of the marketing mix, and you also get success in offline integration.

Integration (offline). When you have an offline campaign, it is good practice to integrate the same design, brand, idea, message, and concept on that banner.

This is about consistency; you must see the same content in the banner and in the display.

What Challenges Do Marketers Face with Display Advertising?

Marketing Downside: *'banner blindness'*

What are the downsides of Digital Display Advertising? We call it "banner blindness." Banner blindness is the user's mental ability to dismiss or disregard ads as they read a web page. If I go on a website, I go to read the content I want to read. If I see that there is a new Toyota Corolla launching on the market tomorrow, I would not care. My attention does not go to read the content about Toyota because I perceive it as advertising. That is called "banner blindness." For example, when you go to Sheikh Zayed Road in Dubai, you are not focusing on every banner that you can see. Your brain automatically ignores advertising because some parts of your brain perceive it as advertising in order to do so.

Click Through Rate *from 0.1% to 0.3%*

What does Click Through Rates mean? It is an important phase that we are going to see many times. It is perhaps the second most important phrase. It is so important that if you went to a tattoo shop and got a tattoo that reads "CTR" on your left hand, you would be on the right path.

Whatever you are doing in digital, every strategy of digital, you are doing it for only one thing: CTR. That is going to be your new Bible for the future. What do you need to do, today? You need to achieve CTR. In any strategy—in Facebook, in Google, in SEO, in Pay Per Click, in Digital Display—you are working for CTR.

CTR is the ratio between "Impressions" (how many people see your banner) and "Clicks" (how many people click). So, a CTR of 1%, it means that if 100 people are looking at your banner, one person clicks on it. 0.1% means if 1000 people looking at your banner, 1 is clicking.

That is still okay. Nobody can expect you to put up a banner and, immediately, every human being would click on it. In Digital Display, the typical Click Through Rates, depending on format, can range from 0.1% to 0.3%.

Now, if you target your banner properly, you can increase this.

Normally, when I launch a campaign, the worst CTR I get is 0.5%. There are campaigns for which I have reached up to 5% CTR. That is crazy! How can I get that? Because I target exactly the perfect audience!

So, if I put up a Toyota Corolla banner, I do not put it up for the 1 trillion people in the market, telling myself, "Every human being going to see my Toyota Corolla Banner!" Traditional marketing will function like this, but Digital Marketing is smarter.

For example, I could target only websites that talk about cars, but only medium class cars. So, if your website is talking about Ferrari, Lamborghini, Maserati, Bugatti, I would not put up a banner there about the new Toyota Corolla. I do not want to put all the effort into making the banner attractive, animated, shiny, with call to action and so on, if it is in the wrong place.

Catch the audience, then you get the Click Through Rate. And the higher CTR, the less you pay! Google and various other publishers reward those who get a better Click Through Rate. If my banner gets more clicks than others, the publisher will show my banner more than others, so I will get more clicks. Hence, I end up paying less for the same number of clicks. And that is very clever!

The Challenges: *Click Through Rate is not the only benefit*

The challenge is that you need to track your ads as accurately as possible. You need to choose your target audience accurately. Historical reliance on Click Through Rate is evolving towards more sophisticated tracking, that considers a range of user actions, such as impact on conversions when users search after seeing a Display Ad.

Ad Dimensions and Positions

Now, what dimensions and positions are there? There are some Common industry ad types for Digital Display Advertising. There are some benefits to having standard types: they are consistent (one set of creative) and generally accepted by all publishers.

Common Ad banner types are Leaderboard, standard banner, Skyscraper, Wide Skyscraper, Island Ad, MPU, Button Ad, Overlay, Takeover, Sidekick, etc. Even after so many years, I never remember all of these!

I do not care, because I know the standard sizes. 300x250 is my superstar number one! This one will always get the highest CTR. Why is that?

Because it is bigger, visibly bigger.

The Skyscraper is also big, but you have to put it on the side. The MPU is 300x250; normally, they put it in the middle and it is bigger. It offers more space, people notice it more and click it more. Obviously, the more space your banners take, the better it is, although you cannot take the entire page.

The Leaderboard is the second best because, normally, it is placed at the top of the page. When I open the page, I see it:

boom! I do not need to scroll down, so eventually people click and they get it. These are the typical positions, as an example. It is not always like this:

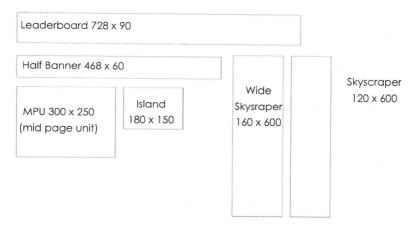

Position and dimensions on the webpage of common ads.
Sizes and names can vary from region to region.

MPU:

- 300×250
- Middle of the page, or right-hand side
- Average CTR: 0.09%-0.13%

Leaderboard:

- 728×90
- Typically located at top of page, and within search results
- Average CTR: 0.08%-0.11%

Wide Skyscraper:

- 160×600
- Right hand side
- Average CTR: 0.09%-0.10%

Island:

- 180×50
- 200×200
- Size can vary
- Location: various

Film strip:

- Content-rich, interactive experience that does not interrupt their viewing of the page

- Brands get a powerful canvas that combines five ads in one 300×600 unit
- Advertisers submit one 300×3000 Filmstrip with five different segments
  The Filmstrip is then served via one 300×600 unit
- Users can explore all segments simply by scrolling, hovering or clicking on the creative

Ad Frequency Capping

There are all these new concepts, although these are not really new anymore, having already been around a few years. One of these is called Ad Frequency Capping, which is:

> *"The limit on the number of times a given ad will be shown to a unique user during a session or within a specific time period of time." (Source: Digital Marketing Institute)*

This concept came out because, sometimes, some people are looking the internet much more than others. You might surf the internet ten minutes a day and be finished; meanwhile, I look at the internet ten hours a day!

Obviously, I would see a thousand banners and you would be seeing only three banners. If I see a thousand banners, eventually, one advertiser can target me repeatedly all day. But I am not going to buy one thousand products just because you show me the ad one thousand times. Say it is Kit-Kat: I am not going to buy a ton of Kit-Kats! It makes no sense, and is going to be a waste. Also, if you bombard me with the same advertising over and over, I will start shunning you.

This is why they introduced the concept of Ad Frequency Capping. It limits the system from showing the same banner more than a certain number of times. And they can decide the limitation. Let us say the cap is ten times a day maximum. Even if somebody is using their computer for ten hours, I can only show that advertising banner for that brand a maximum of ten times in a day. This limits the impressions, so I can get the same banner to more people.

Instead of showing one thousand banners to Christian Farioli and then having nothing left for everyone else, a company can show it to me ten times, ten times to you, ten to someone else, so that at the end of the day it has shown up to hundreds of different people instead of just one. This is why limiting Ad Frequency Capping makes sense.

Target Audience: Who are Your Consumers?

Demographics: *Age, Gender and Social Grade*

The big thing with GDM, or Digital Display, or the different kinds of targeting methods, is that, before, the traditional banner advertising was: "You go to Dubizzle, you put the banner up for a month and it's there." Whoever looks at that, it is there. You think, "Yeah, Dubizzle Dubai is good. Most of the audience is in Dubai."

Not true! 20% to 30% of the people are not in Dubai. They are in Italy, planning to one day go to Dubai and, so, they look at time on Dubai. When they come to Dubai and then leave, they get the banners, but they would never buy from you because they are not based here.

This is why the traditional banner advertising has a limitation. But with the Display Network, you can choose not just what website, but geographically where people have to be to see your banner. So, if I go to a website to check the time on Dubai and I am physically located in Dubai, show me the banner. If I am physically located in Sharjah, do not show me the banner, because I am never going to visit your pizzeria, which is in the centre of Dubai or somewhere. That makes sense. You save a lot of money. You save impressions, and you put all of those to the people that matter the most to you, not only by location, but also by age and gender.

For the Abu Dhabi Science Festival, we did two campaigns: one for kids and one

for parents. The parents are the ones that are going to take the kids to the Festival while the kids might be saying, "No, I don't wanna go this festival!" Hence, the messages were completely different. The parents' message was, "Take your kid. They're going to learn, to dance, to become smart and clever." You think your kids care about becoming smart and clever? No! The kids' campaign was all about robots, laser beams, laser men, and a guy with lightning moulding his head. Then it is, "Mom, Dad, let's go to Science Festival!"

But even with the kids, there was a kind of discrepancy. Three days later, I came up with an idea. I called the creative agency and I said, "Guys, can you split the banner for the kids into two, boys and girls? Maybe the blue one for boys with the robot and the laser, and then the pink one, with, like, Lisa Simpson becoming a famous scientist because she was reading science, books and stuff." Boom! We did it.

This is the idea of Digital Advertising: we can sub-segment to the craziest level! No, we do not need to sub-segment to the craziest level, but just to know that we can if we want.

Geography: *Where are your users based?*
Let us look at Geography. I can target Sharjah, Dubai, Umm al-Quwain, or Ras Al Khaimah. I can target only Ras Al Khaimah

people, and it would go, "Are you in Ras Al Khaimah? There is a special event for you in Dubai. We have a bus that can take you from Ras Al Khaimah to Dubai, and we will bring you back next day." Based on the IP or computer browsing, we know where you are located. In that way, you can target your ads based on geography.

Interests: *As a marketer, you will know your customer. Use this data to feed back into your targeting.*

Interests: this is where things get really crazy. This is Big Brother-level stuff! If you like cars, you will see my ad about the Toyota Corolla launch. If you are not into cars, you will not see it. That is big. I am not into football; I do not care about football advertising. You can push as much as you can, but I will never come to any football match, to anything related to football, be it the new Real Madrid SIM card, or the new special Real Madrid T-shirt, whatever. I do not care, so don't tell me anything. I don't wanna know anything. Thanks to marketing targeted to interests, I do not have to.

Even if I go to YouTube to watch a stupid video, I will see that they are launching the new Digital Marketing seminar event there, because that is my interest.

Purchase Habits: *What do your consumers spend their money on?*

The other targeting parameter is about Purchase Habits. As most of the websites have Analytics, Google knows which users purchase online, and what they purchase online. That is crazy! It is never going to tell you clearly, but, at the end of the day, Google knows which users purchase online, which products, and which services.

That is clever advertising. That is what makes you feel good! Then you think, "There is going to be some advertising, I know that, but I accept it because the advertising that I see is relevant to me."

Consumers Leave a Trail

Everything we have seen is possible because consumers leave a trail, through your IP address, cookies, Analytics, and many other means that Google does not tell you about because then we could shield from them and run away. But I can tell you, the moment you choose Chrome (the Google browser), it starts.

Publishers: Research and Choose the Most Relevant

Choose the most relevant publisher for your target audience!

When you do Digital Advertising, you must research publishers before choosing one. A publisher should normally be chosen based on your target audience because every publisher specialises in a different audience.

Recognise which type of publisher appeals to which audience:

- Relevance to target audience
- Relevance to marketing objectives
- Ad formats accepted (file size, file type, animation, sound, budget)
- Ensure publisher facilitates targeting based on demographics, geography, context, behaviour/remarketing

Planning Tools and Ad Specifications

There are so many different platforms that you can use to choose your target audience. You must contact different publishers and find out their specialisation. There are publishers specialised only in luxury, or only in mobile apps advertising; meanwhile, others specialise in a little bit of everything.

Each publisher provides ad specification and dimensions. They give you some limitations. They tell you, "Okay, my banner is going to be like this, like this, like that, maximum this, maximum that. These are the sides, they can be animated or not." All of this has limitations that you must take into consideration. When you contact the creative agency and you say, "I wanna set a banner like this," you need to give more specifications. Otherwise, the banners are made, then you put them up and you see, "Error, they don't meet requirements." Then you have to come back to the agency, and, in the meantime, you have wasted weeks.

Campaign Objectives

What can be achieved through digital display advertising?

- **Branding:** reinforcing an existing brand.
- **Awareness:** raising awareness of a new brand.
- **Engagement:** user engages with your brand, plays game, watches video
- **Direct response:** complete form, get quote, take action, subscribe
- **Social Media integration:** users join your Social Media platform
- **Lead generation:** build a database of potential customers
- **Conversions/sales:** purchase or other action.

Everyone has a different goal. We should think about our goals and then, based on that, build the entire campaign. Never the opposite. Don't do something because others are doing it!

Think first, "If we have to do it, why do we *have* to do it? What are the reasons? What are the goals?" When you have worked out the answers to those questions, you can plan the campaign to actually do that A to Z. Then you launch it, and then you measure it. You ask yourself, "Are we really achieving that?" If the answer is, "Yeah, a little bit," then okay, you will need to tweak it and relaunch it. Then again you ask, "Are we achieving our goal?" Yes? Good!

For example, to build **awareness** or to do **branding**, I do not care about getting clicks. I do not want to get clicks, because every time I get a click, I pay for it. If I do not want that, I need not put a call to action. I just leave the banner there, without a call to action.

If I put a call to action, there will be more clicks, so I will **engage** and that will drive traffic to my website, and people will see what I am doing. If that is what I want, I will put a call to action.

For **direct response**, I normally make a banner to get you in, right now; that is, to fill out a form and get the chance to win something, to participate in something, to download some-thing interesting for you, etc.

Another goal can be **Social Media integration**. Some ban-ners can have some **integration from Social Media** or **lead generation**; for example, click to register for something, click to download something.

Ultimately, conversions and sales are what you want, but do not expect that just by using banners, you are going to get sales. The number of sales you get will be extremely few, because these are only in the awareness stage.

This is what banners are for: to show potential customers that we exist, just like the banner in Sheikh Zayed Road. However, you cannot put a Kit-Kat on a Sheikh Zayed Road banner and expect people driving to immediately stop to buy a Kit-Kat, otherwise they die! Right?

You do banner advertising for awareness. We do Digital Display Advertising for exactly the same: awareness.

So, when you want to sell, you use other tactics and, eventually, you are going to sell something even with a banner. The main purpose of the banner is to put the brand, the product, the service, or the concept, into the consumer's mind.

Interactivity Scale

Interactivity scale of value for digital display marketing objectives

Now, let us see how interactive the communication can be. We start with delivering impressions. At that point, we are in the **Awareness and Branding** phase.

When the users click to connection, then visit our website, we are in the **Engagement** phase. I am sure that you use and abuse that word in Social Media, right? However, it is not only about Social Media. Even if it is through a partnership, the moment you click and enter my website, you start engaging with my content, and with my company. So, from this moment, you will see the brand of my company over and over, not just in a split fraction of a second in a banner. Instead, you will see insight.

The user then takes action and completes the form. We call this **Direct Response**, when the user has finally done what they are supposed to do. We cannot expect the user to buy online every time, but even when the user books a questionnaire, a spot, a training, a seminar, an appointment with a salesperson, or downloads a form or a company's profile, for us, that is a goal scored. If you download my company profile, it means you are interested in my company in some way. This is why it is called the Direct Response phase.

Next is the **Conversion**, which is when the user makes the purchase.

DMI Interactivity scale of value for digital display marketing objectives

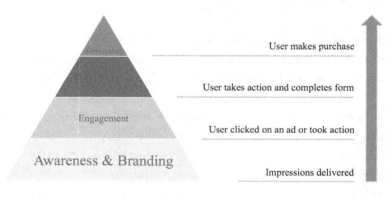

SMART Objectives

- **Specific** – usually a number
- **Measurable** – you have the systems in place to accurately track this metric
- **Actionable** – the actions to influence this outcome are under your control
- **Realistic** – it's reasonable for you to expect to achieve this objective
- **Timed** – you have a deadline for delivering on the objective

Now, as I say and always repeat in all of the digital topics, it is important to have an objective. Why we are doing anything? We need to consider why we are each one of the things we do.

Then there is a concept—coming from ancient traditional marketing, basically from the prehistoric age of the dinosaurs—called the SMART Objectives. I am sure that all of you have seen it a million times. What does SMART mean? It means: Specific, Measurable, Actionable, Realistic and Timely.

If we have a goal with these five characteristics, then eventually we are going to get there. But if our goal is only about, "Um, we wanna sell more." well, that is not specific at all. It is going to be difficult to achieve a goal like that.

Every strategy you use has to have a goal in mind. Remember this interesting point, though: digital goals (such as SEO goals, Pay Per Click goals, Social Media goals, etc.) are good to have, but each digital goal should help to achieve your overall marketing goals. We are not doing Facebook likes just because we want Facebook likes. We need to have the company achieve the overall marketing goals; marketing goals, ultimately, help the company achieve business goals.

What are business goals? You can call it ROI, or revenue, or profit, whatever. If you do not pay attention to that, what happens?

Well, one day, you come into the office and see your boss and you say, "Boss, this post got 20,000 likes, and we even got the Chinese visiting our page. We got 5,000 visits on our website!" Your boss replies, "You're fired!"
And you say, "But . . . 20,000 likes! Look, look! 20,000 likes!"
"You're fired!"
"Why?"
"We haven't sold one single product in the last six months! Stop playing on Facebook and do something else!"

Therefore, even if it is not your direct responsibility—because, in marketing, you cannot be responsible for sales—at the end of the day, you need to consider the bottom line. So, if what you are doing helps get revenue, then good, but find a good way to measure it and to make what you are doing accountable.

When you earn more inquiries, more phone calls, and more media traffic, and can show it to your boss, you are doing your job.

Campaign Budget

On what basis should I buy digital display media?

- CPM (Cost Per Mille): cost per thousand Ad impressions.
- CPC (Cost-per-click): cost per each click on an Ad.
- CPL (Cost Per Lead): cost per each unique contact (email, contact phone number).
- CPA (Cost Per Acquisition): typically associated with a sale.
- Tenancy/Sponsorship: exclusive ownership of a position for a fixed price and duration, and not related to deliverables such as impressions or clicks (e.g. home page takeover.)

Now, here is a little more info about Digital Display. We have CPM, which stands for Cost Per Mille, which means cost per thousand impressions. CPC is Cost-per-click. Only a few of the publishers use CPL (Cost Per Lead); it is very rare. There are some companies that say, "Look, I am so confident about the quality of the visitors I bring, I will charge you per Lead." CPA means Cost Per Acquisition; that is even rarer. It means that I will send you visitors, and you pay me just for those who purchase, or do what they are supposed to do.

Lastly, there is a concept of Tenancy or Sponsorship. For example, I place my banner on your website for one entire month, and it's going to be there day and night. That is tenancy sponsorship, which is another model.

How do I plan my digital display budget?

- Display budget is based on your objectives / goals
- Budgeting factors:
  - » Target Audience
  - » Segmentation
  - » Publisher/Network price points
  - » Geography
  - » Competition
  - » Cost of Creative

What do we use to decide our budget? That is the number 1-million-dollar question! What is your budget? This must be based on the target audience, the segmentation, and the publisher. There are some publishing networks that only serve high-cost clicks. You must also consider geography, competition, and cost of the creative. Even the cost to produce creative advertising may change. If you ask a big creative agency to do a set of animated banners, it might cost you, like, the entire company! If you have some freelancers, it might cost 100 Dirhams, but then not a single human being is going to click that ugly banner.

The point is not to spend money; it is to be smart. It is to use a banner, focused on Click Through Rate.

What does that mean? You use a good banner, or an ugly banner. Which one is going to be better? The right answer is,

"I don't care." I don't care which you like the most, I will use them both. Then, whichever gives me a bigger Click Through Rate is the best, even if everyone else hates it. The bigger CTR is the winner!

Now, obviously if it is more flashy, more shiny, more appealing, then you will probably get more Click Through Rate. Branding people like to be nice, soft, and cool, and that never gets clicks!

Some time ago, I worked with a big branding agency. They gave me a set of banners, and I knew nobody was going to click them. I was right; they got a Click Through Rate of 0.1 or 0.05%. Then I created my own crappy-looking banner, using a free tool, and I got a Click Through Rate of 1%!

It is not about how beautiful it is; we are not evaluating the beauty of the banner. A user has a split fraction of a second, while they are reading a page. If your banner is nice and beautiful, nobody is going to see that! But if your banner is shiny . . . boom, in the face, to the point! They will see it, and more people will click.

Buying Channels

- Direct (Yahoo, ITP, MSN)
- Networks (Google)
- Advertising Sales Houses (Ikoo, N2V, Connect Ads)
- Advertising Agencies (Omnicom, Publicis, WPP, Interpublic)
- Exchanges via DSPs (bear with me, the curtain and wizard behind it will be revealed)

What are buying channels? Where can you place your banner? Through publishers. What are the publishers? You can visit them directly: Yahoo, ITP and MSN. Or through networks: for example, GDN (Google Display Network). Alternatively, you can use advertising sale houses, advertising agencies, or exchanges.

You can even go directly to websites, but I always recommend going for networks or publishers, because they distribute to a much larger audience. So, not only will the people that go to MSN.com see the banner, but also the people that go anywhere else. That way, you get the consistency. You see the same banner over and over in different locations around the internet.

Creative Formats

- Static Ads: typically contain image, text and logo, with no movement
- Homepage Takeover: replace all or part of a publisher's web page with advertising content
- 3D Expandable: contains image, text and logo with movement. Typically, 3 frames.
- Roadblock: combination of ads for the same campaign that appears in two or more placements on the same page.
- Floating Ads: animation outside the ad format, which temporarily interrupt navigation
- Expandable Ads: increase in size as the viewer mouse overs or clicks on the ad
- Catfish Expandable: contains video streaming within the ad
- Synchronised Ads: a combination of ads for the same campaign that appear in two or more placements on the same page and are designed to interact with each other
- Social Media Banner: include dynamic feeds and functionality in the actual ad banner (e.g. comparison, quizzes, games, competition entry)
- iKorner: include dynamic feeds and functionality in the actual ad banner (e.g. comparison, quizzes, games, competition entry)

- Interactive Background: Include dynamic feeds and functionality in the actual ad banner (e.g. comparison, quizzes, games, competition entry)

Static are always the worst. You need to work really hard on it and make it extremely catchy to make somebody click your static Ad banner.

Every few months, there are new banners, formats, shapes, sizes, and tricks. The point is not to know all of them, but to know what you want to convey, and to research and keep using the new options.

If you want to plan something very clever, it takes time. You are not going to just immediately tell the agency, "Okay, I wanna do everything! Bring me everything!" Therefore, it is not going to be easy. You have to focus on one format or another, according to what you want to communicate.

Ad Copy: How to Write an Ad

Now, let us discuss what to write in an ad. Banner Ads and Digital Display are not the same as traditional ads. If you already have a tagline, you may want to use the same tagline for digital. If you have a nice and simple tagline like Nike's "Just do it," that is fine. If your tagline is, "One computer in every desk," or "When does the star shine and the moon and blah blah blah." you cannot put that on a tiny little banner. You need to do something else. Many smart companies create a specific tagline just for digital.

So, what are the main elements of the banner's message?

- Clear call to action (CTA)
- Strong Design (fit for format)
- Context sensitive copy (user & publisher)
- Copy informed by keyword research
- Brand prominence
- Direct and concise language

First of all, the **Call to Action**: You only have a tiny little bit of space. The first thing you need to do is place your logo. The second item you should place is the Call to Action, which states what the user has to do. For example,: get your quotation now, get your insurance now, get your training evaluation assessment now, or get your mobile app now.

Split Testing: Which Banner is Better?

Split testing is publishing multiple versions of an ad campaign, and monitoring the best performing ads. This way, you can include the elements from whichever campaign delivers the best ROI in other creative and iterate campaigns.

- Factors to base split test upon, and what you can learn:
  - » Creative (To which picture does the audience respond best?)
  - » Text (Timeliness and Relevance of messaging)
  - » Call to Action (Concerns and Interests of viewers)
- Advantages of Split Testing:
  - » Better interaction and conversion rates
  - » More targeted and relevant content
  - » Better ROI.

The split testing allows you to deliver and test multiple variants of a banner, each with distinct differences. According to the data from each, you can optimise the design.

The beauty of digital is that you can do split testing. What does this mean? I do not ask which banner is better beforehand. I don't care! I put in both to see which one works better!

Now, in advertising, we know that the face sells more, obviously, but the mentality that you should get is, "If I have any doubts, I'll try them both. My audience will decide."

And after if I see that one of the faces gets more clicks, what do I do? I do a further split testing: I put one with this face and I send to the ladies. Then I do one with the other face and I send to the guys. Then, I do another one with another face and I send to the ladies . . . Boom! We did it.

This is how Digital Marketers should think. You can even change a Call to Action, a message, a colour, or whatever you want. It takes time; I am not saying it is easy. It is cheaper but it is also more complicated to do digital, rather than paying a big agency and putting a banner on Sheikh Zayed Road! You sign the cheque, and it is done. But for digital, you need to work, you need to have your brain working on it every few days, and keep checking, tracking, tweaking, measuring, and analysing. Yes, it is more work, but the results are different too.

Campaign Targeting

There are three ways you can target your campaign:

- Contextual Targeting: Website identifies relevant terms in the site content and phrases, and displays ad where appropriate. E.g.: an article on coffee displays ads from Nescafe.
- Behavioural Targeting: Website anonymously analyses a user's online habits and identifies their interests. Users are then matched to relevant advertisers. This avoids budgetary wastage and irrelevant ads.
- Retargeting: Customers that visit your site and leave without converting are presented with ads for your products on the subsequent websites they visit.

Campaign Tracking

How can you track your campaign? Never by your own experience or by trusting agencies. Trust Google Analytics instead.

Whatever an agency tells you, say, "Okay," and check your Analytics. That is what counts the most.

How to track and monitor ROI:

- Reporting sources include:
  - » The publisher, sales, or ad network (wherever you buy your media)
  - » Internal analytics and reporting
  - » Any offline reports or measures (phone calls, footfall, purchases, coupon redemption)
- Know what reports should include:
  - » Number of Impressions
  - » Number of Clicks
  - » Click Through Rate (CTR)
  - » Conversions

The Digital Marketing Loop

Again, I repeat the Digital Display Campaign Process. You define your customer, publisher objectives, format, budget, media and copy. You configure your targeting and tracking, and go live. Once you are live, you do not stop; you start measuring, analysing and optimising. This is how it is done.

This is why this is a continuative business. You cannot just put digital banner ads on for five days for the special promotion of the month. You need to keep it running. You get branding awareness every day, until you eventually change the banners. People do not like to see the same banner with the same message for 20 years. Of course not! You need to always implement new creatives, new ideas, new things . . . but most of all, you keep it running.

Campaign Optimisation and Iteration

Successful Digital Display advertising is an iterative process. This involves tracking and optimising all aspects of the campaign, including:

- Message/Offer/Product
- Creative
- Publisher
- Ad Format
- Ad Copy

A process of iteration allows you to maximise the effectiveness and ROI of your campaign, helping you achieve your business objectives.

It is never-ending work.

It takes ages to finally tweak and tweak, until I understand what matters the most and what does not. There are some banners that have got a massive Click Through Rate and you look at them and you say, "Really? No way!" Then I realise that the fancy, amazing things . . . nobody cares. I do my crap brand in the face, and I get five times more Click Through Rate!

Conversion: Goals

Luckily for you, we do not measure just how many people click and come to our website, but we are going to see in Analytics how to measure the conversions to our goals. For example, we see that, from that website, we got 10 people clicking and one of them purchased my product. From another website, 1000 people clicked, but nobody purchased anything.

This is what we count at the next level. It is not just to get engagement to your website, but to get conversions. Once we know what converts, what do we do? We cut out all of those websites that drive traffic to our website but get zero conversions.

Nobody knows if those websites got fake traffic and Google did not find out about it, so they still have fake traffic; it does not matter. The bottom line is that we did not convert. If we did not convert, we remove it and focus on those that did convert.

Laws and Guidelines

Be aware that there are laws, guidelines, and conventions that pertain to Digital Display Advertising in your region. Issues to consider are:

- Privacy
- Data protection
- Copyright
- Accessibility

Luckily for you, except for traditional advertising, there are no other rules and regulations. The only thing is that, if you are using Remarketing, you should inform that user behaviour is being tracked and used for whatever purpose in the terms and conditions of your website. There should be a couple of paragraphs explaining this.

You have to add this to be legally compliant about Remarketing. Nobody cares, nobody reads, and nobody knows, but you must put this paragraph in and you will be okay.

This is because, in this age, nobody at the legal level knows what the remarketing is. You do it, and yet, nobody knows what it is!

SEO
SEARCH ENGINE
OPTIMISATION

Concepts

Definitions

Recognise that there are two key aspects to any SEM (Search Engine Marketing):

- Search Engine Optimisation (SEO) is the process of refining your website so that it will be indexed and ranked by search engines, as well as leveraging your links from other sites
- Pay Per Click (PPC) is advertising within search results, and you only pay when the user clicks

These are the "blah blah blah" definitions! For me, the definitions are:

> *SEO is the art of making your website*
> *appear 1st in search.*
> *PPC is the paid (and legal) shortcut for SEO.*

Why do I call it an "art"? Well, even if SEO is something that was born as a task for geeks, there is no a written procedure that you can follow exactly from step A to Z that will guarantee that you are going to be first. It just doesn't work like that.

Also, just because you are first now does not mean that you are going to be first tomorrow. So, while there is a schematic procedure and some steps to follow, there is a little bit of art to it, a little bit of fantasy. When you do everything well, then your position will increase until you reach the top. Otherwise, you can just do Pay Per Click, which is the paid and legal shortcut for SEO.

How do you get to be first in Google? I like this phrase, which was said by an Italian guy who used to be in the United States, "A smile will get you pretty far . . . But a smile and a gun will get you farther." (Al Capone, the famous Mobster)

Sometimes people say to me (probably because I am Italian), "You must know somebody we can make an offer which he cannot refuse. Then he will switch some methods in Google and the next day our website will magically be first!" Unfortunately, there is no such a thing.

I do know a lot of people at Google, not only in Dubai but also in their headquarters in Ireland. I know a lot of experts because I lived in Ireland for few years and worked at Google. Still, not one of them has a clue. I have been collecting information and ideas from all of them and a lot of people they have met working at Google in different offices, in different divisions, in different departments. I have amassed a huge collection of information. Still, not one of them knows the entirety of the secret formula.

As I already mentioned, there are only two human beings that know exactly, precisely, entirely, the secret formula of Google;

they are Larry Page and Sergey Brin, Google's owners and co-founders. But I am sure that if you try to ask them, they are not going to tell you the secret formula. Otherwise, they would be closing up their company the very next day! Despite all this, there are some steps you can take to use SEO to your advantage.

Positioning

In this SEO chapter, we are going to learn how to make your website appear in the organic area. It is not going to happen in one day. It is not like Pay Per Click, where I just put in my credit card, set up my campaign, and in less than an hour, boom! My ad is in the Pay Per Click area.

In the organic area, it is a different game. You need to keep working hard until your website eventually reaches this section. Just like with Pay Per Click, the higher you appear on the search results page, the more clicks you will receive.

Very few users go beyond the first page of search results. It does not matter if it is paid or organic, almost nobody goes to the second page. Therefore, nowadays, it does not make any sense if you tell me, "Ah, I am on the second page. Good!" If you are on the second page, you are in nowhere.

If you are second, you are the first of the losers, because you will get zero clicks.

Know how positioning affects clicks
The proportionality of clicks between organic and paid.

Route to the Customers: *3 hoops*

Any business must jump through 3 hoops in attempting to engage with potential customers through search engines. The key to understanding search engine results is summed up in one word: relevance.

The problem is this: when somebody searches, even if you are first (or second or third) and people click your link, if your website is crap, if nobody answers your phone, if the contact page has a form and when you fill up the form and press okay and the form goes nowhere, you can be first but still have zero clients.

So, make sure the entire path works, from the beginning to the end.

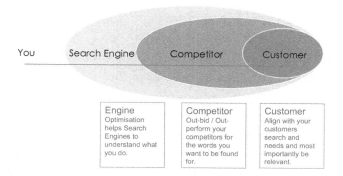

This is the sphere of influence. When people first touch the surface of the Search Engine, they see all of your competitors, alongside your company. When you pass that step, you eventually get the customer. However, it is a competitive endeavour. Most of the job is done by one thing, your best friend—the one you had tattooed on your left hand—the CTR!

Because SEO works this way, the better your Title and your Description, the more people are going to click on it instead of the others, and the more you are guaranteed to stay up there in the rankings. If there is another website with a catchier line and title than yours, then more people will start clicking on it and, after a while, it is going to be first.

Now, that does not mean that, because of the title, your SEO job is done, and you can go to sleep. This is just one of a thousand things that you need to do for SEO. We are going to check out all of them, one by one.

Understand How *Search Engines work*

How does this magic thing of Google work? Well, it works based on Googlebot. Googlebot is a piece of software that runs on Google's servers and does all of the work, like this:

1. *A Search Engine Spider crawls the web.*
2. *Builds an index of the words it finds and their location*
3. *When a user searches, they are searching that index*
4. *The Search Engine presents the most relevant results of the search from the index.*

So, the Googlebot **crawls the web**. It goes to every website of yours, and checks every page of every website, one by one, and reads all the content on your website pages. If you have a 5,000 page website, Googlebot has seen them all. If you have an e-commerce site with 70,000 products, it has checked every product and read every page.

It does this several times a day for every website on the planet. Imagine how much the Google servers are working, day and night, and how many servers Google need to run, to browse all of these websites every single time.

Then, after reading every page of every website, Googlebot **builds an index** of the words it has found in the websites, and writes them down in an index of all the possible words and keywords that it found.

Now, ask yourself, how it is possible that it take 5 seconds to open my website, but when I search in Google, my website appears there immediately? How is it possible that Google is faster than my website?!

The answer is that Googlebot has already been asked and has already created an index. When you're searching in Google, **you are just searching in Google's index**, not across all the websites on the planet.

So, Googlebot has already created the catalogue of who is going to be the first. When I search "Digital Marketing Training", Googlebot already knows the first ten results that will appear. It has already decided the sequence. This is why, when you search, boom! There it is!

The interesting part is—and I want you to tattoo this on your right hand—the Search Engine presents **the most relevant results** of the search from the index. Say I am searching for pizza. Googlebot shows me the most relevant results of the search from the index about pizza. If I am searching for spaghetti, I get results for spaghetti. So, no matter of what any company of yours can do, even if you pay 1 million dollars, if your company does not do pizza, you will not be in the first position when people search for pizza! Even if you pay, you cannot come out first when people search for something else.

This is why it is important to understand this concept. I see companies on a daily basis company that have no clue about SEO. They tell me "Christian, I wanna do SEO for my company and wanna be first when people search Dubai, hotel, restaurant, etc." That is not going to happen, because no one website is the best in the entire universe; not when you globally search for restaurant, pizza, Dubai and hotel! These are such generic keywords. Nobody can put you first for all of them; either you are a restaurant, you are a hotel, or you are the city of Dubai. But if you search for Dubai, there is no way that Google is going to place something else first that is not the city of Dubai. It is therefore important that you understand this topic.

This is what you should put in your mind, so that you understand the mindset of Google. And it is not about tricking Google, it is about finding a way to think like Google. Then you know what to do to please Google. And your ranking will increase a little bit.

On-*site* and off-*site*

There is another important factor: the concept of on-site and off-site. To do SEO, we need them both. I always show the seven secret ingredients to make a pizza on the first day of my seminars. Now if I give you only half of those ingredients, can you make a pizza? No, you cannot. Try to make a pizza without flour, or without water.

Now, if I give you only mozzarella, tomato and olive oil, you can serve them as a Caprese salad, which is very good, very tasty, but it is not a pizza. You cannot say it is a pizza, because it is not. To make it a pizza, you need all of the ingredients.

Now, in SEO, we need all the ingredients. If you put in only one or two ingredients, you cannot say it is SEO, because it is not. The thing is that you have on-page ingredients and off-page ingredients. What does that mean?

On-page is what you do to your website. Your website is your dough, and you need all your ingredients, otherwise there is no point. When we have done all of them, you add some toppings, a little bit here and a little bit there. You continue adding toppings till the pizza is perfect. That is, you continue adding off-site (off-page) optimisation.

The main features that form part of **on-site optimisation** are:

- Code analysis
- Code structure
- Title tags
- Sitemap
- URLs
- Meta-tags
- Alt-tags
- Keywords
- Headings
- Site content

The main features that form part of **off-site optimisation** are:

- Inbound linking
- External linking
- Directory registrations

Now, as you can see, the list of ingredients is quite long for the on-site and quite short for the off-site. But, believe me, most of the SEO agencies only do off-site optimisation because this is the easy part. This is the part they can do by themselves, without needing to modify your website. For example, if the agency does not even ask you for the FTP access to your website, they are not doing on-page optimisation.

To do all of this, you need to modify your website, sometimes a little bit, sometimes substantially. Unless you do that, don't even think you are doing SEO. If you are not prepared to do it, better ask somebody else to do it, otherwise it is going to be a waste of time and you will see no results. Off-site helps, but on-site is the most important.

5P: *Customer Search Insights Model*
Through our searches we reveal who we are.

Now, why do search engines work so very well? Why does Google know exactly what we need, when we search something? How does it give us exactly the results we expect? Because Google knows us. This can be explained using the 5P model.

The 5 P model:

- Person: who the user is, it segments and qualifies them
- Place: location of the searcher as well as their destination
- Priority: the search is an indicator of their timeframe
- Product: indicator of what exactly is important to the searcher
- Purchase: where or how the searcher wants to buy

Google knows the **Person**, exactly who is searching, and because it knows who is searching, it knows exactly what we like and what we want.

It also knows the **Place**. Imagine we are in Dubai during one of my seminars, in a hotel located on Sheikh Zayed Road, and we Google. We get some results. Now, if we go to Milan and search the same thing, we get different results because we are physically in Milan. Now, this is getting better because Google knows where we are based, exactly in this hotel, on Sheikh Zayed Road in Dubai.

Thus, if I search for something, I will get results of things closer to me. If I search "airport", the first results are going to be for Dubai Airport. But if I move towards Abu Dhabi, the search results are going to be for Abu Dhabi Airport.

A few years ago, when you were searching for flights, you had to search "flight from Dubai to Milan". Now, you just search "Flight to Milan". Google knows that you are in Dubai, and you fly from Dubai to Milan, straightway.

Then there is the **Priority**. According to the words that I use, Google know if I am researching, just wandering around, or if I really need what I am searching for, and therefore what is my priority. For example, if I search for something and I write "day delivery", "on time", "online", this means that I am searching for something that I need now. If I search "holiday for next year", it is very different. I am researching, planning, and deciding later. Google knows this.

Let us look at the **Product**. That is the main keyword I am searching for—pizza or spaghetti, flight, app developer, training, etc.—is the product.

Lastly, we look at the **Purchase intent**. If I am mentioning the word "shop", it means I am ready to buy. If I use the words "agent", "agency", "reseller", "distributor" or "supplier", I am looking to buy something. It indicates the purchase intent. Therefore, Google knows I am not wandering around and thinking, I need to buy now.

For example, say your new friend Samantha searches for "agency for adventure holiday in September" and she gets the results. First of all, Google knows exactly who she is: age, sex, and social presence. The place: she is searching from Dubai, so she is based in Dubai.

She is looking for what product? Adventure holiday. What priority? September. So, if we are in May, it is not really a "now" thing. It is not a "today delivery." And the purchase intent: she is looking for an agency. That is all.

Using these easy indicators from the 5P model, the Googlebot mixes it all together and boom! It gives you the results you expect. And amazingly, they are exactly what you are looking for.

Seems, easy? Well, there are actually engineers nearly non-stop behind this. And Google has 50,000 employees!

SEO Process

The process of SEO, again, is an iterative process. First, we start with goals, then on-page optimisation, then off-page optimisation, analysis and again, set new goals and continue.

SEO is an on-going dynamic process with goals, actions, review and iteration

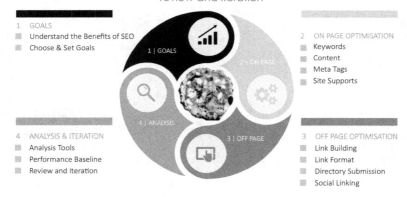

1   GOALS
- Understand the Benefits of SEO
- Choose & Set Goals

2   ON PAGE OPTIMISATION
- Keywords
- Content
- Meta Tags
- Site Supports

4   ANALYSIS & ITERATION
- Analysis Tools
- Performance Baseline
- Review and Iteration

3   OFF PAGE OPTIMISATION
- Link Building
- Link Format
- Directory Submission
- Social Linking

Goals and Benefits

Recognise the goals/benefits of Search Engine Optimisation

What are the benefits of SEO?

Benefits of high listing position in organic search for business:

- Increased click through
- Increased engagement
- Increased conversions

Benefits of high listing position in organic search for your reputation:

- Increased visibility
- Enhanced reputation
- Credibility and status
- Market leadership
- Competitive advantage

If Google places you first, it means you are the best! A lot of you probably think not many people click on advertising and people prefer to click the organic. Well, the truth is, if you are first, you are perceived as "the best," no matter what! And people know you are not paying to be first; you are chosen to be first. Hence, you really are the best!

Now, what do you have to do to achieve this? Ask yourself: Why should I tell my boss, "We need to be first on Google?" Why is important for our business? Why should we put money into SEO?

From the list, choose two goals for your business, and create explicit targets for each one. Write them down here:

_____

_____

_____

_____

_____

_____

_____

_____

_____

_____

_____

On-Page Optimisation

Keywords

On-page optimisation is the process of refining your website so that it can be indexed

and ranked by search engines.

Tools you can use to optimise your website:

1. *Keywords*
2. *Content*
3. *Meta Tags*
4. *Site Supports*

What is a **keyword**? It is a significant word or phrase relevant to the content of your website.

The phrase **search term** refers to the commonly used keywords users type into a search engine to find you.

The Pizza Guide to Digital Marketing

Specify a website, word, phrase or c

Keyword Research

Keyword research means finding the search phrases your customers commonly use.

- Recognise there are **two forms** of keyword research: online and offline.
- Keyword **research tools** allow you to perform filtered keyword research according to the following criteria: custom date ranges, query volume, historical trends, city/country/global; levels of data, related phrases.

Why do I say this? Because you can even do keyword research in a brainstorming meeting, not just using the keyword tool. The keyword tool is very important but I recommend first doing a little brainstorming meeting with your team and your people in different departments because, as I say, only marketers think like marketers. We try to think like a "normal person" but we cannot.

Instead, we ask random people, "What do you call this product?" or "If you wanted to come to our company, what do you think you would search in Google?" Anything that comes out, we note it down. We don't say yes or not, right or wrong; we just write it down. This way, we create a list of possible things, and we keep asking the same question, over and over, to different people. Then we put the list on the Google Keyword Planner.

There are other simple ways to do offline keyword research. One is examining our brochures and all our marketing materials. We read all of them, and we get more ideas. This is because, often in our brochure, our marketing team mentions useful words that give us more ideas about keywords. As we read, we think, "That's right, we also call it that!" By doing this, you can write down as many ideas as possible.

You can even take a look at your competitors. Go to their company website and check what they call their product. Sometimes, they may call the same product something different, so it makes sense to mention all of them, and not just "our way."

Finally, you put all of this in the Google Keyword Planner and that is it. We get a full list of possible keywords. We read all of them and choose the ones that make sense. If we are too generic, no one is going to click it.

Google Trends

Another interesting tool is Google Insights, or Google Trends (the name changes repeatedly).

What does it do? It gives you the seasonality of the keywords; it gives you the trends. That is very useful because it gives you insights into when people are searching for something specific.

For example, if you go on Google Trends (www.google/trends) and you search for "christmas", and then select United Arabian Emirates, this is what you will see:

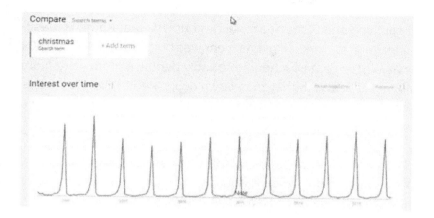

So, if you have a product that is typically sold for Christmas, like Christmas gifts, cards, holiday tours, you can see when people start searching for Christmas in the United Arabian Emirates.

If we select only the last 12 months, we can see people start searching for Christmas in September, and the number of people increases until between December 20 and 26, where you can see a peak. So, October 25th is when we should start pushing our massive Christmas campaign, not because, "Obviously, one month before Christmas!" Nothing is obvious. In this world, what you can prove in numbers, you can do. "I feel I have to start one month before" is not a marketing decision!

It is the same thing for Ramadan. When do we need to plan our campaign for Ramadan? June 7th is when Ramadan starts booming! We can also see that, in Dubai, across one year, if Christmas is 62%, Ramadan is 100%. So, Ramadan is 40% stronger than Christmas in terms of search. If I add Diwali, I can see that it is lower.

I can also check the seasonality. I can see that Ramadan, year after year, is increasing. Last year was crazy! Christmas in 2004 was bigger than Ramadan, probably because there were more tourists . . . and then it goes down compared to Ramadan. This helps me understand when it is effective to start a massive seasonal campaign.

Then, if I change and select Worldwide, Christmas wins. However, we do not care about worldwide statistics, because we have to select the Region where we are based.

If I select India, Diwali wins, Christmas is second, and Ramadan barely shows up. There are also many other keyword tools; some of them are not free, and you just need them when you need something extra that the free Google tools can give you. Anyway, in 90% of the cases, with Google's free tools, you can do more than enough.

Keyword *Tools*

There are many different Keyword Tools. There is Bing Keyword Research Tool, the keyword research from Bing. Don't even think to use it! Do not even waste a single minute of your life on it! There are many other paid tools, like Wordtracker, SEOBook, and WordStream. WordStream is one of the good ones.

You need this kind of a tool, when you reach the top and the basic keyword tool is not enough for you, when you need to analyse more keywords, more data, at a broader level.

There are millions of tools, and every month there is a new one, better and stronger. So, use the Google Keyword Planner as much as you can at first. Then, when you reach the level where you need more, research what are the best tools at that moment.

Google Adwords *Keyword Planner*

Now, let us check out this important Google tool. It is a necessity. Before we look at how to use it and how it works, let us discuss how to choose keywords. You need to:

- Know the sources for keywords within your organisation by:
  » Brainstorming
  » Reviewing marketing collateral
  » Thinking about industry jargon and terms
  » Considering competitors' words
- Recognising and using customer surveys as a way to generate keywords, etc.

Keyword *selection process*

- The keyword selection involves 4 steps: offline research, online research, validation, prioritization
- SEO is not just about courting Google: it is a competitive endeavour
- Rate keywords in terms of competitors, time to achieve positioning and cost of activity
- Long tail keywords: low volume searches that you would like to rank highly for, even though the search terms may be obscure

So, when we get the full list of words, also generated using the Google Keyword Planner, we ponder, "Which ones are good and which ones are bad?" We remove the bad ones; just like we chose only some for SEO, we also cannot choose 1 million keywords. We have to choose the good ones. So, think of it this way, "Is this too generic? Out. Is this too niche? Is nobody going to be searching this? Out. These average ones, good ones, ones in the middle? We'll keep them!" We also prioritise: we choose the ones which have a large number of searches. We want to be first for the keywords that are searched a lot, then for the others.

What do I mean when I say that SEO is not just about courting Google? It is a competitive endeavour, right? It is like when you go to the Olympics. You train every muscle in your body to run faster than your competitors, so you are going to be first. Now, it does not matter if you come first by 1 millimetre or 5 metres. You are first and that is it. If you are second, you are nobody. So, your job is to do every single thing to train every single muscle to be prepared for the race. Here, the race is run every single minute. Every minute, somebody searches. That is a race! 5 minutes later, somebody searches for the same things. That is another race. So, our job is not to be the first, and then just forget about it. Imagine if you said, "Now that I've won a gold medal, I can eat lasagne, spaghetti, and pizza every day, and not train at all!" Well, after 4 years is the next Olympic games. What happens? You lose! It is a competitive endeavour.

We need to do whatever it takes, and keep doing it! Keep maintaining those SEO results. If we abandon it, after a while, we start falling down the list . . . until we disappear completely!

Also, you must rate keywords in terms of competitors. With some keywords, you will know from the beginning that it is going to be very tough, because when you search for that keyword, you see who your competitors are and you think, "I know that's not going to be easy." For example, if you are a software company, and you search "software company", and the first software companies that come out in Google are Microsoft, IBM and Oracle, you think, "I know that's not going to be easy at all!" Do you want to be on top of these companies? It is doable, but you are competing against huge companies with exemplary SEO tactics, a huge number of pages and a huge amount of content! But what if you target a keyword like "software company for Arabic language"? Boom! See, you can be on top of Oracle, IBM or Microsoft. How? Because you are using "long tail keywords."

A long tail keyword is a keyword made with more words. For example, "App company in Arabic language": 5 words. "Arabic app developer": 3 words. Still good. If I want to rank for the word "Hotel Dubai", who is the number one competitor? Burj Al Arab!

So, do you believe that some SEO company can put your Hotel Apartment in Deira first when people are searching for "Hotel Dubai", before Burj Al Arab Hotel? I do not think so! So, chose a keyword that is more suitable for you like "cheap hotel in Dubai" or "beach side hotel in Dubai" or "Dubai Marina hotel beach front". These are keywords that make sense for you, for your customers, and for your business. Because, even if somebody is searching for "best hotel in Dubai", and even if you imagine in your dreams that you can pay Sergei Brin and

Michael Page and you convince them to put your website first, when people click and they see you are not the best luxury 9 star hotel but you are a little hotel apartment in Deira, do you think anyone will ever book a room from you? No! So, you need to be fair, get clicks with the right words, with the relevant words, and then you make a conversion. If I am looking for a cheap hotel and I can see you are clearly a cheap hotel, perfect! I will book from you!

So, the keyword analysis is particularly important for Pay Per Click and SEO. But if you do SEO, it is even more important. This is because you cannot change keywords from one day to the next. In SEO, you will work constantly on the same strategic keywords for months, until you finally reach the first page. And when you are finally on the first page, then you might realise that the keyword you have chosen does not actually bring you any customers, and you have worked for nothing! Therefore, you must do a careful keyword analysis before even start.

On-Page *content updates*
Understanding content writing in on-page optimisation:

- Search engines favor websites that have unique, relevant, and up-to-date content.
- Content updates can contain a broad mix of content: text, photos, videos, slides, etc.

These are the main concepts—you should get these ones tattooed on your forehead! That way, every morning when you go to the mirror, you will see them on your forehead and you will never forget.

Unique content. "Simple! I wanna do an amazing hotel web-site. I will just copy Burj Al Arab's website! They paid a million dollars, I'll just copy and paste . . . done!" Think that will work? No, it is not unique; it is a copy! Say I have a news website. I would just copy CNN and done! Yes, I have made a complete, amazing website, full of amazing content, but it is not unique. That is like when you are writing an exam at school. You copy from your classmate and you do it really well. But the professor will see that the exams are the same and they will expel both of you. The difference is that Googlebot, which enters every web-site 10 times a day, will see which website published the con-tent first, and they will know you copied it because your content was uploaded even just 10 minutes after. Google knows what is unique and what is not. If I copy CNN's content, why should Google send somebody to my website? They will send them directly to CNN instead. Why get a fake? Create an original one!

Relevant content. If I am searching for pizza, I would only get pizza. If I am searching for an app developer in Arabic, I would only get app developers in Arabic. If there is someone else developing an app in Chinese, good, but they don't tell me they are developing an app in Arabic, so for that specific keyword, they will never come up.

Up-to-date content. If I give you the best pizza ever made in Italy, prepared by an amazing pizzeria in Naples and they ship it to you in Dubai, you will get a pizza one month later. Would you eat that? No! Because you like fresh pizza, right?

Google is the same. Why is that? Because users like the same! If you went to a shop and somebody told you, "Oh, I can give you Gulf News Magazine at 50% discount, because it is last week's edition," would you buy it? Do you want to read old news? No, you prefer the new content. So, if your website has up-to-date content? Bingo!

Now, if you have a company doing stock exchange, brokerage, Forex, and so on, you need to publish content not daily, but every minute! If you tell me what happened to the Euro-Dollar 3 hours ago, it is too late. But if you are in the construction industry, or in the crane industry, well, cranes have not changed much in the last few decades. So, if you publish something about six months ago, it is already "wow."

Always remember this: to beat your competitors, you need to be a little bit better than them. You do not need to beat everyone else. You just need to beat your competitors. If you are making a crane website, you need to do a little bit better than other crane websites. Whenever they update the information on their website, you need to do a little bit more.

A content update can be text, photos, videos, slides, and so on. You need to publish fresh Content: unique, relevant, up-to-date. Done!

When you understand the concept of content, you start producing good quality content. It is not free; it costs you to produce good quality content, but it does not cost you a fortune. And when you produce something good enough, you get an audience that reads and listens to what you have to say. So, you need to produce good content gradually, like a good magazine. Not every magazine is good. Time Out Dubai is the best one. Maybe other magazines try to copy it, but the only good one is Time Out.

If you produce good enough content, people will be looking to see the content on your website. However, you cannot think as a marketer. You need to think as a content writer. You need to think as an editor, as a publisher. A publisher publishes a book to give content to readers. I wrote this book not to tell people, "I'm an amazing person! I'm cool!" but to give tips and topics to people, so they can enjoy the content. They would not enjoy it just because you talk about yourself.

You need to do the same in Social Media, and in everything else. Otherwise, you keep posting your boring posts in Social Media, and nobody will see it. To make them see it, you have to pay Facebook to push your boring topic in front of people! This is the big difference. Once you have that concept, then you shift. Then your advertisers start hating you, because you attract more clients than them.

On-Page *content layout*
Understanding content layout in on-page optimisation:

- Know that optimal content layout for SEO includes: page headings, paragraph headings, paragraphs, bold text, links, images, and video.
- Recognise that internal links are important in order to aid navigation and search engine spiders, etc.

Now, I will give you some more tricks when we talk about the strategy. I will give you more ideas, and explain how to easily produce content. But do not forget that, depending what you want to achieve, you will eventually need good, great, and excellent quality content.

One of the reasons why our website looks better to Google is the content layout. Yes, even what the website looks like makes a difference. When a website is so messy that people cannot understand where to go, Google sees that and gives you a minus.

What do you need to include when building good layout content? There should be titles, then sub-titles, paragraphs, etc. Remember that, whenever possible, put your keywords in as many places as possible, and especially in the titles of your paragraphs. Also, when you have a title—also called "h1 Title"—the keyword should be there. Within the paragraph, you have a piece of text, and that should also include the keywords.

When we talk about content, we do not mean any tiny bit of text. More specifically, we mean at least 300 words. If a page does not have at least 300 hundred words of content—not the Title, purely content—it will not be indexed as content. 300 is the minimum.

Normally, people say from 300 to 500. That is what human beings normally recognise as a content. Otherwise, if it is too much, people are not going to like it. But you can use another trick. If you really have a lot of content, you can split it into multiple pages.

Understanding alt tags in on-page optimisation:

- Understand what an alt tag is and how it specifies the alternative text to be used when, for example, an image cannot be rendered, ability to be found in image search, and accessibility.

When there is a picture, it engages the viewer. So, content comprising of images is better. Until a few years ago, Google could not read the text content in pictures. A picture was just a picture.

Now, Google can also read the content of a picture. It does not actually translate pictures, but it is getting close. Despite that, it is still best to have clear texts, titles, pages, etc. Then, in the pictures, you can put what is called the ALT text. This is something for the web developers or webmasters. You, as a marketer, can just instruct your web development team to make sure that the images have the ALT text.

ALT text was invented at the very beginning of the World Wide Web. At the time, if you added a picture, it would take time to load. Sometimes, it even took 30 seconds! So, during all that time, you would be waiting to see the picture. Web developers used to put alternative text so that, while the picture was loading very slowly, you could see what the picture was going to be about. Say they write that the picture is going to be about horse riding in the fields, if I like it, I can wait until the picture is fully loaded. If I do not care, I can move on. This ALT text is what informs Google what the picture is about; if that is your keyword, even better.

Content *balance*

Understanding keyword density in on-page optimisation:

- Ensure consistent subject matter treatment across all the pages of the website.
- Understand what keyword density is: the percentage of times a phrase appears on a page, in relation to the total number of words on a page.
- Understand what Optimal Keyword density is: finding the balance between writing for search engines and humans.

There are some tools that tell you how many times you are repeating keywords in a text. If you repeat them too often, it is not going to work. Some tools, like SEO Book, tell you about what is called the "keyword density." It tells you, out of an entire text, how many times the keyword that you want people to arrive through appears in a text.

There is no clear answer, good and bad. The rule is not to go for these crazy tools that take more time to be learned. The simple rule is to write the keyword as many times as possible, but be proud of what you wrote.

So, according to the English grammar rule, you cannot repeat the same word twice in the same paragraph . . . Listen to me. I do not care about what the grammar rules say. I care about what SEO, Google, and customers say. So, use the keyword as many times as possible. However, the content should be good to read. If you write something like this, as I often say during my seminars, you are producing a big, big crap:

*"Real estate in Dubai is good, because in Dubai there
are many real estate companies, but you wanna buy
a property or rent a property or rent a villa buy a villa
rent a apartment in Dubai and you wanna buy an
apartment in Dubai or you wanna rent an apartment
in Dubai or you wanna buy villa in Dubai or you wanna
rent a villa in Dubai. Where you wanna go, you wanna
go to real estate companies, so which company is real
estate in Dubai? There are many real estate companies. So, you choose a real estate company where it
is. This company is in Dubai."*

Now, the above is a joke, but this is what we call keyword
stuffing. It can be recognised by search engines, and you are
marked as a cheater. And cheaters go out. So, if you were
climbing—slowly, slowly, slowly—and you do something like
this? Boom! Down you go!

The idea, as I always repeat during my seminars is:

"Be proud of what you wrote."

Even in the crazy dream that Google one day places you first
and someone visits your website, if your content is bad, what
will happen? They will close the website immediately. So it is
not just the repetition of a keyword. It should be readable and
as clear as possible.

Don't rely too much on tools

So, there are many tools, but do not rely on them too much.
The tools think they know what Google thinks, but you never

know because the Google Algorithm keeps evolving. There are so many websites that were ranked very high because they used some kind of trick that Google still allowed, but as soon as Google changed it . . . Boom! Down they go.

Have you heard about Google Panda, Google Penguin, and Google Hummingbird? Those are just fancy names for pieces of software that are like Googlebot, but much more sophisticated. They don't browse any page, any website, many times a day. They browse your websites, maybe once every few days. But these new pieces of software, like Googlebot, browse every website on the planet. It normally takes about a month for one of these pieces of software to do this, but they do it with a very high level of sophistication. They browse your website like a human being, checking for freezing, for bugs, for issues, for tricks. If you have been spotted tricking or cheating, someway, somehow . . . Boom! Out! Done! Your website goes from position number 1 to position number 100 in one minute.

Therefore, it is not worth using any tricks, especially those sold by companies that sell you back links and other tricks. "It's only 50 dollars, it's only 15 dollars," they say. Don't go for any of those. It is guarantee that, sooner or later, you are going to go down. If something is so good that it really can put you first, they would sell that for 10,000 dollars, not for 50 dollars. Something for sale for 50 dollars is sold at that price because it is not guaranteed. Or, even worse, it actually works against you.

So, do it properly, and then you will rise. Slowly, slowly, slowly, until you are in first position.

Meta *Tags*

Understanding the importance of Meta Tags in on-page optimisation:

- A webpage is made up of HTML (Hyper Text Mark-up Language)
- HTML is the programming language for web pages and contains several crucial elements for SEO
- A relevant meta tag is an HTML element that provides information about the page
- The four most relevant meta tags are: title, description, keyword, refresh

The Meta Tags are the most important element you have to consider in SEO. Still part of on-page optimisation, you need to change this for every page on your website. Looks like the Matrix movie code, right?

```
<meta name="keywords" content="digital marketing, online marketing, internet marketing, digital media,
<meta name="description" content="Digital Marketing Institute offers professional training programmes
<!-- Place CSS bug fixes for IE 6 in this comment -->
<!--[if IE 6]>
<meta http-equiv="refresh" content="0; url=http://www.microsoft.com/windows/internet-explorer/default.aspx" />
<script type="text/javascript">
/* <![CDATA[ */
window.top.location = 'http://www.microsoft.com/windows/internet-explorer/default.aspx';
/* ]]> */
</script>
<![endif]-->

<!-- Place CSS bug fixes for IE 7 in this comment -->
<!--[if IE 7]>
<link href="/system/css/themes/dmi_theme2012/css/ie.css" type="text/css" rel="stylesheet" />
<![endif]-->

<title>Global Leader in Digital Marketing Education   |  Digital Marketing Institute</title>
```

Now, your job as a marketer is not to write the HTML code or to create the web pages. Your job is to understand what you want to put here. Then you tell your webmaster, your developer, and the company designing and maintaining your website to make sure that your page has Meta Tags.

145

What are Meta Tags? They are additional pieces of information that you declare which Google sees. The most important are: Title and Description.

Above, you can see the browser title: "Global Leader in Digital Marketing Education".

The page title is the one that appears when we search in Google.

Now, it is like if I go to a library and I am looking for a book to lose weight. First, I see all the titles because the books are placed in a vertical position. I spot one book that has a title "The Best Book Ever Written by Professor Christian Farioli." Who is Christian Farioli? I do not know him. I would not even look at the book. There are millions of books and the one next to it is called, "How To Lose 7 Kilogram in 1 Week". That is exactly what I want!

So, I take the book and I look the cover. In that moment, I am reading the next step, the description. But if the title is not good enough, I do not even look at the description. I just skip to the next one. Therefore, in the title, never ever—ever, ever, ever, eve— put the name of your company, because nobody cares about the name of your company. Only the owner of your company and your brand team care about this! Nobody else. So, in the title, put what people need.

The only case where I allow putting the name of your company in the title is when your company name is also the name of your product. If you are looking for a Ferrari, that is a name, that is a company, that is a product. If you are looking for Versace, that is a name, that is company, that is a brand, that is a product. But if you are talking about an event, make sure that the event name also includes as many keywords as possible. Here, in the Page Title that people find on Google, you have only 60 characters to convince them that they need to click on you and not the next one. In these 60 characters, you make the difference between a winner and a loser. With these 60 characters, you build your Click Through Rate.

So, this is the title. In the title, there is more space than 1 keyword because I can put a vertical line, or a simple dash, and I can add a keyword. Sometimes, I put 3 keywords. I put 1 keyword, dash, 1 keyword, dash, 1 keyword. That is my Title. Not any fancy copywriting . . . No! Just 3 keywords: boom, boom, boom! Because even a dog, when they search and they see that this title has your keyword, they click. Think stupid-proof. Not everyone has a master's in marketing, or branding, or advertising from the best university. Normal people look for keywords and they click on keywords, simple as that. Say you are looking for "weight loss," you click on "weight loss." You are looking for an event? You click on "event." You are looking for insurance? You click on "insurance." That is all.

The second Meta Tag is the description. Description in the HTML code looks something like this:

You do not need to understand the HTML code. You just need to tell your developer, "Please, put this Description Meta Tag in this page." This is extremely easy for any web developer to do. It is stupid-proof. Some developers do not want to do it, and not because they do not know. They just do not want to do it because they may need to change the code in a slightly complicated way. However, they can do it. So if somebody says it is impossible, insist.

Now, where does the Description Meta Tag go? It goes in the Search Engine Result Page (SERP). If I change your Description Meta Tag in your websites, you will never notice because, if you look at the website up and down, left and right, there will be no difference. The only difference is noticed by the Search Engine. So, when somebody searches, they see the title, the website and the Description Meta Tag.

The Description Meta Tag length is normally between 120 and 140 characters. Again, people decide to click your website because the title is catchy. "Okay! I read the Title. It is good. Now, what does the Description say? Blah, blah, blah, not interesting at all. Okay, let us see what other websites have to say." They click on the second one. You lost your chance.

The game of Click Through Rate, in SEO, is made up of only two things: title and description. What should we put in the description in those 120 characters? The Unique Selling Point of your company: the reason why should I click your website. Tell me why I should click your website, and not your other nine competitors on the same page. When you convince me with reason within those 120 characters, I'll click on yours. If you fail to convince me, I will click on the next one. If your competitors are more "blah blah blah" than you, naturally I will click yours. But you must play in those 120 characters.

Web developers are the one who add the Title and Meta Tag, but it is a marketing job to choose exactly what to write and where to put it. Web developers have no clue about description. They care about codes, about geeky stuff, not about fancy words or communication. Your Digital Communication expert should do this.

What happens if we leave out the title? Google is so smart that it goes into your website and finds the first title, and uses it as a Page Title. Whatever you have as a title, boom! Page Title. So, you may say, "Then, if we don't do anything, Google finds it, anyway. Cool!" But, eventually, it would not be the best for you. Sometimes, your first title in your first home page is "Welcome! Welcome!" Now, if I am looking for a way to lose weight and the first result is "Welcome"? Well, who cares about "Welcome"? Nobody!

And what about the description? If we do not put the Meta Tag Description, Google

is going to take the first piece of text that it finds in the page and use it as a description. So, what happen with the home page, as most home pages have very little text? Most have fancy pictures . . . and that is it. So, Google goes to the second page, which normally is "About Us." Therefore, sometimes the Description looks like, "The Chairman and Senior Marketing Manager and the CEO are proud to announce that we are a happy company because." And you are done!

So, it is your job here to think, "What do I need to write to make sure that, when somebody searches that keyword and they gets the list, what I have written gets to what they have got in mind?"

Use a Content Management System **(CMS)**

Some Content Management Systems (CMSs) allow you to do this very easily. You do not need a Webmaster. When you create an article, you can add the title and description there. Some other CMSs are not prepared for it, and need modifications because you need to do this for every page of your website. If you have an e-commerce website, with 70,000 products, you need to do this for 70,000 products.

Now, there are ways to help with that. Normally, the Content Management System gets this information automatically. That is, the Page Title is automatically taken from the title that you write

The description is often the same as the short description on your page, but you need to make sure this is going to be something useful. Or you can ask your developer, "Please, run something. Please, add the description and copy the same short description that we have on every page in every product. Copy the same short description for every Meta Tag description."

The developer runs the software once, presses start . . . and boom! One second later, you get 70,000 Descriptions written. But then you need to go through them one by one, and make sure that all the Descriptions make sense and have the key-words and everything you need. Now, to optimise SEO for an e-commerce website is not an easy task, especially if you have products that are not related to each other.

Say I am looking for a dishwasher. I know that Carrefour have dishwashers, but there are shops specialised only in dishwash-ers. So, Google is going to FULL of keywords about dishwash-ers. Carrefour will have some keywords about dishwashers, some about fridges, some about bananas, apple, oranges, fish, meat. It is not going to be easy or feasible to optimise an e-commerce website for that. So what you optimise, if you have an e-commerce website, are sections. You create a dish-washer section, and optimise that page heavily.

At the end of the bottom line, even if the best e-commerce website is completely SEO optimised, the websites that come out first are the reviews websites. Imagine, for example, elec-tronics such as computers.

I search for Asus, the model of my laptop, and out comes a page that is a review of exactly this model of laptop. The review is so detailed, full of content: it is full of keywords, pictures, texts, videos, so of course it is first on the list.

Understanding the importance of URLs in on-page optimisation

Where else we can place the keywords? As I said before, in the URL. Sometimes, the Content Management System creates a URL like this:

1. *www.christianfarioli.com/courses/short-course/ google-analytics-4*
2. *w w w . c h r i s t i a n f a r i o l i . c o m / wp-site?id=3&cat=4&code=4532fd56sdf5*

Which one do you think is better?

The first one is better because it is better for the user, and what is better for the user is better for the whole world. Sometimes, don't try to think too much about what Google would like. No, Google knows that users come first and this is also the main pillar of web usability. Users come first. So, if you want to please Google, ask yourself, "What will my users like the most? Option A or Option B? Option A? Okay, let's do A."

You never know what is happening inside Google. Google works for user satisfaction and usability, so you know that what users like, Google likes. And what Google likes ranks you higher.

Now, we have CMS and we set up. We check with the webmaster to make sure the structure is like your first one. Not every CMS can have a clean structure like this, but, we have recently noticed that the structure is a much larger ranking factor than earlier. Now, they rank you higher if you have a URL like this:

www.christianfarioli.com/courses/short-course/ google-analytics-4

It is a big plus, very big one. Therefore, make sure, if possible, that you have a URL like this. If you cannot, you are not going to design the website anyway, so choose a Content Management System that allows you to have this structure.

This structure also gives you more. When you redesign the websites, if you have a good Content Management System that works in this way, you need not demolish your website and rebuild it from scratch. You can simply change the look. You can change the theme (what the website looks like), but the structure, and most of the content, is going to stay exactly the same. Eventually, I might move the buttons from here to there, or the menu from here to there, or put a bigger picture, a smaller picture, a bigger title, a smaller title, whatever, but the structure will remain the same.

This is what Google likes. Because, every time you redesign your website from top to bottom, you lose SEO. Guaranteed. No matter what, you lose SEO. If your SEO is crap, do it. But if your SEO is good, and you are ranking quite high for many keywords, you are going to lose positions. Guaranteed. So if you try to keep the same logical structure, that is going to save you. You are going to lose a little bit, but not as much. But every time you have a significant web redesign, it makes a massive change.

Now, if you do not have a website, or if you need to develop a website, there are an infinite amount of Content Management Systems that you can use. The one I always recommend is one a lot of web developers don't like, which is WordPress.

WordPress, first of all, is free. I mean, the web developers need to work, right? But the Content Management System is free. It is open source and there are a lot of plugins that you can attach, and you can do whatever you like.

Sure, it is not the safest, because it is free and open source. Sometimes, people can hack into your website from the plugins. I mean . . . people can hack into your website no matter which website you are using, even if you are in the Dubai government! People can hack into all websites. Yes, WordPress is a little bit easier to hack, but it is also the most preferred by Google.

When you do SEO for WordPress and do it properly, boom! When a website is designed with WordPress, you can attach so many things, it is like a turbo boost. You are a normal car and you can put the turbo, the compression, the sleek tyres, the spoiler, and you make the car run like a Formula1 vehicle in no time! With many of the Content Management Systems, making them run faster takes you months of development. Don't bother with that, and opt for WordPress instead.

If you are looking at 10.000 visitors per day, then that may be a bit heavy for WordPress. Still, there are WordPress plugins designed to speed up the website to the max, so that is going to be fine.

The Sitemap

- A Sitemap is a page on your website that provides a map of the website structure in the form of text links to all other pages
- The function of a Sitemap is to help Search Engines find your pages
- The Sitemap should link to every page on your site, and every page should link to it

The Sitemap was a concept invented 10 or 15 years ago in the web, because the websites were so complicated that people used to get lost. When you get lost, you know where you are, and you know where you can go. You click the Sitemap and you have the list of all the sections, pages, and sub-pages of your website, all on one page.

Now, this is good for users, but it is also good for Google because, in one page, Google can see every link of yours. You know that the Googlebot comes to your website and visits your website. It needs to visit every single link on your website to check every single page. When it sees the Sitemap, it knows that it can see all your pages from there. Having a Sitemap like this gives you a plus, but it is only one tiny little plus.

You get a big giant plus if you have a Sitemap like this:

```
- <!--
    Sitemap File Generated by http://www.freesitemapgenerator.com/ at Tue, 24 Jul 2012 11:52:00 +0200
  -->
- <urlset xsi:schemaLocation="http://www.sitemaps.org/schemas/sitemap/0.9 http://www.sitemaps.org/schemas/sitemap/0.9/sitemap.xsd">
  - <url>
      <loc>http://digitalmarketinginstitute.ie/</loc>
      <lastmod>2012-07-23T11:52:01+00:00</lastmod>
      <priority>1.00</priority>
      <changefreq>daily</changefreq>
    </url>
  - <url>
    - <loc>
        http://digitalmarketinginstitute.ie/users/reset_pass
      </loc>
      <lastmod>2012-07-23T11:52:01+00:00</lastmod>
      <priority>1.00</priority>
      <changefreq>daily</changefreq>
    </url>
  - <url>
      <loc>http://digitalmarketinginstitute.ie/about-dmi</loc>
      <lastmod>2012-07-23T11:52:01+00:00</lastmod>
      <priority>1.00</priority>
      <changefreq>daily</changefreq>
    </url>
  - <url>
```

- A sitemap xml: facilitates crawling, indexing, ranking
- It distinguishes between Sitemaps for humans and search engines (sitemap.xml)
- A robot.txt file limits the search engine accessibility to a website

We are going back into the Matrix. This is the XML Sitemap. Your job is not to understand what is written here. Your job is to tell your webmasters, "Please, make sure our website has an updated XML Sitemap." That is it. How do they do it? They Google it. Most Content Management Systems already generate a Sitemap automatically. If not, there are plugins that can be installed to automatically generate the Sitemap.

Because this Sitemap also contains all of the links to your website—every page, including when the page was last updated—it save a lot of work for Google.

How? The Googlebot comes into your website and says, "Ah, how's your website?" And you say, "I have 5000 pages." Big task! It checks page one by one. Page 1, 2, 3, 4, 5 . . . When he reaches page 5000, it says "Okay, bye-bye. See you in an hour."

An hour later, Googlebot returns to see that Page 1 has not been modified, Page 2 has not been modified, Page 3 has not modified, Page 4 *has* been modified. Let me see where. Here! Okay! Updating Index. Back. Pages 5, 6, 7, 8 . . . again 5000 pages.

When there is something like the Sitemap, Google enter and checks. "Let me see the Sitemap," and the Sitemap says, "Nothing has been modified in the last three days." And the Googlebot says: "Okay, bye bye. See you in an hour." It does not spend any energy or resources. One hour later, the website has not been modified. Okay. One hour later, the website has been modified. Where? Googlebot checks on the Sitemap, which says, "Page 436."

"Let us check Page 446," Googlebot says. "Okay, it has been modified. This word has been changed. Okay. Updated. Bye bye. See you in an hour." This addition save a massive amount of workload. Because of this, Google gives you a super plus and a big kiss! After all, this is game changing. This is what you do purely for Google, not for the user, not for anyone else.

Remember you time at school. You write a good exam and score 8. Your colleague writes exactly the same as you, but because he is always interacting with the teacher, he is always engaging with the class, communicating, asking questions, he scores 10 instead. This is what you do in the site. Sometimes, you need to please teacher, not just the public. With this, we make a big difference. Therefore, no matter what happens, this is mandatory. It has to be updated every time you update your contents. It should be run automatically; otherwise you need to do it. There are websites that automatically create the Sitemap, and you upload your Sitemap onto your website. However, it is not going to be updated. I mean, you just tell Google, "Here, look at my Sitemap." But if you do not update the Sitemap automatically and regularly, it will not make any difference.

Now, where we put the Sitemap? Normally it is going to be like:

mywebsite.com/sitemap.xml

We put it in Google Webmaster Tool (now called Google Search Console). That is the best tool you can possibly use to do SEO for Google. It is the tool given to you by Google, so it is certainly not going to damage your website, or your reputation. You need to follow a few instructions, and that is it. Now, this tool is not going to tell you the secrets of what to do; it is just going to tell you some very basic things. If you have a big problem, they will let you know. That is it.

SEO Supports

Webmaster *Tools*
Understanding the importance of a Webmaster Tools for SEO:

- Webmaster tools allow website owners to see how search engines interact with their site
- Common Webmaster Tools: Google Webmaster Tools (Search Console), Bing Webmaster tools

Google Webmaster Tool is not the only option; there is also Bing Webmaster Tool. Do not even open that one, though. I do not even know the URL for Webmaster Tool. I have never used it in my life, but it does essentially the same things from Bing.

Understanding the importance of Webmaster Tools reporting for SEO:

- Webmaster Tools provide reports on: indexation, ranking, penalisation, search terms, errors, location targeting, canonicalisation, etc.
- Submit your Sitemap to Google with Google Webmaster Tools (Search Console)

How does it work?

We can see the number of clicks and it gives us an indication about how our SEO is going, if it is increasing or decreasing, how many URLs there are, but mainly the crawl errors. These are what worry me. To you, it may be look fine, but if there is some error, eventually, other people cannot see your page. But with this, you can identify that before it becomes a problem. That is extremely important.

Off-Page Optimisation

Understanding the elements of off-page optimisation:

- Off-page optimisation is primarily concerned with improving your website ranking
- Things you can do to improve your website ranking:
  - » Link Building
  - » Link Format
  - » Directory Submission
  - » Social Linking

Imagine you contact a company to do your SEO and they do not ask you for the FTP to modify your files and your websites. Basically, they are not doing anything we have discussed so far. How can a company do SEO any of those things? It is impossible! After you have done everything to make the dough, we have to put on the toppings. What are the toppings? Link building, Link format, Directory Submission, and Social linking.

What are they? These things are all part of something called PR. In digital, PR does not refer to Public Relations. It stands for Page Rank. What is the Page Rank? Page Rank is the digital version of Public Relation. Why do we need Public Relations? Because we want to get fans, be popular, and gain trust. This way, others can speak with our company and know that we are a big company.

Page Rank in Google is exactly the same, but in a digital version. How is that? You have your website. At the beginning, Google does not know if your company or your website is trustworthy. So, on a scale of 1 to 10, how trustworthy is your website? Google gives you 0. They say, "Who are these guys? Who knows them? I don't know if they are cheap, if they'll steal my money, or if they even have an office!

Google does not know you, so it will give you 0. Until a company can prove their trustworthy, they are 0.

When we look at, let us say, CNN or CNBC, these have a Page Rank of at least 7 or 8. This means they are very trustworthy. Whatever they look about CNN, you don't question CNN. So when CNN say, "Oh, the Community Development Authority is an amazing company, because they help a lot of elderly people to get easily to Dubai," this means that CNN has a backlink to the Community Development Authority. In this case, not only is CNN a trustworthy source, but they also put their reputation on the line by putting a backlink on CDA. In this case, then CNBC also says, "CDA is a great company, because they did amazing things this year." So Google concludes, "Wow! If these guys are so big and trustworthy, and they link back to CDA. Therefore, CDA must be really big and really trustworthy."

In the beginning . . . there was the Link Building

The more times people link, the more people give thanks, the more the Page Rank gain increases. This was the initial idea that, 15 years ago, got the two guys to create Google. They realised something special that I am going to explain you now.

First of all, Google is not like . . . AltaVista. Have you heard of it? Who has heard about Lycos? Any one heard about Lycos? AltaVista and many others are Search Engines. We call them BG, which means "Before Google."

AltaVista was the first Search Engine ever invented. And what has happened to it, now? You can Google it. This Search Engine was amazing, because it was the only one and was booming! Before, to search something, what did you have to do?

You asked your friends. I used to buy a magazine every week, and there was a review of the best websites so far, and then I would go to a computer and go to the website. But what websites started doing was linking to each other. There used to be some section on the websites, which was called "Useful Links." So, on the Airport of Dubai website, in the Useful Links page, there were links: Airport of Abu Dhabi, Airport of Sharjah, Airport of Qatar, Airport of Bahrain, Civil Aviation Authority of Dubai. Also, on the Civil Aviation Authority of Dubai website, there was a link to Airport, a link to Emirates, many links to the major relevant websites.

This is what started inspiring the Google founders. The previous Search Engines, like AltaVista, only looked for keywords. This made it very easy the people who wanted to trigger the Search Engine. They just filled the website with the keywords and they would win. They were the number ones! But even if the Search Engines worked well, giving good results, at a certain stage, there was an industry that was growing and booming, and saw the potential of Digital Marketing and SEO online. It was the porn industry. The porn industry realised how important it was to be ranked first to get potential clients. So, what did they need? They needed whatever it took to put porn websites first!

There was a time when we used to search "How to cook spaghetti" and the first half of the page was porn websites. How is that possible? There was no way! Then I would read the HTML code to find out how these guys could rank a website that had nothing to do with what I had searched. And I discovered it! They were filling up the website with, "how to cook spaghetti", "how to cook good pizza", "how to cook carbonara", "how to go", "AC Milan", "Milan football".

The Search Engine could not see pictures, so if you took a pornographic picture and called it "spaghetti carbonara", the search engine does not know. As you can imagine, people were getting annoyed. You could not get what you are looking for; instead, you got porn.

Google came in with very strong anti-porn measures and with not only keywords, but Page Rank. You deserve to appear in the results. If you are the big one, you deserve it even more. If I search "spaghetti carbonara", and there is a Page Ranked 1, a Page Ranked 3, a Page Ranked 5, and the Page Ranked 5 normally went first.

Many other Search Engines worked for all the same reasons. For example, they started getting greedy. Running a Search Engine is a very expensive operation. You have big servers, big hosting, etc. Somebody has to pay bills. Who pays bills? Advertisers! At a certain point, Search Engines started placing advertising banners.

You would be searching for something and you would not get the clean results that we are used to on Google. You saw a very big banner! "Toyota is launching the new Corolla tomorrow!" Well, if I am looking for a pizza, I would not care about your banner and I would just keep reading my stuff.

After a while, Search Engines started earning a lot of money. They said, "How can we get more money? We'll put up more banners!" And, after a while, you were searching for something and you needed to scroll down and read the results between all the other advertisements. There was no alternative. It was this or nothing!

But when Google came in with strong anti-porn, no advertising, no banners, that was amazing! The quality of the results was much higher. Boom! In one year, they became the number one Search Engine. This mainly started with the idea of Page Rank. This was a revolutionary idea, a game changer. You can expect that CNN was definitely not linking to any porn website. Therefore, you always know that a high Page Rank means you are a big, good, trustworthy company. Because of this, automatically, boom! All the crap websites were automatically removed. With this, AltaVista was dead. In less than one year, without advertising Google at all, boom! Google became the number one Search Engine.

Plus, they came with a stronger algorithm. For example, many websites were putting keywords on white on white, or black on black. So, if there was a black background, they would write a lot of keywords in black so the user could not see it, but the Search Engines would pick it up and the site would get ranked. But Googlebot became smarter and smarter, and they attacked these tactics. They marked them as cheaters and blacklisted them.

That brings us to where we are right now. Page Rank was the main—and the first—big concept introduced by Google 15 years ago. Now, in all those years, the tricks and strategy involved have multiplied. It is not only about Page Rank anymore, but because it used to be, SEO companies used to base all their strategy on Link Building.

Now, this is one of the things to consider, but it is not the only one. The content, keywords, the Meta Tags; all of these are part of the game. Link Building is not the most important anymore, but it is still good to have because it gives you a start. When you have a new website, if you have no back links, Google thinks, "It's a weird company." It is the same as having a Facebook page with zero followers. That is weird, right?

Now, do not even think of using any tricks. Do not try to game the system. Because every possible game has already been tried 14 and 15 years ago, and not one of them worked. I will give you an example. If, again and again, you are a Page Rank 1, this means you really do not know what you are. Maybe good, maybe bad, I don't know. So one of the oldest tricks was, "Ah, let's create 10 websites and let's send links from those 10 websites to our websites. So we get 10 backlinks." Smart? No! These 10 websites have Page Ranks 0. What is the chance that 10 people decide to open your website, and all of them suddenly link back to the same website that has a Page Rank of 0?! This is called cheating. You remain 0 and you get nothing. Plus, if you want to grow to get Page Rank 1, you need to work twice as hard because now you are a cheater. You are not at 0; you are below that! So, despair.

There were other ideas as well. There were multi-links. Let us say we have 3 or 4 companies. You link to the others and each links back to you. Everyone links back to each other, so everyone generates 6-7 links. Again, there is a link side out. Do not try to do this. The only way you can get a good back link is from a good, Page Ranked website. Any other way, forget it! Don't even think of it, don't even mention it, don't try anything like that!

Inbound *Links*
Understanding the importance of linking formats

How can we build links? There are 4 ways. Recognise different Link Formats:

- Uninformative link: Click here
- URL link: www.vidalsasson.com
- Topic link: hair care
- Keyword link: hair styling like Kim Kardashian (and ensure variety of keywords.)

Let us look at the last one, which is the most important link: the keyword link. For example, say in an article there is "insurance Saudi", or "insurance in Saudi", or "best insurance in Saudi", and it is a link. When you click it, you go to Google area. This is much better because it will identify a specific topic.

For example, "best insurance in Saudi" is a keyword that puts the reputation of somebody on the line. If I asked you, "What does your company do?" and you say, "We are the best insurance company," I would reply, "Ha ha ha! Because you say so?" But if somebody big with a bigger reputation says that you have the best insurance in Saudi Arabia, you really are the best! Then, when I search for "best insurance company in Saudi Arabia", Google will eventually show me your company, because others are saying it is the best in Saudi Arabia, so it should be.

Understanding the importance of quality links

- There is a difference in the quality of inbound linking sites from general directories and classifieds to article sites, up to key influencers and high authority specialised websites

So which websites are better and which are not? This is the pyramid of importance.

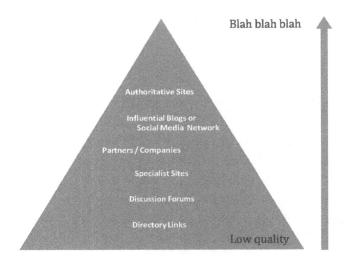

First, look for high quality websites, which are **Authoritative Sites**, websites that people consider trustworthy. It is good to look at the Page Rank, but normally check if it is an authority as well.

Then, go for **Influential Blogs**. Often, these are more popular than traditional media. There are some blogs that have been sold for a lot of money over the past few years, like The Huffington Post. One lady set up the blog and 2-3 years later. She sold it for 7 million dollars. But why was a blog sold for so much? Because it got subscribers. When a blog gets a lot of subscribers, you can sell if for a lot of money!

Influential Blogs is the major choice, because they are not very difficult to convince, and there have human beings behind them. So, you contact the owners, convince them that you have an amazing product, and you publish an article already written by you. Eventually, they will write an article for you, but imagine how many people are contacting influential blogs. The better solution is to get a journalist to write a professional article, and then you submit the article to influential bloggers.

Next, you go for **Networks**, and then for **Specialist Sites**.

Basically, you should try to avoid **Discussion Forums** and **Directory Links**. These mostly provide no value to users. When there are directory links, what is the value? Nobody gets anything. It is much better to choose 3 or 4 big websites rather than 3,000 bad ones. Actually, if you go to 3,000 bad ones, you will probably just go down in the rankings, anyway. But if you choose 3 or 4 big websites and you publish a nice article—full of content, full of keywords, with at least 300 words—then boom! You will go up very fast.

So, remember, it makes sense, just like we do with PR. With PR, you invite a journalist, you organise an event, you talk about your content and, eventually. some of the journalists will write an article . . . but that costs you a lot.

This, on the other hand, is much cheaper if you organise a dinner or little event with Influential Bloggers: they will write a lot about you. Because, when you invite a journalist, they have been doing this for all their life, and they know they are superstars. But with the blogger, they are normal human beings and when you treat them like superstars, they will love you!

One of the first companies that realised the power of bloggers was Nokia, the mobile phone company. Many years ago, Nokia started sending free mobile phones, before the official launch, to key bloggers. Imagine you are a blogger. You are a geek. You like mobile phones. Suddenly, you receive directly from Nokia, the latest of the latest model with the latest features. "Ooh! I got the mobile a week before anyone else!" The people that Nokia itself sent the mobiles to test like to test it. They open the package, and describe every detail about it, and they upload a video.

This is very important: please do not the write articles. Ask a professional to do that. A professional means a journalist, because a journalist knows how to write catchy things that people like. Here, we are not talking about advertising. People love to read articles because they are written for them. So, you need to get a journalist to draft an article for your viewer. That is it.

Remember one important thing: Big Guys! You have to choose famous and influential bloggers. How can we see if a blogger is big or not? Very simple! We Google it and check the Page Rank.

How can you find this out? There are thousands of plugins, if you use Chrome, Safari, or Firefox. Just search for Page Rank plugin. I personally prefer Open SEO Stats plugin for Chrome. I like it because it is complete, and I get a lot of features with it.

What we should avoid in **Link Building**

Be aware of factors that will cause problems with link building:

- Flash content
- Brokers or sellers
- Keyword stuffing
- Duplicate content
- Broken links
- No follow tags

Some factors will cause problems with Link Building, so this is what we should avoid.

Flash content. What is Flash? Flash is a website that appears and disappears like

a flash! I am joking, obviously . . . Flash is a technology that was used to build websites many years ago, because you could add very fancy animations. But the content on flash cannot be indexed by Google, so it is like the page is empty. Don't use it!

Keywords stuffing is when you repeat keywords millions of times without any reason.

Avoid **duplicate content**, especially within your website. Don't make two pages that are the same, Or have the same titles. With two different articles, each must have its own title. If we make a mistake like this, Webmaster Tool is automatically going to tell you. You will see: "Problem, warning: duplicate content". Then you know what is duplicated and you delete, edit, or fix it.

Broken links are also seen as bad usability. Broken links is when you read, " . . . and to check this out, click here!" And you click . . . Error. This is because the same "click here" has been indexed by Google. That is bad. Demerit.

No follow tags is another thing that your Webmaster must know, but it is a minor thing.

The most important things to avoid are duplicate contents and **Keyword stuffing**. Put a keyword as often as possible, but do not stuff it. Apart from that, simply follow the Webmaster Tool.

Whenever Webmaster Tool highlights an error, problem or warning, you can find a way to remove those warnings. The warnings are not a big problem, but if you remove the warnings, you will get another plus.

Understanding content link building techniques
Content link building techniques:

- Creating articles
- Blog posts
- Videos and info graphics for publication / distribution on other websites
- Understand the importance of your web presence in link building: ensure you have presence on all major online platforms (social media, YouTube, Twitter, Facebook) as your listing there may be found in search before your own website
- Links within Social Networks have been included by search engines as influences of ranking
- Directories link building: submission of listings, press releases or product catalogues to directories
- Sponsorship + promotions link building: sponsoring activities and charities, running competitions
- Widget link building: Creating a piece of functionality that other websites can use on their websites
- Be cautious of link buying offers, as paid links are generally in violation of search engine quality guidelines

Now, let us talk about Links within Social Networks. Facebook has Page Rank 9, but not because you put a backlink to Facebook. No, it is because, when Social Media came in, Google started revising its algorithm. Facebook has a Page Rank 9, but if you check the Page Rank of every Fan Page on Facebook, the results are "unknown." It is the same story for big pages. Even Jennifer Lopez, the Queen of Facebook with 45 million likes, has a Page Rank "unknown".

What can you do to build links? You submit links to directories listings, but you need to check which directory listings have a Page Rank. There are many directory listings that are absolute crap, and using those makes no sense.

Be careful of link buying offers. Whenever someone is sending you a link or a backlink, 99% of these are in violation of Google policy. So, you should never go for it. It does not matter how much you pay for it. Normally, every link billing offer is mostly crap. If they sell you a back link for 10 or 15 dollars, it is complete crap!

Analysis

Tools

Understand how analytics can help with reporting and measuring a sites SEO performance:

- Analytics Tools enable you to track and measure the Search Traffic to your website
- Common analytics tools such as, Google Analytics, Stat Counter, Omniture, etc.

There are many analytics tools that help you doing SEO. And you can measure, and track, or whatever you need to do. There are many tools, but I prefer Google Analytics: firstly, because it is Google and secondly, because it is quite accurate in terms of filtering good traffic from bad traffic.

There are softwares browsing the internet, and many analytics platforms cannot recognise that software. They think it is a normal person, but that is not true. So, you may think, "Oh, we got one hundred visits today." However, it may not be true. It may be some software checking it out, so you get a fake number of views. But with a big platform, they normally filter out most of the bad traffic.

Baseline

Understand what metrics are needed to analyse SEO performance

The criteria against which you will measure your website's performance:

- Can it be found?
- What Page?
- What Position on the Page?
- Is it technically complete?
- Who is above you?
- Traffic from each Keyword?
- Conversions from each Keyword?
- Keywords used to find your site that brought organic traffic to the site
- Record your performance to rate the effectiveness of your SEO activities

If you are doing SEO, or if you have a person, a team, or a company doing SEO for you, you have to measure your website performance based on this.

First of all, ask the question: **Can your website be found?** Because sometimes, even many times, new companies put their website out and tell me, "Christian, even when I search for my website, it does not come up: How is this possible?" Sometimes, the SEO is done so poorly that this happens.

Next, what page? What position on the page? I can give you another trick here, to check which pages have been indexed by Google, and how many pages your website has in total. If you type "*site:mywebsite.ext*" in the Google search bar, you will see the pages in your website indexed by Google, along with the title and the description of each page. Here is an example:

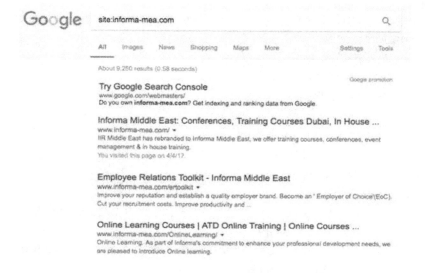

In this case, I can see that the Informa website has 9,250 pages indexed by Google. Then I see the home page with the title and description, followed by every other page. This is every possible page listed. You got the point? So, if you are optimising or trying to understand what is going on, you can see exactly every page, every trend, every title.

Then how do you rate your SEO? Is it technically complete? Are they doing all the things that we have discussed?

Who is above you? That is especially important. If it is a massive company then, to some extent, they deserve it. But if there is a very little company, like a little garage, maybe you are doing something wrong, and you can do better.

You can also check whoever is above you: what is their Page Rank? Is their Page Rank 1? If so, you can easily beat them just by tweaking a little more. The Page Ranke is 8? That means you need do something different. Focus on another keyword.

Do you get traffic from each keyword? Have you checked Webmaster Tool or Analytics? How much traffic is each keyword generating? When you see that you are ranking very high for a keyword but you are getting very little traffic from that keyword, or even more importantly, very little conversion, you are wasting your time.

Conversions from each keyword? This is what I just mentioned, and it is even more important. If you are number one, and you get 50 clicks but 0 convert, that is bad. So, it is good to rank first, but if you don't convert, don't focus on that keyword. The ones that convert are the best keywords for you!

If the situation is, "Yeah, I'm converting and I'm in position number two, I'm good," you need to do whatever you can to get to number one, because this is your best keyword. You are going to bring much more revenue to your company by using it properly.

Check which keywords are used to find your website that brought organic traffic to the website. The Webmaster Tool will tell you about keywords that possibly you do not even expect. For some reason, people are entering your website from that keyword, and you have no idea why. But it is like that. If people are coming, let us get them to come even more. You did not know that there was a gold-plated mouse making people enter your website, but now that you do, use it!

Record your performance to rate the effectiveness of your SEO activities. When you have a platform like Analytics, it is easy. You can go to the history, and see how your performance is during the month, the week, etc.

Keep in mind that, every day, new people are creating new websites, and more people are doing more SEO. So, wherever you are right now, every year is going to be more difficult to maintain the same position. If you are first now, it is easier to maintain that position, rather than wait two years, realise you are nobody, and have to start again. If you are number one, keep it that way. If you are not, try to make it happen as soon as possible because everyone else is doing exactly the same.

Analysis *and review*
Understand ongoing tasks needed to boost SEO performance:

- Maintain a weekly and monthly calendar of website performance against baseline
- Record any notable events that would drive organic traffic to your website: PR, marketing, competitions, etc.
- Assess the impact of your activities, spot any trends, and identify remedial action
- Understand why it is necessary to schedule a monthly keyword research exercise to ensure you are being found for the right keywords and phrases

What tasks do we need to do, on an ongoing basis, to keep and boost the SEO performance?

Make a weekly and monthly calendar of the website performance against baseline. For this, I have another tool for you, which is called the "Page Speed Test":

https://developers.google.com/speed/pagespeed/insights/

We put in the website, we wait a few seconds, and it gives us the speed and usability test based on mobile and desktop. If it is red, you have to work a little bit on it. If it is yellow, it is just acceptable. If ti s green, it is perfect. Now, the main aspect that makes the difference is when you leverage the browser caching. This is when the web developer enables some caching functionality that speeds up the website a lot. This also optimises images. Even an image that, to us, looks amazing, is eventually too big. Normally, if a website is not well optimised, many images can be compressed a lot (only the size, but leaving the same resolution, look, and feel, so nobody notices the difference) to save a lot of space and make the page load faster. That is always guaranteed to help. You will learn many tricks, but normally the browser caching and images are the first in need of being optimised.

On mobile, it is exactly the same, because on mobile, you see everything smaller. So you do not need the same high quality picture, you just need a smaller one. In traditional Content Management Systems, this can be complicated. This is work needs to be done manually. You have to download all of the pictures from your server, and then optimise all of them crazily and re-upload. Alternately, if you are using a Content Management System like WordPress, you can use plugins that automatically compress the images.

There are a lot of things in this field, but it gives us an idea because Google recently announced that, in terms of SEO, you get ranked higher if your website is fast. Now, in major user experience flow, it is still speed.

Sometimes, people open a website and it takes too long to load. It takes 10 seconds, 8 seconds; it is still too long. It needs to be faster. How can you make it faster? First, compress the images. Second, follow some of the recommendations. Now, you cannot do everything, because some of the things are physical, and some of them depend on the CMS. But the more of the advice you follow, the faster it becomes, and soon, the Rank rises.

The other thing that has been announced since April 2018 is that the website has to be mobile friendly, otherwise your SEO is going to go down.

SEO Golden Rules

Now, this is the recap of everything we have learned so far for your SEO strategy. Once you have done all of this, you are the King of the Planet! You may say, "Oh, it's

easy!" Be careful: it looks easy, but it is not. Every one of these things involves a lot of attention to detail. But these are the best things you can possibly have:

- Fresh Content (Unique yes/no, blog curation)
- Relevant (Keywords, Titles, Texts, Metatag, URL, Images)
- Google love Google (Tools, sites, blog, YouTube...)
- Navigability
- Site Structure (Sitemap)
- Links (Inbound, Anchor)
- Mobile Phones Friendly (mobile sitemap)
- Videos & Links
- Social Media Links
- TIME on site (Interesting Content, better than competitors)

Fresh Content

First of all, fresh content. If you create content, create fresh content. Do not copy others. If you do not know what to write, use content repurposing. Clever companies use the concept of repurposing. One example is the weather forecast in the United States. When you go to United States and you watch the TV, you can see hundreds of channels about the weather forecast. Everyone in the USA is getting crazy about weather forecast! You need only one, right? But the weather forecast is just one little piece of content.

When the content is "It is going to rain, tomorrow," what more can you say about that? Nothing. But they got clever! For example, when I was in the USA, on one of these channels was a lady in a bikini and high heels, with a tight T-shirt, giving the weather forecast. And when they say, "Tomorrow it is going to rain," you see a big shower on her dress that makes her T-shirt very tight. It is the same piece of information, repurposed into different content. So, whatever information you repurpose, in a crazy way, in a funny way, in a curious way . . . you can get traction. It is not important what you say, but how you say it. If you say it in the same, boring way that magazines are saying things, you will get no clients, no traction, no SEO. You will get nothing.

Relevant

Remember, the Keywords are at the centre of your Digital Marketing work. Where do you put the keywords? Everywhere! In Italy, we say, "We put them in like parsley. Everywhere!" Because, in whatever dish we cook, we put in some parsley. Absolutely everywhere!

Whatever you do, you have to put in the Keywords. Everywhere. Even in street banners, put in the Keywords! Say you took a picture and are about to post it. Wait, wait, wait! Before posting, let us see the name of the picture. Put the Keywords in the jpg file name. Especially in titles: Page Title, Paragraph Title. Put it in the text, the paragraph, the Meta Tags, the URL, the images, in the videos, the PowerPoint presentation, the pdf file. Wherever you can, put it in.

Now, I can tell you even more. YouTube is also listening to the content of your videos. There is a voice recognition software, and you can get subtitles automatically generated for your video. On YouTube, you can use the functionality called "Enable automatic subtitles." Now, this content is indexed. Therefore, video content is also being indexed in terms of words used. If I use keywords, keywords, keywords in my video, eventually, people on YouTube searching for those keywords will find my video.

So, whatever you do, wherever you go, even on the street, you have to keep your keywords in mind. This is what people look for. This is the tendency now, because of Google. We look for keywords. We don't read the entire content anymore, because we recognise the common keywords. So, your life is going to be a keyword, now.

Google love Google

This is a crazy, clever concept! I learned it from a guy who was working for Google, at the main headquarters in San Francisco. He was a speaker at an event and he came out with this concept. Imagine you own a multibillion dollars company, and one of your accountants left. You need to hire a new accountant. You have a list of many accountants who would like to work for your company, and you have a son. He has just finished university, has a first degree in economics, and is looking for a job. Who would you put first? Your son! There we are. Google does exactly the same.

When you search for a video, out of all the video websites, which video comes out first? YouTube! It is such a coincidence that YouTube is owned by Google! Such a coincidence that Google shows you all Google properties first!

And, when you go to YouTube, you keep seeing advertising—still from Google. Then, from Google, you click, you go to some other places—possibly owned by Google again. Now, there are some blogs owned by Google itself. A popular blog platform is Tumblr. So you can guess that, when you put up a backlink or write an article in that platform, you get a big hug and kiss from Google! So, every few months, I do something: I search which companies Google has recently acquired, and whatever they are, I try to use as many of them as possible.

Many years ago, many companies said, "No, we're not going to put our corporate video on YouTube, because it is only for stupid videos. We are a serious company and we cannot be on YouTube."

If you use YouTube, your ranking increases. That is it.

Navigability

If your website is easy to navigate, it is a big plus. That is not easy to do, though. "Okay, I want an easy to navigate website!" Okay, you can pay a million-dollar company like Leo Burnett or something, and they build an amazing, easy to navigate website. Or, you get a free WordPress website. Same thing.

Site structure (Sitemap)

The Sitemap, mainly the XML Sitemap, is the most important. This is the number one priority.

Links

This includes links, inbound links from other website to your website, and eventually anchor links or internal links. You can have a section of your website where you talk about, say, App development, and the word "Arabic App developer" is linked to your home page. So, even within your website, you have a nice article, and you link some of the keywords back to other pages on your website. Now, don't create a mess, because when you are creating internal links, there should be only a few, good links and not a bunch of backlinks. You should put maximum one or two links per article to specific sections of your website that talk about that topic. Don't link to the home page randomly for no reason. Link only to the relevant pages!

Mobile phone friendly

After Android acquisition and after April 2015 when Google announced that, if your website is not mobile friendly, you are out, this has become important. Also, in 2012, Google purchased an Italian company (Move Mobile) that helps you to transform your website very easily into a mobile friendly one. If you have a straightforward website, there are some tools that, kind of automatically, transform your website into a mobile friendly one.

For videos and links, possibly put videos on your websites: obviously just YouTube video, not everything else. It has been statistically proven that if your website contains a YouTube video on the home page, the chances of being first increase by 45%.

Social media links

At very least, make sure you register on every Social Media Network and make sure that, in every description or the "About us" page, you put your website's full URL.

Time on site

This is one I came up with by brainstorming reverse engineering ideas, people, and things: time on site. Exactly when YouTube came out, it was clear that if you put a YouTube video on your website, in a matter of one day or less, your website would appear on the first page. We were thinking, "That's unbelievable! That's impossible!" It is true, in one day! Then they changed the algorithm a little bit.

Still, the idea for me was clear. Google always focuses on telling you "Content is King." You need to provide good quality content. Now, how can Google know if something is good quality content or not? The answer is: time spent.

If I write an entire page full of stuff, but you enter my website and immediately leave, that is no good. A lot of content does not equal good. CNN has a lot of bad content; people want to cut it. But when people stay on your website longer, they visit more pages, which means the website is good. When you don't get bounce rate, when you enter in the website and you stay, and you read, and you click, then it is a good website!

Google, thanks to Analytics, knows that, and thanks to Google Chrome as well. Even if you do not have Analytics on your websites, but people come to your website and browse from Google Chrome, it knows which websites people browse. And it knows that, when people are searching for insurance, and they go to this website, that website and that website, but they spend a lot more time on one of those websites, it means they prefer the content on that website more. So, here we are. Bingo!

Clearly, when you put a video on your website, people stay longer, even if it is a small video. If it is a 1-minute video, instead of staying 1.5 minutes like on every other website, they spend 2.5 minutes on my website because they click play and they watch. After 1 minute, the video ends, they continue reading, they leave, they do whatever

they want. But amazingly, boom! I increase time spent on my website by one minute! This is why, whatever you are doing, keep the user on your website, especially on the home page, because people usually just spend few seconds there just to understand what your company is about. But if you have enough content, or a video, then people will stay longer.

My secret is to write 300 words on the homepage. Whether people read it or not, I don't care; it's not my business. Some of them want to read and they read. And it is not extremely long. It is more than anyone else, though, because nobody puts 300 words on a home page. I put it. Still, it is not a huge amount of text. Decent, with a good title, good paragraphs, good content, good enough. Some people may skip it, fine. But still, because you see the paragraph and the title, you know that the website is going to be talking about that topic. That means you are going to spend more time to see what the website is about. You know this is going to be what you wanted; you know that for sure.

When people spend time on your site, boom! You are number one! You write interesting content, at least better than your competitors, and you win! Remember, the look and feel of the site works only for the first 5 seconds. You get the perception that it is good or bad very quickly. But even websites with no graphics are good, and Google is teaching you that. Look at Google's home page. There are no graphics, there is nothing. There is only one box in the middle asking you what you want. You search, and you get the results, which is only text. Therefore, the fancy graphics, at the bottom line, are not really worth it.

PPC
PAY PER
CLICK

Concepts

Definitions

Definitions of **Search Engine Marketing**:

The process of placing "pay per click" ads in search engine results pages.

Definition of **Pay Per Click**:

The revenue model adopted by search engines whereby the advertiser only pays once a user clicks on an ad.

What is Pay Per Click? I call it the shortcut for SEO. When you don't have time to wait for SEO, you pay Google and you are first, or almost first.

When we talk about SEM, or Search Engine Marketing, we also talk about Pay Per Click. Now, for me, SEO and Analytics are related to Pay Per Click. Why is that? SEO, because I just told you that Pay Per Click is the shortcut for SEO. Analytics, because, especially when you are paying per each person coming to your website, you want to know how much you are paying and how many people you are getting there, and want to know how many of those purchase the product from you. If you get a thousand people on your website and nobody buys anything, you are just wasting money.

SEM is an on-going dynamic process with goals, setup, management and review & Iteration.

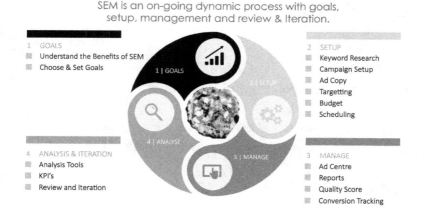

1   GOALS
■ Understand the Benefits of SEM
■ Choose & Set Goals

2   SETUP
■ Keyword Research
■ Campaign Setup
■ Ad Copy
■ Targetting
■ Budget
■ Scheduling

4   ANALYSIS & ITERATION
■ Analysis Tools
■ KPI's
■ Review and Iteration

3   MANAGE
■ Ad Centre
■ Reports
■ Quality Score
■ Conversion Tracking

Search Engine Marketing **Process**

How does the Pay Per Click cycle work? First of all, we set goals. Remember that before you start any digital marketing channel, any digital marketing campaign, or strategy whatso-ever, you always set some goals. These must be aligned with marketing goals, and with business goals.

Once we have set the goals, once we know why we are going to do Pay Per Click, we setup the entire account, we do the keyword search, setup the campaign, write the text, choose the targeting, decide the budget, and schedule the campaign. Then, we manage the campaign, looking at the numbers and the reports: what is working and what is not. Next, we start tweaking it, and finally, we analyse and finish tweaking the campaign. We then set up new goals and the circle continues.

All digital campaigns work this way. There is no such a thing doing setup once and then forgetting about it. As you know with Social Media, where you need to post on a daily basis, you don't just post random things. You plan and you post based on what works. This is why the analytical part is always important, not just on your website, but on any platform that you use. Because, after six months, if you post 720 posts, obviously there will be some that had amazing success, and others that got absolutely nothing. So, after six months, you check and understand which were the best posts. What you can do? You can either repeat them, or just find some similarity and post similar things. In digital, we do the same. We launch a campaign, then we check what is working, but we do not need to wait six months. Usually, we do it on a weekly basis, or on a monthly basis maximum. So, that way, we will keep implementing and improving.

Now, we are going to talk about the concepts of SEM, goals, campaign set up, campaign management, campaign analysis and, luckily for you, laws and guidelines that are pretty much nothing. Actually, in the last few years, a few laws and guidelines have come out, but almost nothing, so you are still lucky.

Search Engine Marketing **Definition**
What is the definition of SEM?

"The process of placing Pay Per Click Ads in Search Engine Results Pages" (source: Digital Marketing Institute)

So, we place Pay Per Click Ads in the Search Results Page. Pay Per Click, by definition, is:

> *"The revenue model adopted by Search Engines whereby the advertiser only once a user clicks on an ad." (source: Digital Marketing Institute)*

Recognise that there are two key aspects to any SEM (Search Engine Marketing) strategy: SEO (Search Engine Optimisation) and PPC (Pay Per Click).

Here is a little more about the definitions and concepts involved:

- **Search Engine Optimisation (SEO)** is the process of refining your website so that it will be indexed and ranked by search engines, as well as leveraging your links from other sites
- **Search Engine Marketing (SEM)** is advertising within search results, and advertiser only pays when the user clicks
- **Strategy Considerations** when to apply PPC:
  - » Filling gaps where organic reach is weak
  - » Strengthen visibility
  - » Early and immediate access to market

Positioning

Now, we are going to see when it is good to use Pay Per Click, when it is good to use SEO, and when it is good to use both, because positioning works for both. SEO and Pay Per Click are in exactly the same league. Somebody searches something and the search results come out. Some of the results are paid listings, some are organic listings.

How many results are there? Now, until a few months ago, there used to be three paid results on top and then eight results on the right, so a total of eleven. It has not always been like this. At the very beginning, when I started doing Pay Per Click in 2003, there was only the lateral one and there was only a few Ads (maybe three) because nobody was doing Pay Per Click.

It increased, but normally almost nobody clicked the lateral advertising. So, Google added one line of advertising. But it did not put the one that paid the most there; it put the best Advertiser there. Now, I am going to explain you what

I mean by the best advertiser, and how to make sure you deserve the first position. It is based on what is called the quality score.

After a while, Google realised that it is good to be on top, but if you are on the right instead, you get nothing, and companies were not ready to give more money for this. So, they started putting two results on top and the others on the right, until they later said, "Let's put three paid ads on top and the others on the right." Now, they scramble the concepts, because if you are on the right, you get a really, really, extremely low number of clicks. This is why the system changed, and now there are four ads on top and zero on the right. That is just for now; nobody knows what it will be in three or six months, or one year.

Now, what happens if there are five advertisers? What happens if there are twelve advertisers? Before, they were on the left. Now, they mix them: if there are four, sometimes, you are fourth, sometime, you are not there, sometimes you are there. They give a little bit of possibility to all of the advertisers to be there, but they make you appear there more often according to, again, the quality score.

This is the game: how to make sure that, if we pay, we are going to be there? The good thing for you is that, if you are not there, for sure nobody is going to click, and you do not have to pay. That is a guarantee. But if you want to be there because you want to get clicks, you will need to learn what you need to do.

Know how positioning affects clicks

- The higher a listing appears on the search results page, the more clicks it receives
- Few users go beyond the first page
- Increased enquiries and sales
- Better brand awareness online
- Valuable market information

The concept of positioning is a very clever thing. The higher a listing appears on the page, the more clicks it receive.

Few users go beyond the first page. I don't know if you remember when the last time was that you did not find what you were looking for on the first page, and you had to click on the second page. It was probably days or weeks ago, right? If you think about when the last time was that you did not find what you needed on the second page and you had to go to the third page of Google, you probably would not even remember, because 99% of the time, the results are on the first page. If you are not on the first page, you are nowhere.

But the concept of positioning is very interesting because it says that the higher a listing appears, the more click it receives. But it is not just about clicks; it gives you better brand awareness. Because, where do we start reading? We start reading from the top. If our result is at the top of the page, everyone is going to read it, even if people do not click. Everyone is going to see our name, brand, company, and products for free, because if people don't click, we don't pay.

Also, they give you a business advantage because now it is not about television advertising any longer. It is a Google centric world. This means that whichever website Google places first is the best for us! Before, whatever they put on television used to be good. The big brands were on TV; not anymore. Now, the big brands are those that appear on top of Google, because we trust Google more than our mother, brother, sister, nephews, nieces, teacher, doctor. When you feel a pain, you Google it, right? So, imagine that a doctor studies all of their childhood, plus five years of medicine, plus three years of a master's degree in medicine, plus crazy exams, plus two years of internship to become a doctor . . . and you Google it! How sad is that? And even if the doctor tells you, "You need to take this medicine," 50% of the time, you Google it just to be sure, because Google is more accurate than your doctor, right?

Why is that? Why do you think we trust Google more than all these people? There is a reason. Google, with time, has gained our trust. How is that possible? I will give you an example. You just met me yesterday; you don't know if I am a good person or a bad person. You spend a day with me. If you say to me, "Ah, you are Italian. Could you recommend a good Italian restaurant?" Now, you don't know if I am going to tell you the truth or if I am going to tell you a bad choice. You don't know if I am going to send you to some dodgy place and they are going to steal all of your money, or to a place where you get poisoned, or if I will send you to a restaurant where I have some shares, and they give me a commission for all of the clients that I send there. You cannot know. But, if I send you to a place and you have a lovely meal, the next day you think, "Yeah, Mr. Christian was right!" Then, the day after, you ask me, "Where can I eat the best spaghetti?" Again, maybe you just got lucky with the first one, but if I give you a reply and you go to that restaurant, eat the spaghetti, and think it was really good, the next day you will probably ask me where you can get great lasagne, or something else.

So, imagine if you were able to ask me 100 times a day for several years, and 90% of the time I am right? You would trust me blindly! You would not even question if it is good or not to ask Christian where to get medicine. You know that I am right.

This is why we trust Google so much. Plus, for some reason—for some magical reason—whenever we search for something, the first few results usually give us exactly what we are looking for. We do not even understand why, but we take it for granted.

Common Terms

Key search terms

- **Common Terms:**
  - » CPC (Cost-per-click)
  - » PPC (Price Per Click)
  - » Paid search
  - » Paid Search Engine Marketing (SEM)
  - » CTR (Click Through Rate).
- **Common PPC tools:**
  - » Google Adwords
  - » Bing and Yahoo Adverting
  - » Search Alliance

CPC stands for Cost-per-click: because we are paying for it, we need to know what CPC is. If we work with an agency or if we hire somebody doing SEM, or if we are doing SEM, this word is something that you use on a daily basis: CPC (Cost-per-click).

Some people use the word PPC to say Price Per Click, but that is wrong. Why is this? You have to know this is not an exact science; there is no PhD about this. This is a common sense terminology.

Paid Search is the area where the paid advertising appears. Sometimes they call it Paid SEM or Paid Search Engine Marketing.

And our best friend is the CTR. You have to tattoo CTR on your left hand! Seriously, most of the strategy works around the CTR. When you ask me, "How can I be first?" I can tell you that one of the most important things you need to get is CTR; not more money, not larger budget. Just get more CTR. We are going to see how.

What are some common **Pay Per Click tools**?

The most common one is Google Adwords, which is the platform that allows us to put money and setup everything to make sure that Google is placing advertising in the Paid search area.

There is also Bing and Yahoo advertising. What is a Bing? It is a search engine by Microsoft. Usually people say, "When it's not Google, it's Bing," but what is the percentage? Bing is around 3% to 4%. Google 95% to 96%. Is it worth doing a Bing campaign? No. I can tell you who use Bing: people who are not technology savvy. Don't spend even one minute of your life on it because it is not worth it.

I call the people who use Bing "grandpa." Why is that? Because when grandpa goes to the supermarket, to Carrefour, he sees a laptop on special offer of 600 dirham. "Amazing! Finally, I will buy a computer!" Grandpa buys the laptop, goes home, charges it up, switches it on, and there is an icon for Internet Explorer. He opens it, and there is a search box. He searches and the result comes out with Bing. Now, the next time that his grand-child comes to visit grandpa, they will say, "Grandpa, don't use Bing and Internet Explorer. I'll put Google Chrome on for you." Grandpa does not understand what is going on, but from the next day, he also uses Google. Even he is out of the 4%.

There are Search Alliances and other Search Engines, but we do not care about them.

The only exception is if you are targeting China because Google does not work in China, so you need to do everything on Baidu, which is the Chinese copy of Google. The Chinese copy of Google works pretty much the same: last year, their revenues were more than $7 billion.

The User Journey

Pay Per Click Marketing provides acess to the complete user journey.

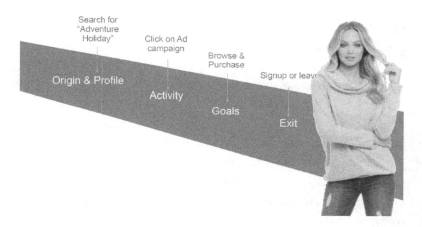

Always think, when you plan a campaign, that the campaign is not everything. In Digital Marketing, you need to think about what happens before and after.

When people search on Google, they normally click on PPC or on organic results. Now, because you do an amazing Pay Per Click and your result appears on the top, or you do an amazing SEO and your result appears first, it is not guaranteed that that is enough. It is good, but it is not the entire big picture, because yes, you get the user clicking, but what happens next? They may click your website, and the website takes too long to load.

Some users click back. If they go to your website and they do not find the information they are looking for, or the information is too confusing, they leave. If they do not understand the language, they leave. If they go to the product, they like the products, they call you and you do not answer the phone, they hang up. And then what do they do? They click the next one.

Just because you are first does not mean your job is finished, because you don't want to just get clicks, you want to get clients. You have to make sure that the entire process works. Normally, the customer can find the phone number, or where to put in their credit card, or shopping card, or whatever to pay. But what if they go to the contact page and they do not understand, or there is the only an 800 number and you are based abroad so you cannot use that number, or if you have some people answering the phone in a way that is not helpful or is boring? It does not work.

Do not expect that you are going to get a lot of clients because you place your company first. Make sure that something happens after they click. Even when people browse through your website, it should be designed with the main criteria to make it easy to understand, to clearly explain what your product is, what you are offering, what are your benefits, and the Call To Action (CTA). Then visitors reply to the Call to Action and go to the contact page, they should easily be able to contact the company, or download the document and so on.

This is an important concept because a lot of clients hire people or suppliers to do Digital Marketing and then they don't see any increase in sales. They tell me, "We are selling exactly what we were selling before."

You need to measure what is going on, but you need to make sure that, after people come to your website, they know what to do.

The beauty of digital is that we can see the entire user journey in the digital world. For example, we can see that the user searched for something, clicked an ad, browsed the website, and eventually purchased and left, or left without purchasing.

We track what is going on so that we know at what point the user finally decided not to proceed with the purchase. At least then we know what stage the customer got to. That means we can tweak, we can change, we can try some trick to make sure that the next one is possibly going to buy something.

Benefits of PPC

Key Search Terms

- More than anything else, it is the level of **Intent** revealed by the user that makes PPC marketing work, as the user is self-qualifying
- **Relevance** factor and reaching the right people who are interested
- **Timing** factor and reaching the right people at exactly the right time
- **Qualified** nature of the Visitor: A combination of the above means that a visitor referred from search is likely to be of a highly qualified nature
- With Pay per click (PPC), you **only pay for the clicks you get**
- **Accountability**: it is highly transparent and measurable
- **Visibility** in search results is within your control

The main benefit of Pay Per Click that companies still do not understand is the **level of Intent revealed by the user**. When I am in Sheikh Zayed Road and I see a banner, the banner is in my face. I do not want to see that, but you it put there! When you put your advertising in a magazine, I do not want to see that either. But in search, when I search for something, I have an intent: I want to search for that thing. It make sense for you to put your advertising in front of me.

The **Relevance** factor. If I'm searching for pizza, this means that I need pizza.

The **Timing**. If I am searching for a pizza now, I would not care about pizza in one hour. I will have eaten my pizza. You can advertise all of pizza that you want, I would not care. In one hour, I want to search for a second-hand car, and that means that I have been looking for a second-hand car. It is not like when I watch a football match, and I see an ad for a car repeatedly. When I have time, when I want, I will search for a car, and I will see the ads.

The **Qualified nature of a visitor** is a combination of the above. When I was in sales in Oracle, they told us about the concept of a qualified customer. A qualified customer is somebody who is a decision maker, has a budget, and has a need. A combination of the three is called qualified. When somebody is looking for something and they are clicking on something, we do not know 100% if they have a budget for it, but most probably they do. If somebody is searching for something, they need the thing; we cannot be sure that they have the entire budget to get it, but possibly, yes. So, of people coming to our website from Pay Per Click advertising, 99% are qualified.

With **Pay Per Click,** we only pay for the clicks we get. If I give you a business card, it costs me 1 dirham. What guarantees do I have that the person I give it to is going to check out my website? Possibly one out of 20. This means it costs me like 20 dirham to get a visit to my website, and that is just for the printing. After that, there is distribution: I need to move around, meet people, attend events, give away a lot of business cards. Business cards are the cheapest and easiest form of traditional marketing. With Pay Per Click, my website is up and running. Anyone who is looking for something can click and see my website, and I pay only for those. I do not pay for those who I distribute business cards to, they look at the card, and they do not go to my website. Those are free. I only pay for those that go to the website. That is a very cool system for advertising.

Goals and Benefits

Recognise the goals/benefits of Search Engine Optimisation:

- Benefits of high listing position in paid search for **business**:
  - » Increased Click Through Rate
  - » Increased engagement
  - » Increased conversions
- Benefits of high listing position in paid search for your **reputation**:
  - » Increased visibility
  - » Enhanced reputation
  - » Credibility and status
  - » Market leadership
  - » Competitive advantage

What are the benefits of Pay Per Click? There are benefits for the business and for the reputation. For the business, because we increase the Click Through Rate (CTR), we increase engagement and we increase conversions. More clicks, more traffic, more conversions: that is a guarantee.

But for the reputation, it is a very important factor, because a company increases its visibility. Even if I do not click, I can see you. Enhanced reputation: whatever is placed first is the best. It is all about credibility and status, market leadership and competitive advantage. The first always get more than the second and is perceived better than the second.

Sometimes there are companies that call me and say, "Christian, I have seen my competitor, a tiny little company, and it appears on top of me. Our revenue is $20 million dollars per year, and I appear nowhere. But the first few companies are run by people that started their business last year." This is the perception. This is competitive advantage.

Goals Exercise: *Set up your goals*

Choose 2 goals for your business and create explicit targets for each:

- Click through
- Engagement
- Conversions
- Visibility
- Reputation
- Credibility and status
- Market leadership
- Competitive advantage

Now, I am asking you to do the same exercise I propose during my seminars. The exercise is that you have to think about your actual job, your actual responsibility, and you need to choose two goals out of these for your business. You are going to write why you chose them here.

If tomorrow you are going to meet the chairperson of your company and you say, "Now that I have been to Digital Marketing, we are going to start the Pay Per Click campaign."

And the chairperson asks you, "Why do we need to do it? Why do we need to pay Google? Google is free. If we're going to pay, what do we get from it?"

You need to tell them two reasons why you need it for your business. There is no right and wrong. Every business, department, division has its own requirements, but you need to choose the two and write why you chose them here.

My first goal is:

_____

Why?

_____

My second goal is:

_____

Why?

_____

Now, do you think you were right or wrong? You were right. Even if you were wrong, you were right. Why is that?

You could have a good goal or a not so good one, but even the not so good one is not bad. This is because if you have a goal in mind, sooner or later, you are going to achieve it. Having a bad or wrong goal is better than not having one at all. If you do Pay Per Click just to do Pay Per Click, or if you pay an agency to do Pay Per Click and you don't even know why you are doing it, that is wrong!

You need to do things with one reason in mind, so that you can measure, and you can keep working to achieve that. Your goal cannot be "to put our keyword first," because there are thousands of keywords. Which one do you want to be first? All of them! Why? For what reason? You need to be specific. You need to understand why you are doing things. Once you know, you work on achieving that.

My opinion is that, normally for 99.9% of the company, the main reason that you should choose to do something like Pay Per Click is to get conversions. Bottom line, if I bring you 25,000 visitors a day to your website, why would it be beneficial? You may have many reasons, but the conversion is what you can easily measure and put on the table of your boss or anyone else and say, "I'm the person who got 1,000 conversions a day."

To get traffic to your website, there are an infinite number of tricks, good and bad. I can buy cheap fake traffic. I can get people browsing and clicking on your website for nothing. I can use pop up advertising. I can make your website appear in every pop up, no matter where you go. Sometimes, I am shocked to see Qatar Airways still doing pop ups. I go to some website and the pop up is for Qatar Airways! Do you think I suddenly decide to book a fight? Of course not, I close all of them! So, 99.9% of the time conversions are what you should go for, even if you are not selling anything.

Here's another concept. A guy behind Barack Obama's Social Media campaign in 2007 gave it to me. What do you think the President needed to be elected? What did he need? Conversion. The main goal for the digital campaign of Barack Obama was to get donations. He did not have rich friends who could give him a million dollars to sustain his campaign. He only had ordinary people. Through Social Media, he convinced people to give him small donations, even $5.

His website was a political website, explaining his ideas, his concepts, his news, his scheduled appearances, etc. and there was a main button on top right, red, bold faced, which said "Donate." That is the reason why he needed people to come to his website. That is why he built the website in the first place: to get donations.

That website got a bounce rate of 3.5%. If you know Analytics and use the bounce rate, you know 3.5% is crazy!

So, the idea is: even a politician is looking for conversion. If you are a hospital, what is a conversion for you? Patients booking. I go to the website, I see the hospital, I like it, I make an appointment. If you are a lawyer, I go to the website, I go to the contact page and I contact you. Any business can have a conversion, even if you are a non-profit company. You get donations? That is a conversion. Bottom line is, if you generate leads, you are doing well. If you cannot prove what you have done in the eyes of people, you are just someone who is playing on their Facebook all day, right? But if you get conversions, nobody can say anything.

So, choose the conversion as the main goal. And then, for the second, choose it from among the others. The bottom line is, you will go for all of them, but you cannot go for all of them at once right from the beginning. So, choose conversions first and the second depends on your business. Soon, you are going to go after all of them, and you do not need to spend crazy money to be the first. You will notice that some of the keywords you target convert a lot. Other keywords may get clicked but conversion is zero. Then what do you do? You do an analysis and you see what is going on. Then, you invest in keywords that convert more. Simple.

Pay per click

Keyword *Research*

- Start with customer and work backwards
- Keyword Research is the fundamental starting point for any campaign, and allows you to look at what people are actually doing right now
- Keyword Research Tools allow you to consider competitors when planning your own campaign
- Be aware of the information that is available about competitors and the requirement for competitive research about the following: visibility, ad copy, landing pages, positioning of ads, overall approach, etc.

Pay Per Click starts with keyword research. Even before launching a start-up myself, I used keyword research. A few years ago, I set up a jet ski rental company in the area of Ghantoot, far out of the digital world. Back then, we just did little bit of analysis because, a few years ago, jet ski rental got banned in Dubai because the son of a Sheikh unfortunately died in a jet ski accident. Ghantoot is just on the border between Dubai and Abu Dhabi, but it is officially Abu Dhabi. So I said, "We can get the licence there," and we set up a jet ski rental in Ghantoot. We did some calculations and said, "This is amazing! Nobody has asked to rent a jet ski in Dubai; either you go to Sharjah or to Abu Dhabi." In Abu Dhabi, the first place will be Ghantoot, and there is no competition.

But, to decide whether to start the company up or not, I used the keyword tool. Yes! To decide if it was worth it for me to set up a business for jet ski rental, I used the keyword tool.

People search online before purchasing offline. So, if there are enough people searching for something, it makes sense for me to set up the business, because nobody in Ghantoot is going to pass by and say, "Oh, there's a jet ski rental company. Let's rent a jet ski." Otherwise, I would need to do traditional advertising everywhere and that would cost too much. But, if there are enough people in Dubai searching for "jet ski rental", "rent a jet ski", "jet ski hire", "hire a jet ski", it makes sense for me to set up a company. Because I say, "We're 20 minutes from Dubai Marina." You don't even need to know that is Abu Dhabi: you know it is 20 minutes from Dubai Marina. If I want to go to Dubai Mall, it takes me 40 minutes, so travelling 20 minutes is fine.

It is a long way—around 30 kilometres—but because it is all highway, and only takes 20 minutes, so I did everything. I called the company Ghantoot Water Sports, but I called the website "Jet Ski Dubai only 20 minutes from Dubai Marina".

Now, only few people know that it was not Dubai but Abu Dhabi, but who cares? The important part is that I do not care even about the name of my company, because we got the licence, and the licence has to be called that. I have never even mentioned that it was Ghantoot Water Sports. It was Jet Ski Dubai for everyone else.

I never focused on promoting the name of my company. I don't care about the name of my company. I care about what people are searching for, and I want to be known for Jet Ski Dubai.

Google PPC

Starting a Google Ad Campaign

- Planning: There is a process for running a Google Ad campaign
- Identify the four different steps involved:
  - » Plan
  - » Setup
  - » Build
  - » Track and monitor
  - » Repeat
- Be able to describe the ultimate goals for your PPC campaign
- Know where to find Google's online tutorial supports, and know what the resource is called

Research

Keywords

- Keyword research is the process of defining the search terms we most want to target
- Recognise that keyword research identifies the scale and volume of searches being performed for a particular phrase

Tools

Google Research Tools that are available:

- Keyword Research Tool
- Traffic Estimator
- Google Trends Timeline

So, how we do keyword research? With the Keyword Research Tool.

There have been many tools from Google to do that. Some of the tools appear and then, after a while, they disappear, and then there is a new one, and then after a while that disappears, and there is a new one again.

The one that works now is called Google Keyword Planner. That's just for now; tomorrow nobody knows if it is going to be something else.

Keyword Research tool

- What the Keyword Research tool does: for specific keywords, it allows you to look at search volumes, in particular, geographic locations over a particular timeframe
- Use the Keyword Research Tool to find the research volumes for a specific keyword, in a specific region, over a specific timeframe

If you just Google it, Google Keyword you will see the first result is Keyword Planner. Now when you open the Keyword Planner, you have four options. Now we are going to go to the crazy things. 99% of you will need the first option.

The first option is search new keyword using a phrase website or category. What does that mean? We tell Google some of the keywords that we think make sense for our websites and Google will give us a lot more similar ones.

You just write the first keyword you have in mind, you choose the target (the country), then you push on the "Get ideas" button. First of all, you get a chart, telling you every possible synonym, and the tool tells us how many times in your country your keyword has been searched each month.

Then, we click a keyword idea and we get suggestions. And for each synonym, you can find out how many times it's searched for each month, so you can choose which keywords are more strategic for your company and for your business. This tool gives you a lot of ideas to expand your reach.

Campaign Process

Set-Up

Steps to setting up a campaign

- First key steps in building a campaign:
    - » account setup
    - » keyword selection
    - » campaign architecture
    - » search term bandwidth
    - » ad copy
    - » landing Page
    - » bidding
    - » targeting options
    - » setting targets / budgets
    - » conversion tracking

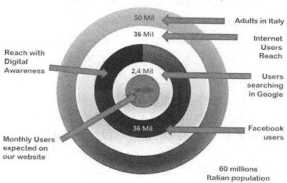

Digital Target Users Example in Italy

When we run a campaign, it is like trying to shoot at a target. However, we have many arrows, not just one. The overall chart is the total number of people that have internet access, which is possibly just like everyone else. This is so you know how many people there are, but we are not going to target all of them. We are going to target those who meet some requirements: they are in the right location, the right gender, the right age, etc.

How can we target this with awareness? This is the brand awareness phase. We can build brand awareness through Facebook, Google display campaigns, or any other medium. Even if they search on Google, we can get them through awareness.

There is a more inner circle of the people who have a need and search for it. These are our favourites because these are the ones we can just show off to. We get them with what I call Inbound Marketing: people searching and finding.

Finally, those in the centre are the ones that finally convert.

If you have enough people in the searching phase, you do not need a big awareness campaign, because you just need to give them what they are looking for. If you are selling an expensive premium product, you probably have enough people searching for it, and you are okay. But if you organising doing an exhibition, you need to get much more. There are not enough people looking for "horse exhibition." Even if you get all of them and you invite them to the exhibition, you are going to have one hundred people, and then everyone else is not going to do anything, so they really need to go for the awareness phase by building awareness through a Facebook and Google display.

But do not forget that the ones searching are the easy ones whom you can grab immediately.

What are the steps to do a Pay Per Click campaign? We set up the account by simply going to adwords.google.com. The way the account set up works also changes from time to time. Normally, you select the keyword, structure the campaign, and search term bandwidth. First, we go for the big search terms (the ones that got a lot of searches), then we go for the small ones, or the longtail keywords. Next, we write the proper text, choose the Landing Page, decide how much money we are willing to pay for the click, choose a targeting option, budget, and once the campaign is up and running, after a while, we can set up the conversion tracking.

This is very important for many reasons: one, because we are paying for each click and we want to know which ones of those converts, and two, because after we have the campaign running for a while, we need to choose the conversion optimiser option, where you are actually going to tell Google, "Okay, I have done it."

After a while, when you have been generating some conversions, you tell Google, "Please do your things, change the number, change the cost-per-click, change whatever you need to change, to make me get as many conversions as possible." And because Google has enough statistics to know which keywords convert, it changes the number accordingly to get you more conversions. This is why it is important to choose a conversion, and to set up the conversion properly from the beginning.

How to set up a **Campaign**

- Account Structure: understand that a Google Account structure is built on Campaigns, Ad Groups and Ads.
- Advantages of good Ad Group Organisation: simplified management, optimisation and reporting, improved performance in terms of lower cost per click, and higher quality score from Google.

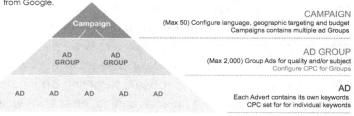

We structure the campaign in this way. At the top is your account, where you put your company details. Under one account, you can have as many campaigns as required. Under each campaign, you can have different groups. Under each group, you have different ads and different keywords.

Now let us understand how these things work. We have one account and we have different campaigns.

Each campaign has a budget, and a target. What does that mean? I need to decide how to split my campaigns. I could have only one campaign; that is fine. But it makes sense if I split the campaign to win.

For example, I have one campaign for the UAE, one campaign for the United States, and one campaign for Europe. Alternately, I may choose to split a campaign per product. It is up to us to decide how we want to split.

However, it is important that we structure the campaign correctly from the beginning, otherwise, after a while, as we expand our campaign, we will see a mess. We will not understand what is going on, and we will get lost.

Therefore, it is important to allocate budgets for different campaigns. Then, if a campaign finishes, or is not working as expected, we can pause it while continuing the others. Each campaign also has targeting. As I said, the targeting can be typically geographical targeting. Also, for each campaign, within the targeting, we can also choose the type of campaign. A campaign can be Search or Display. What does that mean?

A search campaign is what we call a pay per click campaign. A display campaign is banner advertising. Banner advertising campaign does not appear on Google search. It appears on other websites with some banner space. Both still work under the same Google Adwords platform.

Now, say we have decided that we will create one campaign and we are allocating 10,000 dirham a month to it. Good. Then, within one campaign, we can create more groups. What does it groups mean? Normally, we don't create one ad that fits all. That is why we say that is easy to place a banner on Sheikh Zayed Road, because it is just one and the agency does not need to do anything.

Running Pay Per Click campaign is more complicated. It is not one banner or one message that fits all. Not at all. Because we are targeting different keywords, different ideas, and different options, we have to write different messages. We divide all of those messages into groups. For example, we have a campaign for holidays. You are looking for travel, specifically travel to Asia, you have campaign with a nice message, which is going to say, "Travel to Asia". If somebody is looking for travel to Italy, it does not make any sense to have a message "Travel to Asia". They are not going to click it because they are looking to travel to Italy. Therefore, I need to get a campaign that advertises travel to Italy. If I search for travel to Asia, you are going to show me a nice trip to Asia. One message does not fit all. We need to create more ads.

Out of each group, we can even different ads that target the same keyword. So, if I am searching for travel to Asia, I can decide to write many ads, and the system would keep rotating. If I am advertising travel to Asia and I can show sometimes message 1, sometimes message 2, sometimes message 3, we will see which one works better. One can be "Visit Asia and its beautiful cities". The other one can be "Go to Asia and have fun". The last one can be "Go to Asia and experience the local culture and cuisine", whatever. At the end of the day, nobody knows what is going to convert more and what is going to get a higher Click Through Rate. We use the three of them and, after a while, we see which one got more clicks.

This is how you should think as a pay per click. Forget that one message fits all. I know that there are many agencies and companies that do the simple things. But the simple things do not give you results.

- Account setup: create an account using Google Adwords
- Configure currency, time zone
- Configure payment options
- Configure user logins

Once upon a time, you used to go to Google Adwords, put in your email and password, and that was it. Now, you do not even need to put in your email and password. You just get it from your Gmail, and you are in.

The only thing that you need to set, when you set up a new account, is the time zone and currency. Once you have chosen the time zone and currency, you cannot change them. Even if you call Google customer support, there is no way. The only way to change the currency is to close the account and open a new one. Now, in my opinion, if you are in UAE, always chose UAE Dirham, because if you choose dollar, you will pay more. I have seen this with some accounts. Keep it in mind.

Keyword *selection*

Keyword Match Types: Broad Match, Phrase Match & Exact Match

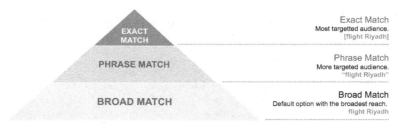

Keyword Match Types: Broad Match, Phrase Match & Exact Match

Before setting up an account and getting the campaign live, there is one thing that you need to understand. We have been talking a lot about keywords, but in Adwords, there are some distinction between different types of keywords.

There are **phrase match**, **broad match**, and **exact match**. What does it all mean? If I am searching for a *"holiday in Asia,"* then if I chose exact match, my campaign will only be shown if it targets exactly the words *"holiday in Asia."*

For example, if I put the keyword [Flight Riyadh] between square brackets, when people search for *Flight Riyadh*, my campaign comes out, but when somebody searches for *"Flight to Riyadh" or "Best flight to Riyadh,"* this campaign does not come out because it will come out only when you search exactly for *"Flight Riyadh"* as it is. Similarly, if somebody searches for *"Riyadh flight,"* the campaign does not come out. This is why it is at the top of the pyramid, because we get exactly what people are searching for.

But if you put your phrase between quotes—"Flight Riyadh"—it comes out even if people add something before or after. Let us say with the brackets somebody searches for *"best flight Riyadh"* or *"Worst flight Riyadh"* or *"Flight Riyadh and Jeddah."* In this case, the campaign ticks the criteria and your campaign comes out, even if people add something before or after, but not in the middle.

Then there is **broad match**. Broad match means, if I use the keyword simply as it is without any brackets, and in my campaign, I use the keyword as it is, *flight Riyadh*, then the system will give me anything that includes both words: *flight and Riyadh*. So, if I search for "best *flight to Riyadh*," "*I want to go to Riyadh*," "*Which flight do I need to take*?" the campaign comes up. Anything that contains both will work.

This automatically includes synonyms, even if you do not want it too. So, if you want to do it like this, automatically you get every possible synonym, but sometimes, unfortunately, you get synonyms that do not really mean what you want to say. So the only way to get around this is, instead of using this broad match, you use what is called the moderator. This is where you put the plus symbol ("+") in front of the word if you want to get exactly that word and no synonyms. They use *"holiday"* automatically to go search for *"vacation"*, but if you put *"+holiday"*, you are sure the word "holiday" has to be there. This way, you get exactly that keyword without any synonyms. And I recommend you do that because it is good to get synonyms if you are doing an awareness campaign. For an event too, it makes sense. However, if I want to get specific people, the synonyms get you a lot of clicks for nothing.

Negative Keywords

- Negative Keywords: exclude irrelevant search queries
- Understand what Negative Keywords mean: words or phrases you do not wish to be found for
- If a user searches for "phone", they may not wish to see "phone booth" or "phone company"

Now, we need to understand what our negative keywords are and where to place them. For example, a few months ago, I had a guy in my class from Saudi and he worked for a date company. It is the largest date company in Saudi and he was getting a lot of clicks, but almost nobody was calling on the phone. Why was this? We did the analysis and we discovered people were looking for dating websites—they were looking for wife or husband, girlfriend, boyfriend, not the fruit! But a date reads the same as a date!

If you are looking for a synonym of dates, you get people coming to your website who are not the people you want. So, knowing that, include enough negative keywords to try to avoid that as much as possible. There is never a guarantee that you are going avoid all of them, though.

For example, in real estate, if people are looking for real estate agents' jobs, okay, put job as a negative keyword, then your website will not come out as a result. But if somebody looking for a job is searching for real estate companies, and they are going to contact all of them, you cannot avoid that. You are going to get some unavoidable ones. That is part of the game.

Ad Copy

Creating Ad Copy

- Well-written ad copy is critical to success.
- Qualities of well-written copy:
  - » clear
  - » concise
  - » direct
  - » explicit CTA (Call to action)
  - » attractive
  - » simple
  - » compelling
- It is best to trial multiple ads until you find the ones that work: different wording, CTA, different Landing Page, etc.
- Appreciate that there are different criteria against which an ad is shown: keyword relevance, content quality, and budget
- Understand what Dynamic Keyword Insertion (DKI) is, and that it will change your ad based on the search phrase

How do you write your message? For me, this is the most important part because, based on your message, you get Click Through Rate, so a well-written copy should be clear, concise, direct, with an explicit Call to Action, attractive, simple, and compelling.

It looks simple but it is not simple. To do something simple is very complicated. It is like with websites when people ask, "I just wanna do something simple. Look at Apple website, how simple is it?" To make something simple is very expensive. iPhone is the simplest phone to use, and it is also the most expensive. So, doing simple advertising is complicated but this is the idea behind it.

Ad guidelines

- Character limits with Ad words are strict and must be respected
- Use of special characters, trademarks, exclamation marks, content
- Constraints on capitalization, issues with grammar/ spelling, use of phrase "Click" or "Click here", overuse superlatives, etc.
- You cannot run description lines into one another

There are some things that you cannot use, like special characters. You cannot do something like ***wow wow wow special promotion***. Special characters are not allowed; otherwise, you can do visual spam.

You also cannot use trademarks: you cannot use the words Amazon, Microsoft, Google, Sony, etc. because they are trademarks. If you want to use these and others, you need to fill in a special application form. You need to show that you have the permission to use that trademark. It is not easy.

Now, sometimes people make spelling mistakes. Earlier, if I wanted to target spelling mistakes, I had to imagine every possible spelling mistake, and write keywords with spelling mistakes. Google now does this automatically so, if the user makes a mistake, Google recognises that they are looking for your keyword and they show your Ad, anyway.

And if you have any doubt, there is the AdWords Policy Center that you can read. It changes all the time because they add more and more stuff. You can see what you can do and what you cannot do. Normally, just give it a try: if you cannot do something, you will get a message saying that you cannot do it.

Landing Pages

Good Landing Page

- Understand what a Landing Page is.
- Attributes of good Landing Pages:
  - » relevant content to search
  - » product
  - » title and image prominent and visible
  - » clear Call to Action (CTA)
  - » minimal clicks to conversion

Now, say the ad is good. After the ad, there is the website. And what is the first page where you land from the search? It is called the Landing Page. A Landing Page is the first thing users see after advertising. It needs to be good. What does a good landing page have?

First of all, it must have relevant content to search. If I am searching for a specific product, send me to a product page, do not send me to the homepage of your website. The title and image have to be prominent and visible, you need a clear Call to Action, and minimal clicks to conversion. These are the requirements of the best Landing Page, according to Google itself. If you make a Landing Page like this, you get a big plus from Google because your Quality Score depends on your Landing Page.

So, we have seen that the Click Through Rate is very important, the next thing is the Quality Score. This is the score that Google gives you to tell you how good or bad you are, for each of your keywords. Based on that, your ad will go higher or lower, and you will pay more or less. One of the reasons why your Quality Score is high is because you have a very good Landing Page.

Targeting

Options for campaign targeting:

- time (time of day, week)
- location and language
- network and devices

Budgets

Can I pay more to get first in Google PPC? Wrong!

Everyone thinks that being first in search is about paying more. That is wrong! Everything is about the Quality Score. This is very important because your job—if you are doing Pay Per

Click—is to increase your Quality Score as much as possible. **Google Quality Score** is everything, and it depends on:

- The historical Click Through Rate (CTR) of the keyword
- Your account history, which is measured by the CTR of all the ads and keywords in your account
- The historical CTR of the display URLs in the ad group
- The quality of your Landing Page
- The **relevance of the keyword** with the ads in its ad group and the matched ad to the search query
- Your account's performance in the geographical region where the Ad will be shown
- CPC of the keyword (okay, money matters . . . a bit)

Historical Click Through Rate is crazy! Historical means, for example, you do a bad campaign, you get a bad Quality Score and a bad CTR. Then you hand the campaign to me. Even if I change everything, it is going to take a while until you can even improve your score because, historically, it has been doing badly, so it takes time to fix it.

Your account history is measured by the CTR of all the ads and keywords in your account. Say you do one keyword well, one ad very well, and one campaign very well, but you have one terrible campaign, the terrible one is going to bring down even the good one. So, the entire account needs to be done perfectly, not just one or two campaigns. This is done to avoid the situation where people were creating campaigns just to tackle competitors. For example, if people are looking for Toyota Corolla, and the Nissan advertises PPC and shows an ad that says, "Nissan is the best car", nobody is going to click it because they are looking for a Corolla. Hence, this campaign will get a very low CTR and, because of that, even the good campaign is going to be affected.

The historical CTR of the display URLs in the ad group. There are clever people and they say, "You set up the Toyota Corolla account, I set up the Nissan account to tackle competitors, so your account is going to be clean and my account is going to be dirty, but we do not care because we are doing it for awareness. But they used the same display URL, so even the other account got affected.

The quality of your Landing Page is an important one because so many Landing Pages are not designed according to Google standard, so they get a low Quality Score.

The relevance of the keyword with the ads in its ad group, and the matched ad to the search query. Each keyword needs to be relevant.

Your account's performance in the geographical region. If you run a campaign in an area where, on average, the advertisers are crap, even if you do a bad job, you will be doing amazing. If you do a campaign in UK or in the United States, you need to be top class because you compete against top class advertisers.

The CPC of the keyword. At the end, as the last point, money matters a little bit. But it is not the most important at all. The Quality Score is a ratio from 1 to 10. If you get a Quality Score 1, you pay 100 times more to beat a quality score 10, so money is the last point of the program.

Campaign Management

Quality *Score*

- Recognise the success parameters in Quality Score:
  - » relevance
  - » correlation with ad
  - » specific Landing Pages
- Recognise weaker position:
  - » somewhat less relevant keywords
  - » keywords not always correlated
- Recognise poorest position:
  - » random keywords
  - » little correlation
  - » no relevance
  - » not coherent with Landing Pages, etc.

What do you need to get a good quality score? Relevance, correlation with advertising, specific Landing Pages.

What do you need to avoid? Less relevant keywords.

What do you need to completely avoid? Random keywords, little correlation, no relevance, not coherent with Landing Pages.

Say you are advertising with Toyota Corolla, and you go to Nissan Altima. That is totally not the right thing to do. There is only one option that you can do in that case. It is a very tricky one but it can be done to target your competitor. It is very subtle. I need to find a good way to not spoil the reputation of your company. I am Nissan, you are looking for a Toyota Corolla and I drive you to a Landing Page that is a Toyota Corolla Vs. Nissan Altima comparison page. And in the ad, as you are looking for Toyota Corolla, I mention "Toyota Corolla Vs. Nissan Altima." People that see this say, "Huh, let me see. I wanna see the Toyota Corolla. Let me see the competitor," and you click, and you go to a Landing Page that has Toyota Corolla mentioned in the title and everywhere, so it is relevant. But this is Nissan's website. I compare the two cars fairly. That is fine. You get CTR, matching, relevant, you get the Quality Score . . .bingo! You need to convince your boss that you want to do a campaign like this.

Conversion **Tracking**

- What conversion tracking means, and how it allows you to track outcomes based on Adwords traffic
- Conversion tracking requires code to be applied at the last unique step in the online process: e.g. product purchase, website inquiry, download, etc.

We set up the conversion tracking to make sure that when someone does what they are supposed to do, we know about it. When someone fills in the form to send a request, this is a conversion. When someone fills in the form that will download the brochure for the Digital Marketing training, that is a conversion. When somebody goes to the contact page or requests to be contacted to find out more information, that is a conversion.

When somebody goes to the contact page and they click to see the phone number to make a phone call, that is a conversion.

Conversion tracking can be done in two different ways. One of them is directly using AdWords, but I do not recommend you do it that way. The better way to do it is in Analytics. Basically, when you are in AdWords, we just measure the conversion for AdWords.

But I don't want to measure just AdWords; I want to measure the conversion for all of them, even when people come to my website from SEO, Social Media, email marketing, or SMS. I need to know how many of those convert, so it is better to set-up the conversion from Analytics. Then, whatever person comes to my website, when it converts, I know about it.

Cost Per **Acquisition**

Cost Per Acquisition

- Cost Per Acquisition (CPA) is a function of Conversion Rate and relates to the cost of paid clicks to achieve a sale
- Factors which impact cost per acquisition:
  - » Ad copy
  - » Campaign architecture
  - » Bidding strategy
  - » Landing Page
  - » Call to Action

When we have enough conversions, we can move to the CPA model, the Cost Per Acquisition. What does it mean? It means that I measure how many times people convert, and I decide that I am happy to pay a certain amount per each conversion.

If I am selling a laptop that costs 5000 AED, I know that each laptop that I sell I make 1000 AED profit. So let us say I make 1000 AED for every sale. Every click cost me 10 AED per click (CPC).

After a small number of clicks, I will sell a laptop and get my profit. Now, sometimes there is more competition, less competition, sometimes the market is stronger, tougher, or easier or whatever. Eventually I can say, "Look, I can spend up to 500 AED in pay per click advertising for each laptop sold. I'm happy to spend up to 500 AED."

So, I set a cost per acquisition at 500 AED and then Google will change all of the numbers, the bidding, and the Cost-per-click on the different keywords, groups and other stuff to make that they get as many conversions as possible. And, statistically, I will not spend more than 500 AED per each conversion. But to get to that level, you need to have enough conversions in your account.

Normally, with at least one month of conversions, the system can understand the numbers and play with them.

Usually, you play with the numbers, but, after a while, if you have a lot of products, it is going to take forever. I know companies that have 5,000-6,000 products, even 70,000 products. You cannot check every keyword one by one and change a little of the CPC. Once you know the conversion, you decide the Cost Per Acquisition, and the system does it for you.

That is a really good thing, because when you reach this level, you put as much money in as you can! You know you put 1 dollar into advertising, you come up with 3 million dollars in sales.

You have no limits.

ANALYTICS

Power and Control

Many years ago, when there was no Digital Marketing, no Facebook, no Google, nothing, the tyre company Pirelli came out with the tagline:

"Power is nothing without control." (Pirelli)

When Carl Lewis won the medals at the Olympics, they bought high heel shoes, they printed huge banners, and they stuck them around all of the biggest cities. And this was the first time that a tyre manufacturing company started giving interviews, because everyone was buying cars—even fancy cars like Ferrari and Lamborghini—but nobody cared about tyres. They cared only about the car. The tyre was never considered a cool topic. Pirelli was the first one to reinvent and rebrand the concept of tyres. This was the tagline and the message that has been running with Pirelli for decades.

Having seen that, I came up with my own tagline:

"Traffic is nothing without Analytics!" (Christian Farioli)

If you cannot measure what you are doing, there is no point even starting. Everything is related to Analytics because whatever you are doing, you need to check if it makes sense, and if you are sticking with your plan. Also, before planning your strategy, if you already have Analytics running on your website, I recommend you to have a look and find out what is working and what is not. This way, you get an idea on what to change and what to keep.

Web Analytics Definition

"Web analytics is the measurement, collection, analysis and reporting of Internet data for purposes of understanding and optimising web usage." (Source: Web Analytics Association)

But let us see a simplified definition. For me, Analytics is:

- How are users getting to the website?
- Who are those users?
- What are they doing on your site?
- When and where are they leaving?

Analytics Providers

Not just **Google Analytics**

- Adobe/Omniture Sitecatalyst is one of the most robust and customisable, albeit also one of the most expensive
- Many analytic systems nowadays specialise in specific functions, such as mouse-move heat maps or real time data
- There are pros and cons for each system, but Google Analytics is suitable for most with a nice balance of functionality, user friendliness, and low/no cost.

What are analytic providers? There are literally hundreds, probably thousands, of them. These are some of the most famous: Adobe Sitecatalyst, Coremetrics, ClickTale, Webtrends, Sitemeter, Yahoo Web Analytics, StatCounter, and obviously, Google Analytics.

Every few months, every start-up in Silicon Valley launches the latest of the latest analytical platform, claiming to be the best, the strongest and most powerful, etc.

Now, which one do you think I always choose? Google Analytics!

Why Google Analytics? Because, as I already said you, Google loves Google. Google Analytics integrates perfectly with

Google Adwords, Google Webmaster Tool (Search Console), and Google Keyword Planner.

Google Analytics was created in 2004. Actually, it was another company that was bought by Google and it became Google Analytics. Even after so many years, Google Analytics has never been static. Every few months, they improve some functionality, they increase something, or they add some new way to measure things. It may not be the most advanced platform, but it keeps advancing.

Say, one day, you have this choice: "Look, there's a platform that gives a little bit more. It costs me a lot of money, but it gives me a little bit more insider info because of this or that." Fine. You buy the other platform. Then, sooner or later, Analytics is going to integrate all of the possible functionalities that marketers need. So if you buy a platform that does not evolve fast enough, you have ended up with nothing.

One more important thing is that Analytics has existed since 2004 and there is a lot of data inside. If you choose to go for another platform, you start collecting data from scratch at that moment. Then, after 2, 3, 4 years, if this company fails and you need to change the analytical platform, you lose all of your past data.

So, for me, it is quite a good idea to choose a platform that is going to be quite stable. This is why I continue with Google Analytics. Plus, it is free. So if it is cheaper than pizza, why not go for it?

Analytics Process

Analytics is an ongoing dynamic process with goals, setup, management, and review and iteration.

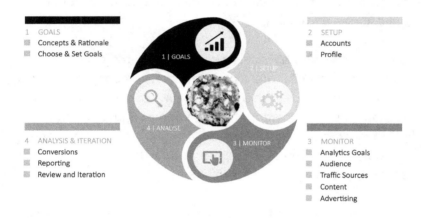

1 GOALS	2 SETUP
▦ Concepts & Rationale	▦ Accounts
▦ Choose & Set Goals	▦ Profile

4 ANALYSIS & ITERATION	3 MONITOR
▦ Conversions	▦ Analytics Goals
▦ Reporting	▦ Audience
▦ Review and Iteration	▦ Traffic Sources
	▦ Content
	▦ Advertising

How does Analytics Process work?

We decide why we need to do Analytics, then we set up the account. We start monitoring and analysing our goals, which means our conversions, then the audience, traffic sources, the content, and the advertising. After that, we make some decisions. We tweak and come back to set up new goals.

> *"Collection, measurement and analysis of digital marketing & website data."*
> *(Source: Digital Marketing Institute)*

Benefits and Goals

Recognise how data collection may be carried out online:

Measurement is important:

- as a source of "Market Reality"
- as an aid to running effective campaigns
- as a basis for making informed decisions

The Benefits of Analytics:

- get closer to the customer
- accurately gauge user experience
- gain insights from real customer experience
- increased accountability
- focus and prioritization of resources
- conversion rates and enhanced ROI

Why do we do analytics? It is a source of "market reality." When I finished university in 2001, my IT Engineering thesis was about web usability. To study how accessible a particular website is and what was not easy about it, we asked people to do a task, for example, "Get the phone number of the company." Everything was tracked on the computer, and we found out where they were clicking around to find the phone number.

We were measuring the mouse, the time, and also where the user was looking. That was an expensive task, all just to study how long it took them to find the contact page. Then, if you move the contact page button, you need to think of a new subject. You cannot use the same one, so you need to do a big survey with a lot of people to find out how people find things easier to do. So while it was easy to say, "I just need an easy website," it was extremely complicated and extremely expensive to make an easy website at that time. This is why only huge companies could afford big usability laboratories, like Microsoft, Xerox, Apple, etc.

Nowadays, thanks to tools like Analytics, we do not need to interview people using surveys. With Analytics, we get the source of market reality. We do not care about things we hear sometimes, like, "Yeah, here, the culture says this . . . the culture is different . . ." or "Yeah, I feel that we need to change the website because it is old." With Analytics, we get the real deal.

It is even better as an aid to running an effective campaign. If we spend money, we want to be sure that the campaigns are perfect. Measurement is important as a basis for making an informed decision, not, "Yeah, today it's going to rain so we have to change the website."

What are the benefits of Analytics? We get closer to our customers. It is like we step next to our customers and we see what they are doing. This is something that even big supermarket chains are doing. They place cameras inside the stores, on top of their ceilings, and they watch what people do from the moment they enter to the moment they exit. There are even tracking systems analysing where they go, where they look, etc.

With Analytics, we do not need to buy expensive tools and toys; it is already there. We get and track the user experience from A to Z.

When we gain insights from real customer experience, we increase accountability, we focus and prioritise our resources, we know what works and boom! We put more money into it.

Finally, we measure conversion rate and enhanced ROI. ROI is what we started with. Every senior manager, even if they have no clue about digital, social media, and anything else, will give you more budget when you prove that whatever you're doing is bringing a ROI. This, for me, is the most important point.

The User Journey

Analytics tools provide access to the complete user journey: from the origin of website traffic to how users navigate and interact with a website to how users exit.

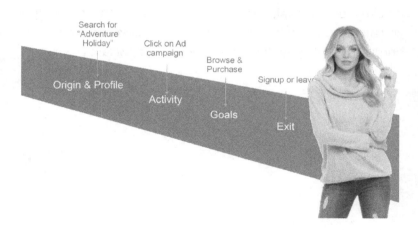

THE USER JOURNEY

Pay Per Click Marketing provides acess to the complete user journey.

Let us look at the User Journey. You already know it. What happened before? Somebody searches, and when they click, they go to our website. Now, even if you get 10.000 people a day on your website, not all of them are going to buy, right? Most of the reason why people do not buy from us is either because they do not trust us enough, or we make life too complicated for them. If the system is too complicated, users will leave without purchasing, but they are not going to tell us. So if only 10 purchase something, we do not know why the other 9,990 did not purchase, and we have no way to ask them because they already left our website.

Like our friend Samantha. She searches for something; she clicks SEO, advertising, or something else; she goes to our website; and then browses our website. She spends only one minute or two and then decides to leave without purchasing. Now we think, "Oh, we got Samantha onto our website and she didn't purchase anything. Why was that? " Now, we cannot send anyone outside the supermarket to ask her, "Hey, can I ask you just why you didn't purchase anything?" We cannot do that online too, but we can see exactly what is going on inside.

How Analytics Works (Tech)

The technical steps involved in tracking a user on a website:

1. *User types in a web address in their browser*
2. *This triggers a request to the website's server*
3. *The page is served to the user's browser*
4. *Each page of the site contains a piece of code from Google (JavaScript) which is executed when the page loads*
5. *This places a cookie on the user's computer*
6. *The data is sent to Google servers*
7. *The data is processed*
8. *Reports accessed later by the site owner through the Google analytics interface*

How does this magic thing of Analytics work? When somebody types a web address in their browser, there is a trigger and a request to the website server. The page is served to the user's browser, so the server sends the page to the user, and the user sees the page on their screen.

Now, each page of the website contains a little piece of code from Google. It is a little piece of software, or JavaScript. This thing runs on the user's computer. Every time you come to my website, my website has a tiny little code from Google that runs on your computer, starting a recording. When you enter into my website, your behaviour is recorded, one by one, click by click.

Also, this piece of code on top places a cookie on the user's computer. Now what is a cookie? It is not the biscuits that you eat as a snack. The cookie is a little file of text. Once you browse my website, it runs and creates a little file on your computer. Don't worry, it is exclusively text, so there is no way that any virus or security breach or hack can come from a cookie. The cookie is the safest thing that exists, at the moment.

Again, in theory, you should inform users about cookies in the Terms and Conditions of your website, just for privacy, because I am creating something on your computer and by some laws and regulations, you should inform the person that this is happening. Now, this is happening all the time. When you look at your cookie folder on your computer, you will see there are hundreds and thousands of cookies. Most of the websites where you go—at least 90%—create a cookie.

All of these recordings of data are sent to Google server. Whatever you are doing, the little software is recording and sending all of the data to Google.

Google processes the data and shows you everything in an easy-to-read form. Imagine how many people are coming to your websites every day, how many things they are browsing, how much they are clicking, how many places they are going. This generates a massive amount of data. All of this is sent to Google.

I remember many years ago, when somebody in the organisation needed a report, the CFO informed the IT team that he needed it. The IT team checked with a database administrator to run a query to interrogate the database, and extract the data. When all the data were extracted, they sent all of this data to the data analyst, the person that counts the data and put the things in an easy-to-read form—that is, creates charts and stuff. Then, that person sent these back to the CFO. One week later, the CFO got the final report of the essays of the month. This takes a lot of people, effort, and time. Nowadays, you just login to Analytics and see exactly what is going on, instantly.

Accounts

How to Setup and Configure Google Analytics Account:

1. *Access www.google.com/analytics*
2. *To register, you may have to setup a Google account. To access Analytics, you can use your Google Adwords login*
3. *Add your account information: domain name, time zone, data sharing settings, etc.*
4. *Agree to the Google User Agreement and understand what the implications are for your website's privacy policy*
5. *Download and implement the analytics code snippet*
6. *Adjust account settings: default page, exclude URL query parameters, e-Commerce site selection, apply cost data, setting up site search*
7. *Link Analytics with Webmaster Tools and Adwords*

How do you create an account? Simply go to Google.com/analytics, register, and that is it. Then, if you already have an Adwords account, you are leading them both.

When you register, Google Analytics immediately gives you the code. This is 5 or 6 lines of text, and nothing else. You need to place this in every single page of your website, not only the homepage.

Generally, if you have a CMS, there is a special feature to place a piece of code in a special location, and this automatically goes to every single page. This is it. Most of the CMS already have an Analytics code section. If not, ask your web developer, or your web design company, to find the way to do it. This is the easiest of things. If Google Analytics is missing even one page, it is not going to work.

Goals

Three Steps in Goal Creation and Configuration:

What are the simplest ways to set up goals for Analytics? First, we identify our KPI: what we are going to measure, and what we want to get out of this. Then, we configure the goals in Analytics, and link to all of the other tools, especially Adwords. If you are using Adwords, you need to be able to measure the outcome of it; not just how much traffic they are getting, but also how much traffic converts.

Identify **KPI/Objective**

Key performance indicators for your business should form your goals:

- A goal within analytics is a measured user action that counts towards a Key Performance Indicator (KPI) for the business
- Common goals: inquiry form completion, brochure request, newsletter sign up, subscription, file download, completed purchase, increased spent time, etc.

- Goals can be setup around areas such as: visitors, content, leads, conversions, etc.

How do you identify KPI or objectives? For example, how do you find out how many forms got filled in, how many inquiries got added, how many people signed up to download a newsletter, how many subscribers you have, how many people download your company profile, your file, or your trial, or how many purchases they are making. If people spend a certain amount of time on our website, it means they are interested. Therefore, I want to measure those people as well. We decide what we are going to measure, but we can measure pretty much everything.

For example, leads: when people fill out a form, there is a lead. How do we work this out? We can measure Analytics. We set up the goal and the Analytics, so after a few months, we can see, "Okay, 10,000 went to our website, 1,000 signed up for something, so we got 1,000 leads." Now, if those convert or not—that is not your job. That is a sales job. You have done your job, which is generating leads.

Types of **Goals**

These are some of the types of goals that we can measure in Analytics. We have some primary goals and secondary goals. Primary goals can be around sales or leads. We have conversions, transaction, lead conversions or conversion values. For us, a lead is worth 10 dollars.

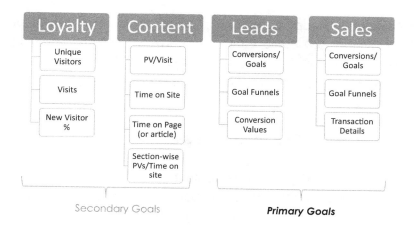

Loyalty	Content	Leads	Sales
Unique Visitors	PV/Visit	Conversions/ Goals	Conversions/ Goals
Visits	Time on Site	Goal Funnels	Goal Funnels
New Visitor %	Time on Page (or article)	Conversion Values	Transaction Details
	Section-wise PVs/Time on site		

Secondary Goals   *Primary Goals*

Additionally, there are secondary goals: secondary reasons why we need to use Analytics. For example, for content consumption, for engagement, to see how many page views, to see how much time our visitors spent on our website, or how much time they spend on a specific page, article, or section of our blog. Lastly, there is the Visitor loyalty: how many unique visitors there are, compared to the returning visitors.

In marketing, there is a clear rule that says, "Keeping a client, costs you 30 times less than acquiring a new client." That is a simple, average goal. It is not the law that it is exactly 30 times, but on an average, that is how it is. After all, if you don't know me, you don't trust me, and you have no idea about who I am, it takes me time, effort, and money to convince you to purchase something for the first time. After you have done it the first time, it is easier for you to buy again. Also, I don't need to blast you with display advertising, PPC, and every possible thing. I can simply send you an email: "How are you? Eid Mubarak, Merry

Christmas, Happy New Year!" And when you are in need of something, you come right here. It costs me almost nothing to maintain a client. This is why it is important to know how many people are coming back and how many people you are getting new.

Set some goals and KPIs

- Think of the types of content across the three websites
- What goals should they use to help judge if their website and digital marketing activity is effective? What would be the most important primary goal and secondary goal?
- How do you think these goals should be measured?

Let's test out a few of these ideas. We will examine three different types of websites and will see what the different goals and KPIs are for each one.

Bayt.com

Bayt.com is a portal for jobs. You register and you can see companies posting jobs, and you can apply for them. Let us say it again, clearly: conversion is what matters most. We do not care about anything else but conversion. So, what do we measure for conversion for bayt.com?

When people register on this website, they become a candidate and put their CV online. You could say, "We got one million CVs on our website, good." But are you making any money out of that? "No, nothing." So for us, that can be a conversion that we are going to measure, but it is not the one that we are going to focus on. Even if you get 1 billion people registering on your website, you still make zero. Because, who pays? Companies posting job ads. So, company registration when they post a job request is the revenue. That is the gold that we are looking for.

Then definitely, as a secondary conversion, we need to get CVs. If you want to have a company paying you, you need to have enough CVs to make it worth it for them. Nobody is going to register and pay to post a job when there are no candidates on your website. So candidates are secondary. They are important, but they are secondary.

Eventually, if you have a lot of candidates, since it is not easy to get a job, we can do some upselling. "I can write you a CV, I can help you do this and that," and we can make money in another way.

Also, on these kinds of websites, there are sometimes some advertisements. Out of the advertising or premium posts, they can make a little bit of money as well.

FlyDubai.com

This example seems to be easier, but many times, most people go the wrong way. Why is that? Because people in marketing are too focused on crazy words like engagement, rate, ratio, and so on, and they forget about the most important things. When you have an e-commerce website, the only thing that matters is conversions—not even conversions, but transaction details. What do you prefer to sell—10 flights from Dubai to Bahrain or 5 flights from Dubai to Australia? Flights from Dubai to Australia, right? Similarly, transaction details are more important than conversions.

Say, I sell electronic products. You ask, "How many electronic products did we sell today?" 100. "Oh, good!" Yeah, but what we sold was 100 mice: we made nothing. Tomorrow, we sold 20, but what we sold were 20 laptops. That is money! So if you have an e-commerce website, transaction details are the only thing to work for.

What is the secondary goal for Fly Dubai? This depends on your marketing strategy. Normally, the number of returning visitors makes sense as a goal, because if people buy from you once, and then they never come back to your website, that is a problem. If you try to spend much more money to get more clients to come back to your website, but you lose many of the clients you already have, this is a problem.

I know that in marketing people say, "Ah, this year, we got 20% more clients than last year!" Good. Sometimes I ask, "How many clients you have lost? How many clients were your clients last year but are not this year?" They all look at me like, "Ah, good question." That is much more important than knowing how many more new clients you got.

Dubizzle.com
This example is the most complicated because Dubizzle has a lot of different streams of income. One of the ways they make money is with premium. You post a job? It is free. You want to

sell your laptop? It is free. You want to sell a table. It is free. But if you want to highlight your job, you need to pay.

So, they generate traffic from people who are buying and selling anything, but they realise they cannot make money out of these customers. If you are selling your laptop, if would be lucky to make 1000 dirham. You are not going to pay a commission to Dubizzle to sell a 1000 dirham laptop. But, to get a job, there is money to be made. Or, if I sell a car, there is money to be made. If I sell an apartment, there is lot of money to be made. There is why some categories are paid categories.

Then, another stream of income is advertising. Dubizzle invests a lot of money in advertising. They generate this revenue through their traffic.

So, what is the point of that? When I go to Dubizzle and I search to buy a car, if I finally buy a car, Dubizzle makes nothing from me. I could browse the website for one month, and still Dubizzle would make nothing from me. But people that post and have a car for sale? That is a goal. How many people post only cars, real estate, and jobs? This is important for Dubizzle.

Then, for the secondary goal, we have different things. When you are on Dubizzle, if you want to buy a car—say, a BMW—you choose the model, you see many of them, and you can click to send the message or to show the number and call the person. Have you ever thought, "Why do I need to click to see the number?" Why is the number not already there? That would create usability flow. I need to click to see the phone number, so why not just put it there?

There are many reasons for this. The most important one is that Dubizzle knows that you are probably not going to call that person. I can browse Dubizzle day and night, and look for a Ferrari or Lamborghini day and night, but I could be a 15-year-old kid just dreaming that I would become rich and buy a Ferrari. So, every day, I browse for a Ferrari and just keep dreaming.

This is a lot of traffic, but Dubizzle needs to know what kind of product and service people really want to buy. It is definitely not a Ferrari. They like to browse it, but probably only one million people click to see the phone number, or they enquire. But people browsing maybe, Nissan, for example? There are more than enough of them, and most of them are going to click to see the phone number, to fill in the form, and make a purchase.

This is why it is important to use tracking like that. Another reason is that there are engines that scrape the web, automatically going inside the website and searching for any kind of mobile number. They extract the mobile numbers, and can send a massive SMS forward to those numbers. To avoid that, making it so you need to click to see the number prevents the software from scraping your site.

The most important thing we need to measure is what people are really interested in. In the beginning, every possible thing was available on Dubizzle. The most important portal of real estate at that time was a property finder. That was purely, exclusively a property website for agencies and for individuals.

Everyone was posting rent and sale. But Dubizzle saw the potential of real estate, and they saw with analytics that a lot of people were into the real estate section. They rotated it, so they did not put real estate below, they made it prominent . . . boom! They put it on the home page, not because everyone had noted that real estate was booming, but simply because people were putting real estate there, and Dubizzle put real estate on their home page.

After checking the statistics for a while, it turned out that many people were looking for real estate. Many were looking to buy and many were looking to rent. So, what did we do in this case? We put two major sections on the home page: buy and rent. This is what people want, not what I think people want. They browse this section most of the time. Why would we keep it hidden? We put it straight on the home page. That was an important business decision.

The same thing happened with cars. So many people checked out and bought cars, so Dubizzle thought, "Let's put cars on the home page. If so many people are buying cars, let's make a little bit money out of them!"

Goal **Configuration**
Setup and Configure Goals in Google Analytics:

- See Main Profile Page to find the Goal Creation area
- Different types of goals within Google Analytics:
  - » URL destination goal
  - » Time on site goal
  - » Page/visits goal

» Event tracking goal
» Social interaction goal
- Goal Setup steps:
  » Add a goal name,
  » Select a goal type
  » Add the goal conditions

We have seen how to set up goals, account, profile, how to monitor, and how to analyse. What can we measure as a goal? What can we track as a goal?

URL destination: when people reach a place, we say "Goal!"If we are a magazine online, we need people to read more. Time on site: when people spend more than two minutes, we say "Goal!"

This is done on a single page. This is the only page you need to set up to choose how to track your goals. You give the goal a name, you put in the URL that you want to track as a goal, and you are already done.

Eventually, we can do what Google calls a goal funnel. This is another crazy clever concept.

Goal **Funnels**
Setup and Configure Profiles & Filters. A goal funnel:

- is a series of pages leading up to the goal page destination URL
- is often used when there are multiple steps in a transaction process
- provides valuable guidance as to where visitors leave, where information is unclear or inadequate, or where the online process has good flow/bad flow

The idea of the funnel is that, in digital, we have a lot of visitors coming to our website (from PPC, Social Media, SEO, or any other strategy) but only some of those make a purchase. The others get stuck in the middle of the funnel. Sometimes, there are elements that will make customers exit the funnel, without reaching the important stage, which is the conversion.

Now, to give you an idea, let us say that we have 1,000 visitors coming to our website in a month. Good. Now, first things first, you have the bounce rate. Let us say there is a 50% bounce rate. That means that, after less than 1 minute, you no longer have 1,000 visitors; you have 500. Then, after a while, people look around, they don't know what they want, they don't understand. So, after a while, you have 100 visitors. Finally, out of this, some of them decide to purchase the product. Let us say half of them. Out of the 50 who decided to purchase, some of them they left immediately, some of them eventually, some found it too complicated, or the transaction did not go through (there were some errors). At the end of the day, we have 5 customers. Good.

Now, as it is now, if we get 2,000 visitors, we get 5 customers. How can we increase that? The bad way is, "Let's spend double! Let's do . . . double SEO, double PPC, double Social Media, double Twitter, double YouTube!" Amazing, we spend twice as much, but if we are lucky, we get 1.7 times the number of customers. So it is not 5, but maybe we get 8.

At the end of the second month, you say, "Boss, we increased sales, now we should spend more money." And the boss says, "No, instead of 10,000 dollars a month, we are spending 20,000 dollars a month just to get a few more customers? No, no, no! There is something wrong!"

What do normal companies do? They say, "Let's change the website, The fault is with the website." Wrong!

Now, what would a smart company do? What would a smart digital marketing manager like you do? You get a bigger funnel, so you get a bigger output.

What does this mean in our strategy? First of all, you work to reduce your bounce rate a little bit. Even if it brings only 10%, with a new funnel, instead of a 50% bounce rate, we get only a 40% bounce rate. This means that, in one minute from 1,000 visitors, we get 600. Straight away, we can get 6 clients instead of 5. We just increased by one more sale a month without spending a single dollar!

We work on an additional website, but monthly, it is going to be exactly the same. For our products, we can enhance the pictures, the description, the Call To Action, and then instead of 20%, we get to 30%.

After two steps, increasing 10% in one step of the funnel and 10% in a second one, we have almost doubled the number of new customers. Then, in the purchasing phase, with the shopping cart, we polish the experience and remove whatever is unnecessary. We make sure the process is fast, easy and smooth for everyone, so instead of 10%, we convert 20%.

Then, from 5 sales a month, we jump to 18 sales a month, without spending one single dollar into more traffic, but just by shaping the funnel. This is an amazing idea.

I heard about this several years ago, and little bit later, Google came out with the funnel visualisation. It allows us to visualise our goals using a funnel method. How do we tell Google about these things? In the same goal page. When we put the goal in, we also set goal funnel. Click goal funnel and set it up, step by step.

Contact Form

118 visitors finished | 17.11% funnel conversion rate

Contact Us Page
652

	652		562	
/	263	(exit)	244
(entrance)	82	/	80
/courses/type/professional-diploma-in-dig..	15	/contact-us/	46
/about-dmi	12	/contact-us	21
/courses/postgraduate-diploma-in-digital-	11	/about-dmi	11

90 (13.80%)
proceeded to Contact Us Submission

Contact Us Submission
90

0 · 0

90 (100.00%)
proceeded to Contact Form

Contact Form
116

	26	17.11% funnel conversion rate
/masters-registration/	13	
/masters-registration	8	
(entrance)	4	
/courses/type/postgraduate-diploma-in-di...	1	

Out of 652 people who come to the contact page, 90 go to the
next step. 562 leave. Out of those that get to the next step, all
of them fill in the contact form. Nothing lost. This is the idea
that we can measure step by step: where are we losing people?

I always say, during my workshops, that we need to make people go inside your shop, look around, see every possible thing.
Wherever they go first, we can see where they are. The most
important part about this is the purchasing step. If they skip,
we can see where they are skipping, because the only thing we
care about is that they go to the cashier. We make sure to close
every possible exit. They are forced to go inside, like IKEA.
When they are at the cashier, they have to pass the cashier and
buy something.

This is the point of doing the funnel visualisation: to find out where your customers are abandoning the purchase or conversion.

So, in this way, you increase your leads simply by doing something better, not by spending more money. Then, when this is perfect, we spend more money. We do more Pay Per Click, more SEO, more digital, more Social, more everything, and we get more and more and more. And then, out of 1,000 visitors we get 18 instead of 5. That is a big difference. When we get 18, boom! Now, open the tab, spend big on massive advertising, and we get an ever-increasing number.

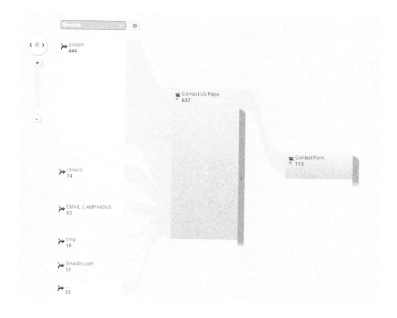

This is another visualisation: the goal flow. This is important because it tell us, out of our final goals, where the users came from: from Google Adwords, Google direct, email campaign, Bing, LinkedIn, etc. Here, we see the ROI of our conversion, and we see that a massive number of people that we send to the Contact Us page mostly drop out. Only a few fill the form. Perhaps filling the form is too complicated, too long, or we ask for too much information. So, we remove it, and we check if we need to increase this. It is a big drop. When I see a long questionnaire, it is always a massive drop. You don't need to be a genius to understand that. But your management needs the long form to be filled. The solution is to find a way to, instead of having one big step, splitting them into 2 or 3 smaller steps. Instead of asking 20 questions, ask 3 questions, then 7, then 10, for a total 20 questions. That way, you will get a lot more people contacting you.

Reports

Standard *Reports*

- Appreciate the wide range of reports available within Google (70 plus)
- It is possible to generate a report to cover any of the main sections within Analytics:
  - » Visitors
  - » Traffic
  - » Content
  - » Goals
  - » E-Commerce
  - » Adwords
  - » Event tracking
- View common reports: visitors overview report, geographic report, new versus returning visitors, mobile devices, visitor flow, traffic sources

Finally, we can also do old-school reporting. All of the things that we have seen so far, you can also get them as a report, a traditional, standard, old-school report. When your boss tells you, "I want a report on my desk, Sunday morning 10 o'clock." What do we do? We program such that we receive an email every Sunday at 9 o'clock. We get the email, we print the report, and we go to our boss, "Boss, I've been working all weekend to get the report done. But look how amazing it is!" And you do the same story every week…

Reporting **(Advanced)**

Real Time Reporting

- Recognise that Google Analytics includes real time reporting: provides a snapshot of current activity on your website: visitors, content, traffic sources, goals
- Appreciate the benefits of being able to track how current live events are impacting your traffic (radio, TV) etc.

Now, a few years ago, some companies used to say, "We need a better analytical platform, because we need to analyse people on the same day." Google analytics data used to be supplied after each 24 hours. Today, you can see what has happened until the end of yesterday. Once the day is finished, all data are collected, analysed, and displayed. Somebody says, "I want to know how many users are on my website, right now." And so, real time reporting was implemented. Now, on the left side, you will see the reporting in real time.

It is very clever to measure offline advertising. I will tell you why. Because you see where your users are, and how many users are on your website right now, and how many users have been there, minute by minute.

If a radio ad running in Dubai, and the radio is saying, "Now, check out our website for our amazing promotion," you can be there in Analytics and see how many people take action and go to your website at that specific moment. At 8 o'clock at night, a TV show is broadcast in Abu Dhabi, and you can see people in Abu Dhabi—tick, tick, tick, tick—going to your website. Then, you start measuring the conversion of your TV ad or radio ad.

Intelligent reporting:

- Access the Analytics Dashboard to find 'Intelligence'
- Various features are available in 'Intelligence': ability to set alerts, ability to monitor and manage user activities
- What setting involve alerts: (e.g. set a traffic alert if your traffic drops below expected, page bounce alert if bounces reach high levels)
- Recognise different alert types: bounce, traffic, page views, etc.

Customised *reporting*

We can even build custom reports based on every possible crazy thing, and we can put an email address, so we can automatically check daily data, or monthly, quarterly, yearly—whatever we need in the report. This can be good as a way to keep a history. It is constantly written every month. When you check Analytics, by default, they show you last 30 days. This way, we can choose the month of January, February, March, and compare it, but some people still like to get it old-school in their email. So, there is a report sent every month. Then, you can make the old-school comparison: how does this month compare to the same month last year? There are people that like to keep a record in that way.

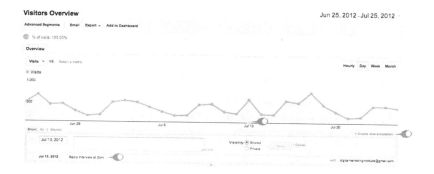

Another funny thing that you can do is adding annotations, on the chart itself, and write something. For example, we are launching the latest Toyota Corolla, today. After six months, one year, two years, you come back to Analytics and you check the notes. "What was the campaign that we did last year that was very effective?" You come back and you see, "Ah, this was the campaign where we launched the new Toyota Corolla. What was that campaign that we used to launch the new Yaris? Oh yes, this was very bad. Don't do that. Let us do something else, instead." So, even if people working for you leave your company, you have a useful, simple track of everything in your Analytics.

Profiles and Filters *(advanced)*
Setup and Configure Profiles and Filters:

- Create A Profile within Google Analytics to help group customer segments together (origin, source, pages viewed, etc.)

- Apply a Filter: Commonly used filters are: IP addresses, traffic to directories, page title, campaign, country, e-commerce, etc.
- Add a new profile to your website
- Add a meaningful name to the profile
- Create a new filter based on the profile
- Create additional filters and edit filters

Different types of filters

- Predefined filter excluding IP address
- Custom Filter Customer Segmentation
- Setup Users and Permissions
- Grant access to others within your Google analytics account, and apply different permission settings
- Be aware of the security risks of granting administrative access to another user

You can even set up profiles and filters. I can exclude traffic from being tracked, for example, from specific countries or specific IP addresses. If I have a bank, the customer service division are people who stay on the website day and night. Whenever somebody calls and asks, "What's the credit card rate," these people check on the backsides of the creek, because if their rating is 75%, they get the promotion! Thus, the customer service staff is using the website day and night. That would generate massive traffic. However, that is not good traffic, because it is not client traffic. Therefore, you want to remove all of this to make sure the one that you measure and analyse is only the clean, pure one. You do it by setting up a filter that excludes some IP addresses.

If you have a local business and your website is developed and maintained by a company in India, you can exclude Indian traffic. That way, you are sure that you are not going to get any statistics that are not from real visitors.

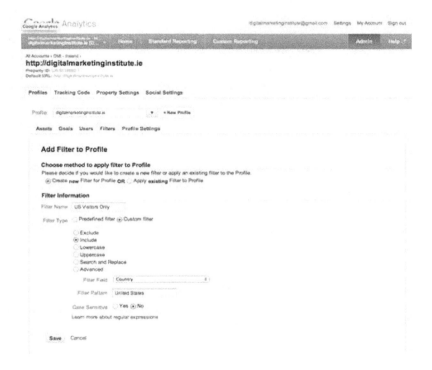

You can also create a filter to make different profiles. You can have one filter that gets only UAE traffic, and another one that gets only Saudi traffic. So you can say, "Okay, the marketing manager of Saudi? I measure you by this. The marketing manager of UAE? I measure you by that. The marketing manager of India? I measure you by that." And I see 3 completely different charts. It is like having 3 different accounts on the same website.

Finally, if you're crazy enough about analytics, you can even get certified!

Analytical people use data to make informed business decisions based on solid data and trends.
Never a feeling!

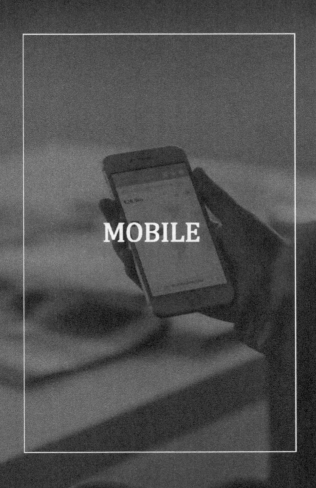

MOBILE

In this chapter we are going to discuss mobile, and I want to talk you about . . . pizza! Do you need a pizza? Okay, you can Google it. When you Google pizza, what happens? Watch this video:

https://www.youtube.com/
watch?v=rJsApM0N4zc

This was a video introduced when Google purchased Android, and they began to focus every possible effort and innovation on mobile. This tells you a lot. It tells you that when you are doing SEO, you cannot pretend that when people are looking for pizza worldwide, your pizzeria website is going to come out as a result. It is not going to happen. If I am based here and I search for pizza, I get results from here. If I am in Milan, I will get a pizzeria near Milan. Thus, SEO is a challenging task.

Related Topics

Related to mobile marketing, we have: Display, Social Media and Analytics.

Analytics, always. Display, because we can do digital advertising the same way, or slightly differently, on mobile, and we can do advanced Social Media on mobile. We can do also what is called SoLoMo: Social Mobile Local.

Which mobile do you have? Which one is the best? We have already said that the best mobile is the one that your customers have. I remember, a couple of years ago at a big event at the World Trade Center, there was a stand with a quote from the eminence Mohammed bin Rashid Al Maktum, minister of defence and prime minister of the United Arab Emirates (UAE):

> *"I want UAE Government services to be de-*
> *livered to the public through mobile phones."*
> *(Mohammed bin Rashid Al Maktum)*

Public services, the most boring and time-consuming activity in the history of humanity, is finally on mobile phones. That is really impressive!

Mobile Marketing Process

Effective Mobile Marketing is an Iterative Process

What are the mobile marketing processes? Let us see the steps.

First, we see the opportunities, challenges, risks, characteristics, trends, and devices. Then we optimise: app development and mobile websites. Then we advertise: SMS, mobile advertising, proximity marketing. Last, we analyse the results: tweak and go back to the opportunities.

We are going to discuss the mobile revolution, mobile optimised websites, app development, SMS marketing, mobile advertising, proximity marketing, mobile commons, emerging trends, laws and guidelines.

Now, you think mobile marketing is a simple little thing BUT there are so many topics in it! These are just some of the main topics. Every week, an American comes up with a new crazy idea, one that is better, faster, cheaper, and stronger for mobiles. You do not need to run out and get everything. Find out what makes more sense for your business, and try to implement some ideas that can be clearly measured, reused, and adjusted overtime. It is not about doing something one month, and doing something else the next. Nobody can guarantee that you are going to launch a new mobile trick for a campaign and it is going to work instantly. But if you can measure it properly, you can adjust it. Then you keep going on and on and on . . .

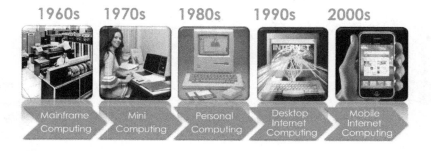

The tech cycles tend to last 10 years. Every 10 years, there is normally a major change. The change for the year 2000 was Mobile Internet Computing.

Mobile Marketing Definition

"Any marketing activity conducted through a ubiquitous network to which consumers are constantly connected using a personal mobile device." (Andreas Kaplan)

Global Mobile and **Online Commerce**

(US$ billions / % of respondents)
2009 v. 2015

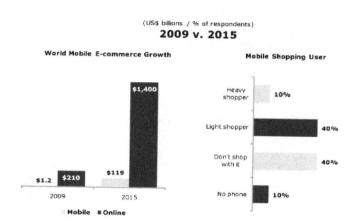

World Mobile E-commerce Growth

Mobile Shopping User

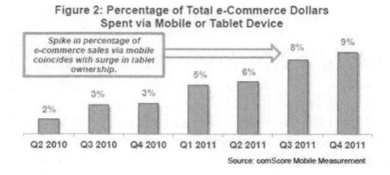

Figure 2: Percentage of Total e-Commerce Dollars Spent via Mobile or Tablet Device

We can see that the number of mobile phones is increasing crazily, and the number of mobile shoppers is also increasing crazily. Every few quarters, there are more and more dollars spent through mobile devices. It means that people are purchasing more from mobile devices.

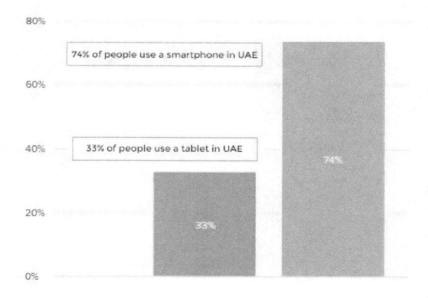

Most of the people in UAE have smartphones, but there are a decent number of tablets around as well. That is also not to be underestimated, because while on mobile you have a little screen, you can show a nice, big website on a tablet.

3i Principles

3i Principles are the foundation tenets of the Digital Marketing Methodology:

- **Initiate**: start with the customer and work towards your digital strategy
- **Iterate**: continually learning from engagement with customers, and applying this on an ongoing basis
- **Integrate**: integrate digital channels coherently and in terms of traditional marketing activities

The principles are always the same. Initiate, iterate, integrate. Whatever we do, even from mobile marketing, we do on a recording basis.

Consumers are driven more and more towards mobile because of the freedom and control it provides them over their experience.

Mobile Consumer Evolution

The range of activities and services available to consumers through mobile devices has evolved along the following route:

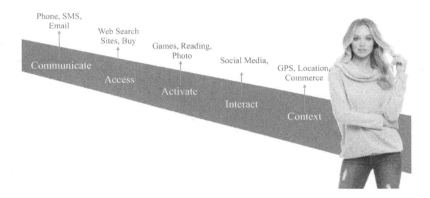

The consumer journey starts with just a communication, with SMS and phone and, eventually, an email. That then goes to web, search sites, and purchasing. And then games, books, photos, social media, GPS, commerce.

Communication Zones

Depending on the consumption channel, users apply personal preferences and etiquette and expect marketers to do likewise.

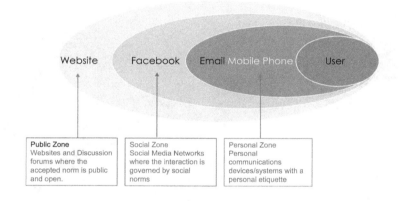

Public Zone	Social Zone	Personal Zone
Websites and Discussion forums where the accepted norm is public and open.	Social Media Networks where the interaction is governed by social norms	Personal communications devices/systems with a personal etiquette

Let us check out the communication zones. This means how near or far the different communication channels are from us. Our beloved websites are the farther from us. Facebook is much closer, because it enters into the personal sphere. Then, even closer, we have email, and even closer than that, we have the mobile phone. Why? Because it is with us all the time.

Characteristics of the Mobile Medium

Mobile is important because of the dynamic between immediacy, mobility, and interactivity.

Immediacy

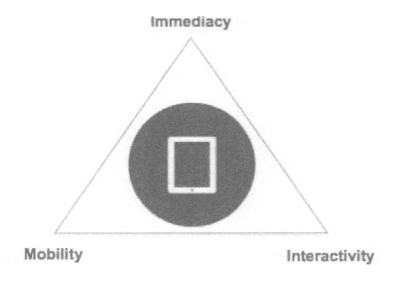

Mobility   Interactivity

Those are the characteristics of any mobile device and any mobile marketing activity. No matter if you are doing SMS marketing, proximity marketing, or any other crazy thing, these are the characteristics:

- **Mobility**: the key characteristic of a mobile device is that we carry it with us as a mobile computer distinct from a desktop or other computer
- **Immediacy**: the mobile device is always on, always checked, and always acted upon
- **Interactivity**: capable of interactivity with people and systems by means of live data

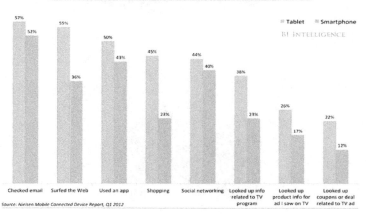

Source: Nielsen Mobile Connected Device Report, Q1 2012

Mobile is the third screen for advertising, the first and second screens being the TV and the computer. Now, funnily enough, even if we spend most of the money on traditional TV advertising, what do people do? While watching TV, they use their mobile. Most of the time, what are they doing? Email, then surfing the web, then apps, shopping, Social Networking, looking up information related to the TV program, looking up product information they saw on TV, looking for a coupon, deal, or discount related to TV. You can imagine, if we do this while watching TV, why put advertising on TV? Nobody is going to look at the advertising. You are just going to take your mobile, and when the advertising is finished and the movie continues, you (probably) put your phone down.

New Opportunities

With mobile, your business can:

- Rank in mobile search: SEO
- Advertise: PPC and Display
- Interact: Social Media / Geo Tagging
- Communicate: Email / SMS
- Sell: Mobile Site / App / M-Commerce

All with consumers chosen based on where they are and what they are doing.

With mobile, your business can rank in mobile search. Since April 25 last year, if you have a mobile-optimised website, you can rank in mobile SEO. If you do not have a mobile-optimised website, the chances that people will find your website when they search from mobile are tiny.

We can do advertising, pay per click, and display. We can even do specific advertising: in Google Adwords, we can set it up to do advertising specifically only for mobile. So if you search from desktop, you get one message; if you search from mobile, I can send you a different message.

Mobile Fit

Is Mobile Marketing appropriate for your organisation?

- **Usage and Adoption**: Are your customers using mobile?
- **Culture**: How is mobile viewed in your region?
- **Preferences**: How is mobile used in your region?
- **Risks**: What are the risks to your brand on mobile?
- **Integration**: How will you integrate mobile with your existing marketing activities?
- **Skills**: Do you have the skill set required to conduct mobile marketing?

There are some things to consider. Even if everyone has a mobile, we need to know how our customers are using mobile. Say you are selling to Central Africa, where people do not have a mobile. That is a different game. What is the culture of mobile like in your region? What are the preferences? What are the risks of putting your brand on a mobile?

Integration: how will you integrate mobile marketing with existing marketing activities? Because it is not just about mobile. You will learn later in my book how to integrate all the channels, all the aspects, all the strategies together. Another important question is, what are the skills that we need to learn? Or, what kind of skills do we need in the people, or the company, we hire for mobile marketing?

Mobile Goals

What do you want to achieve with mobile marketing?

- **Business Goals**: lead generation, sales, cost reduction
- **Customer Service Goals**: satisfaction, referral, repeat business
- **Product Goals**: product research, design, enhancement
- **Communication Goals**: communicating brand personality, reputation management
- **Marketing Goals**: branding, awareness, engagement, response, lead generation, conversion

Why do we need to do mobile marketing? It depends. We may have business goals to generate leads to generate sales, reduce cost, or provide customer service.

Now, the latest trend is this: big companies started offering customers service support on WhatsApp, because today everyone is on WhatsApp. And it is so easy . . . If you call me and you say, "Look, I have a problem with my mouse . . . I don't know, there is a light. There is a message that I don't understand."

Instead of spending one hour of explaining and trying to understand what you mean and what I mean, I say, "Can you take

a picture with your mobile and send it to me on WhatsApp?"
Then I can see it. "Ah, easy! You just need to put a new battery
in." So easy, with one picture.

You may have product goals (product research, product design,
product enhancement), communication goals (communicating
the brand personality or our company reputation), or marketing goals (branding, awareness, engagement, response, lead
generation, conversions).

It is up to you to tell me what is going to be your goal for mobile.
It is not going to only be selling more. Sometimes, you do a
campaign to get customer service, communication, or something else.

Potential Risks with Mobile

- Intrusiveness
- Breach of privacy
- Bad campaign
- Annoyance
- Brand damage
- Irritation
- Saturation
- Data protection issues

The main risk is the intrusiveness, because you cannot send an SMS with promotions and amazing discounts every weekend. It happened to me, so I called the company many times, I insulted them repeatedly, and finally, they removed my number. So, for a month or two, I was okay, and then suddenly—ding ding ding—more SMS. That was crazy!

Even email marketers think, "It is free to send email. When we send 1 million emails, somebody will reply! And if you don't reply, who cares?" No, you should care.

Because our beloved Apple does not send email spamming messages telling you how amazing the iPhone 6++ is and you should buy it now immediately, with 20% discount. They do not send you the same email five times a day!

If you are intrusive, people will not love your product.

The other risks are breach of privacy, bad campaign, annoyance, brain damage, irritation, and saturation. If there are too many people sending you the same message, even a good message is not good anymore. I remember, a few years ago, it was nice to receive "Merry Christmas" or "Eid Mubarak" from your bank. Now, every year, I receive so many SMS, so many emails, and so many things about Eid Mubarak, Happy New Year, etc. Now it is not cool anymore.

We need to check if what we want to do is not outdone by other people. It is cool the first time. Even many years ago, when telemarketing was something new, it was okay. Now, every day, somebody calls from a bank or from some company trying to sell you something.

That has become saturated, so it is better to change. Otherwise, "Oh, this guy! No, no, no, I don't wanna buy anything from you." Even if you are very kind, your company is very kind, your brand is very nice, when you do the same things that everyone else is doing in a saturated channel, people perceive you as a boring company, boring people, boring salesperson. Maybe you are not, but this happens because you are doing it in a saturated market.

The last risk is data protection issues for mobile devices, because it is related to privacy and it depends on the laws in different countries.

Reaching the 5 Types of M-Shoppers

Often, we think that people who have a mobile also shop online using mobile.

In the United States, they are so advanced at tracking and sub-segmenting customers that even among people that purchase online with their mobile, they distinguish between five personality types. Imagine how crazy that is. You know that a percentage of people that have a mobile also purchase online. Out of those that purchase online, we can distinguish 5 personality types:

1. **Exploiters**: These are the smallest group of M-Shoppers currently (6%). They are the most likely to visit a showroom. But retailers would be wise to try to entice this group to still buy from their organisation, by improving the effectiveness and efficiency of their website. Apparently, this group is almost as likely to buy it from their site as they are from a competitor. Mobile Strategy: Vouchers, Mobile Payment Processing
2. **Savvys**: This group knows what they want and how to look for it. They are the second smallest group (13%), but the best group for targeting with mobile experiences. Because they are comfortable with their technology, the

savvys are the best group for testing loyalty programs, offers, and new programs through their mobile devices. Mobile Strategy: Vouchers, Information Apps, Loyalty Programs, Mobile Payment Processing

3. **Price Sensitives**: Slightly larger than the Savvys (at 19%), this group responds to both types of experiences: retail and mobile. They do not always use their mobile devices when shopping, and usually respond well to store promotions. This is a group to target with X and Y. Mobile Strategy: Vouchers, Loyalty Programs

4. **Traditionalists**: This group poses the least threat of showrooming of all the groups. That is because they are mostly using the phone to consult with friends and family, or to look up online reviews (sound like anyone you know?). Traditionalists are likely to interact with your company in the store, on the website, and through an app. They are also likely to respond to a QR code. Generally, however, this group (which is about 30% of the market) is going to buy in the store. Mobile Strategy: Information apps, loyalty programs

5. **Experience Seekers**: As the largest group in the study (at 31%), the experience seekers value the customer experience more than price. The group shows retailers that there are lots of opportunities to expand the mobile experience with their shoppers. But they also show that retailers must also provide an excellent in-store experience. Mobile Strategy: Loyalty programs

Mobile Role in the Mix

What is the mobile's role in the mix? On one side, we have Customer Engagement. On the other side, we have Brand Awareness. So, what do we want to do? We want to make sure that we can direct our customers in as many directions as possible. With email, we get engagement but not much brand awareness; with mobile, we get everything.

This is an interesting chart that tells us what we get according to what we want to achieve, and what is the best strategy to use. Mobile is exactly in the middle of all of them.

Convergence

Device functionality begins to come together in one device:

- SMS
- Camera
- Music
- Phone
- Browser
- GPS
- Email
- Office Applications
- Social Media
- Gaming

Mobile Optimised Website

A mobile optimised website is a variant of an existing website that is optimised using style sheets to facilitate presentation on a mobile device. (Digital Marketing Institute)

Users that browse to a website using a mobile device are automatically redirected to the mobile version of the site.

The best way to check how our mobile is performing is with the Google Page Speed Test, which tells us how fast the mobile version of our website is. It tells us if there are problems. That is very important.

The most obvious difference between desktop and mobile version website is that, in mobile, most of information is removed, and only the key information is left. Also, the font size automatically increases. We should not need to zoom in, scroll down, and move around too much. Mobile is perfectly user friendly, and we get the information we need immediately. Normally, on a good mobile website, not all the information is displayed, only parts that people on the move need. Do not forget to put the most important of all of them, which is the call button, that thing that when you click it opens up the conversation. Otherwise, you have to copy the number, go out of the website, and paste the number to make the call. Too complicated. Having a call button is good, and you can also track the calls.

Today, for most websites, 50% of the traffic is on mobile. There is no excuse.

On top of that, especially from mobile, if you ask a person to fill in a form, nobody does this. Even if you put just 3 questions, it is too much, so you have to be careful because these are customers that you are losing. It is much better to allow people to sign up to your mobile website through their Social Network accounts (Google, Facebook, LinkedIn). Why ask me for my name and my email, if there is a way for you to know it already? With the social login, I just click, and you automatically get my details; I don't need to write anything, and you are sure that the details I put in are correct.

Advantages *of mobile websites*

Immediacy – Mobile Websites Are Instantly Available:

- Apps, on the other hand, require the user to first download and instal the app from an app marketplace before the content or application can be viewed

Compatibility – Mobile Websites are Compatible Across Devices:

- A single mobile website can reach users across many different types of mobile devices, whereas native apps require a separate version to be developed for each type of device

Upgradability – Mobile Websites Can Be Updated Instantly
- You can change the design or content of a mobile website and the changes are immediately visible; updating an app, on the other hand, requires the updates to be pushed to users, which then must be downloaded in order to update the app on each type of device

Findability – Mobile Websites Can be Found Easily
- Mobile websites are displayed in search results, making it easy for qualified visitors to find you; in contrast, the visibility of apps is largely restricted to manufacturer app stores

Shareability – Mobile Websites Can be Shared Easily by Publishers, and Between Users
- Mobile website URLs are easily shared between users via a simple link (e.g. within an email, text message, Facebook or Twitter post); an app cannot be shared in this fashion

Reach – Mobile Websites Have Broader Reach
- Because a mobile website is accessible across platforms and can be easily shared among users, as well as search engines, it has far greater reach capability than a native app

Life-Cycle – Mobile Websites Can't be Deleted
- The average shelf-life of an app is less than 30 days, according to some research. Mobile websites, on the other hand, are always available for users to return to them

Time and Cost – Mobile Websites are Easier and Less Expensive
- Mobile website development is considerably more time and cost efficient than development of a native app, especially if you need to have a presence on different platforms (requiring development of multiple apps)

Support and Sustainability
- The investment considerations of app vs. website do not end with the initial launch; properly supporting and developing an app (upgrades, testing, compatibility issues and ongoing development) is more much more expensive and involved than supporting a website over time

Features of good mobile optimised websites

- Usability
- Legibility
- Image Size
- Site Navigation
- Page Structure
- Scrolling
- Version Redirection
- Integration with Phone functionality

Good optimised mobile websites are usable, easy-to-read, they have good image sizes (visible but small in terms of size), and they are easy to navigate. Now, there are standards. Everyone knows that if you see a little thing on the right and you tap on it, this is a menu. It is a common thing nowadays.

The page structure has to be very simple. It has to have scrolling and you have to choose how to make your mobile website appealing. Many websites, for example, when you open them with your tablet, they think you are on your mobile, and they show you the mobile version. And it does not look nice on tablet. So, you need to make sure that the system detects correctly if you are navigating from a tablet or a mobile, and show you the right version of the website.

Also, the good mobile websites integrate with all the phone functionalities. The main functionality that you want to use is the call, right? This is the number one thing that you need. Everything else, I don't care. What is the main reason you are interested in people going to your website, from your desktop or your mobile? To convert.

Either I fill in a form or I send you an email or I click . . . and I call. Then when I call you, you reply, and you ask me for the information you need. But don't ask me the information before I have even contacted you, when I don't know if I even want to consider you as a potential supplier. Why are you asking me for information before I have even decided that, and giving me nothing in exchange? You are going to make me waste time giving my information, before even knowing if I want to do business with you?

I remember, one day I called an insurance company that was supposed to be huge in Dubai and they told me, "We don't give any information on the phone. You need to come to our office." What? In the world of internet, you cannot give me any information, not even via the phone? No, sorry, you can tell your boss that you have lost the Farioli family, including its kids, because I will never come to your office. Bye-bye! I do not know how much money an insurance company can make out of a family in a lifetime, but they lost it. If you want to work this way, and if you want to force me to come to your office just to answer some basic information, you can wait. I do not know how many people are going to come to your office.

Also, you need integration with phone. This means you need to be sure that what happens on the phone works. If you get a lot of phone calls and then everyone is asking you the same question, and you say, "No, you need to pass by our office," then bye-bye, let us count how many clients you lose because of that.

Before, not mobile optimised:

After:

O'Mahonys Mobile Digest - October Issue

The Bloody Meadow by William Ryan

Captain Alexei Korolev returns...Following his investigations in "The Holy Thief", which implicated those at the very top of authority in Soviet Russia, Captain Alexei Korolev finds himself decorated and hailed as an example to all Soviet workers.

The Bloody Meadow
by William Ryan (save €2.38)

Captain Alexei Korolev returns...Following his investigations in "The Holy Thief", which implicated those at the very top of authority in Soviet Russia, Captain Alexei

Case Studies

It is important to understand that people on the move have different needs. They don't need the same long story.

Mobile Website   Standard Website

They need a short story that normally is: benefit, benefit, benefit, and Call to Action (CTA). Boom, boom, boom, go!

Gifts

Advertisers A and B both operate within the gift space. They have similar product offerings, and **both receive in excess of 10% of their traffic through the affiliate channel from mobile handsets**.

Advertiser A has a fully optimised mobile experience while Advertiser B directs visitors through a mobile device to the standard desktop version of the site. As a result, **Advertiser A** experiences a much better conversion rate through mobile handsets—converting at 5.3%.

As the customer journey through Advertiser B is not optimised for mobile, there is a higher drop off rate and conversions have suffered. **Advertiser B by contrast only converts 1.3% of its mobile traffic.**

Footwear

Advertiser C has a mobile optimised site in place whereas advertiser D again directs to the standard desktop version of the site.

With the ability to seamlessly browse products, add them to your basket, and complete the transaction without any need to resize the screen, **Advertiser C has a conversion rate of 3.2% through mobile handsets whereas Advertiser D only converts barely a third of that rate.**

Apps

"An app is an application, typically a small, specialised program downloaded onto a mobile device."

Mobile apps are still booming, and they started on July 13, 2008, when our beloved Steve Jobs launched the iPhone 3 and introduced the App Store. This was the beginning of the revolution. In 2008, only iPhone 3 users could use apps, until they introduced the iPad. That was another boom: bigger screen, bigger apps. Soon iPhone 4, iPad2, iPhone 5. Immediately all kinds of apps flooded the market. Shopping, dating, whatever it is, every sector was growing. The number one benefactor was hospitality.

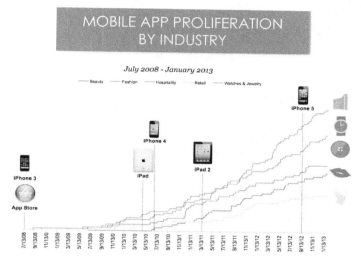

Mobile apps proliferation by industry

Why Do People Use Mobile Apps?

Drivers of App usage:

1. *Apps allow you to customize a phone to your specific set of wants and needs*
2. *Apps can offer users a rich and interactive experience*
3. *When done right, apps make people's lives easier; the best apps identify a need or problem that average people have and seek to provide a solution to meet that need*
4. *Follow the Crowd: "Everyone else seems to the using them and I'll be left out if I don't figure this out"*
5. *It is perceived as Cool/Fashionable*
6. *For Entertainment and Games*
7. *Because the mobile web can frustrate some users due to the lack of mobilisation, and apps provide a more phone centric experience*

Watch this video made by Axe in Japan: it is a campaign done a few years ago, and they called it "the make up call." That, for me, was a genius brilliant idea, and it got several awards.

https://www.youtube.com/ watch?v=q6isqDG0lEk

This video makes you want to install an app and use it every day. And what the app does is that it reminds you to use the product! They also built it with traditional ads. You cannot make an app and just think, "I made an amazing app, and everyone is going to know." No, nobody is going to know. It is like a website. You may have an amazing website, but who is going to know about it? Nobody, if you don't promote the website. So, Axe promoted the app with every other channel. This way, their users learn about the app, like it, use it, and want to keep using it every day. And they want to be sure they use the app, otherwise the lady gets angry! And at the end, bottom line, the lady is telling you to remember to use the product.

That is really crazy! It is a genius thing. Of course, it might not work everywhere. I agree with you: you cannot do this in Saudi!

#SoMoLo: Social, Mobile, Local

So let us talk about #SoMoLo. This crazy concept is not reinventing the wheel, just shaping the wheel into a different shape. Sometimes, you don't need to create crazy things: you just need to be smart, clever and creative.

- **Social**: Social customers seek advice from friends, family, and other buyers every time they make a purchase decision

- **Mobile**: with smart phones and tablets, SoMoLo customers are on-the-go. They seek information from every location
- **Local**: SoMoLo customers use location apps such as FourSquare to make the most of their surroundings

This is the area in which mixing different strategies can get you a better outcome than the sum of the individual parts. We have seen how to do Social Media many times. Still, every day somebody tells you that there is new trick to do in Social Media. Well, that is just Social Media.

In Mobile Marketing, we have seen even more tricks, ideas, and topics, in addition to old-school Local Marketing, which is banners or whatever you do in your business or your shop, or in front or around your shop to attract customers.

The difference is that Local Marketing, which has been done for centuries—even before marketing was invented—relies on customers passing in front of your shop and you finding a way to convince them to come in. Even the simple board in front of your restaurant that says, "Special promotion of the day 35 dirham lunch," is Local Marketing.

Some clever people came up with the concept of mixing the three strategies to create something amazing. I like the phrase that says,

> *"The future isn't about mobile. It's about mobility." (David Armano, Edelman Digital)*

The point is, the future is not the mobile device but what you do with it. First, when somebody interacts with you through this device, remember that they are on the move or they are in the middle of something. This can be good or bad. If they are in the middle of something and you force them to interact with you, you are never going to get anything. But in the moment that they are okay with it, then they can interact with you, even when they are in the toilet!

Special Apps *to post on Social Media*

During my seminars, when I explain mobile, I take a picture with my smartphone: a selfie with my students. Then, in few seconds, I show them live that I can publish it simultaneously on different Social Media platforms. They always say, "Oh, how did you do that?" Simple, I use an app: Buffer.

Then I say to my students, "Okay, guys. What should we learn from this simple exercise?"

Two things:

First, posting on five Social Media platforms can be very easy, much more than you can possibly think. Maybe when you post, you open every platform, you think about what to post, you look at the moon, the stars, the planets, and after two hours, you know what you are going to post, and you write, and you change your idea, and then you need to open every platform, and change, and do, and "na na na na na"! Sometimes, sharing a simple picture with a simple question is easier than you may think.

Secondly, there are many apps that allow you to simultaneously post one thing in several platforms. One of those is Bufferapp. com, a system where you link different Social Media accounts, and you post on your walls through Buffer. You can plan for the future or you can choose a posting frequency: let us say, I post twice a day, in the morning at 9:30 and in the afternoon at 4:30. Good! Whatever you want to post, you send it to Buffer. So, in one day, you could draft 10, 20, even 30 posts and then, every day, at the perfect time, it posts for you. Boom, boom, boom!

Another tool, the first and most advanced software to post in Facebook and other Social Media, is Hoot Suite. Buffer is purely for posting, not for engaging or for follow-up. It is only to post, and you can do the same from your computer or your mobile.

So in two seconds, I posted on five Social Media platforms!

Now the game is the following. If I want to get people commenting on my post, I will need to think a lot and create something amazing, unbelievable, and share it and also pay for the advertising, otherwise nobody is going to see what I post.

When you have local marketing, or a local event, you have people next to your shop, your place, or your event, so there are many tricks that you can do to eventually get people engaging with your comments or content. One of the simplest is the one I do with my students during my seminars: I take a selfie and then ask my students, "Guys, can you engage with my Social Media accounts a little bit?" A little bit, that is it. This gives my Social Media a little bit of a boost.

Virgin Radio *case history*

Virgin Radio is an awesome example of this. The radio saw that the internet was getting more important, and people were starting to download podcasts, stay online, and listen to music online. The radio was afraid that, one day, you would go to your car and you would not listen to the radio anymore; you would listen to a podcast, or put on YouTube, or play your own music in the car. In order to increase the engagement, many times, radio stations post stuff and, on the radio, tell you to go and check it out. They would say, "Hey, we just posted a crazy picture! Go and check it out on Facebook/radio and comment: you can win a prize!"

What do you do? You go on your mobile, you check, you comment, you post, you laugh, you reply, whatever you do. So, even when you switch off Virgin Radio because you have left your car, you at least already like the Virgin Radio Facebook page. Then they follow you even when you are not listening to their radio. They make you engage on Social Media.

The radio are very good at this because they learned what engagement means long before the social network was invented. The radio has never been just playing music and that is it. When you just play music, there are 1 million stations that do the same. But the good ones are those where there is a speaker who engages with the audience and says, "Hey guys, have you ever left your girlfriend by SMS? Tell us your story!" And then you send the SMS, or you call: you engage.

People like to hear other people's stories. They have been doing this for the decades. Now, there are Social Networks, but when you know how to do a proper radio show, you can do well on Social Network too. When you know how to do both, you combine, and you multiply the results. Imagine how many likes Virgin Radio is getting for free, without advertising.

So, if you are smart and you come up with an idea that mixes the Local Market with Social and Mobile, you win!

Wiman *(Social Wi-Fi Router) case history*

I will give you another example: the Social (Wi-Fi) Router. A few years ago, I came up with the idea of building a Social Router. One week before starting the project and getting people working on in, I spoke with a friend of mine and he told me, "But there is already one. There is a company in Italy that already did this."

"Are you joking? After six months of planning, you tell me that somebody already did it and it's working?"

"Yes, that's it."

It was a company that was awarded by Tech Crunch, and it was called Wiman. This was the absolutely first Social Router. How does it work?

You put it in any cafe or any public place that you want, connected to the internet. You give people a way to access the internet. When the customer checks with their computer or their mobile, they see "Free Wi-Fi." Great! They connect. When they connect, a page opens that says, "To get free Wi-Fi, you need to login with your Google account or Facebook account."

So, you don't need to ask the person at the counter, "What's the password?" and they reply, "I don't know, I'm new," or "I don't know, the password has been changed."

You just login with your own Facebook or Google account, and then you can browse the internet. At the same time, the system clicks "Like" to the place's Facebook page. So, for the cafe, bar, or restaurant, I let you browse the internet for free, but this is not a cost to me. Rather, it is a marketing tool, because the more people browsing the internet at my place, the more people like my Facebook page. And who actually likes my Facebook page? Not some random person in South Africa that nobody knows and never comes to my place. No, it is a real customer of my business, someone who knows my store and has visited it. This is priceless, because you build a community of people that are the real community of people around you.

That is the amazing concept of SoMoLo. It is not just one thing, it is many systems and tools that came out a couple of years ago with the idea of SoMoLo. So, when you have a strategy, don't think in compartments, like, the Social media compartment should only do Social media, the mobile compartment should only do mobile, traditional advertiser only do banners, etc. Find a creative way to mix them, and you will see the results.

The Big Decision: App vs. Mobile Website

Apps

- Platform specific
- Does not always require internet access
- Can leverage the features and functions of the phone: Camera, GPS, Accelerometer, etc.
- Generally built for a specific purpose or use

Mobile Website

- Platform Agnostic
- Will render on any handset
- Uses standard, recognisable interface and navigation
- Generally built for a wide range of uses

When you have reached the limitations of what a website can do, an app allows you access to the functionality of the phone to provide a specific service or function.

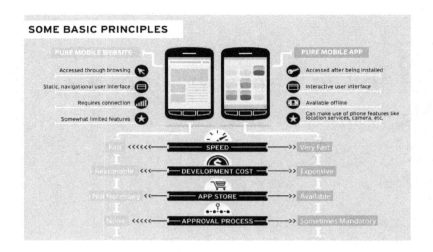

In this infographic, you can see the big differences.

With a pure mobile website, you access through the browser, every browser can work. It is static, requiring a connection, and has somewhat limited functionality. You can use the phone, and there are few little things you can do, but not everything. The mobile App can work after being installed, but you need to install it first. Sometimes, we check a website and, two seconds later, we leave.

You need to install the app first to use it. It has an interactive user interface: amazing, you can add all of the special effects that you want. It is available offline, even when there is no internet connection, or when you are working in a country where 3G internet connection is not easily accessible.

It is big here now, but two years ago, few people had the full 3G connectivity, and most of them had a limited 1 gigabyte, so they could not browse, send photos and videos online; they did not have enough data. Apps can make use of phone features like location services, camera, etc. With an app, you can do whatever you want with your phone.

What about characteristics? In terms of speed, mobile websites are fast, but an app is much faster. In terms of development costs, mobile websites are reasonable, but an app is expensive. In terms of the app store, for the mobile website, it is not necessary, but for the App, it is often mandatory, and an approval process is needed. Sometimes, there is a tiny little thing in your App that is not approved.

Therefore, if you are launching an event and you need an app for a specific time, you need to have the app ready quite a long time in advance. You need to make sure it is ready, tested, and works for many devices.

When to Use an App

Interactivity/Gaming

- For interactive games (think Angry Birds), an app is almost always going to be your best choice, at least for the foreseeable future

Regular Usage/Personalisation

- If your target users are going to be using your app in a personalised manner on a regular basis, then an app provides a great way to do that

Complex Calculations or Reporting

- If you need something that will take data and allow you to manipulate it with complex calculations, charts, or reports (think banking or investment), an app will help you do that very effectively

Native Functionality or Processing Required

- Mobile web browsers are getting increasingly good at accessing certain mobile-specific functions such as click-to-call, SMS, and GPS. However, if you need to access a user's camera or processing power, an app will still do that much more effectively

No connection required

- If you need to provide offline access to content or perform functions without a network/wireless connection, then an app makes sense

Mobile App Platforms

Apps platforms include:

Android, iOS, Blackberry, Windows Mobile,

- Apps are specific to the platform that they are built on. Many companies create apps for multiple platforms (Rovio, Skype, etc.)
- Companies also make their platform decisions depending on the number of their users that use the platform and the critical mass of apps on that platform
- Each platform has its own app store:
  - » iOS – Apple App Store
  - » Android – Google Play Store
  - » Windows Mobile – Windows Market Place for Mobile
  - » Blackberry – Blackberry App World

Attributes of an Effective App

- Built around a specific need
- Clear utility value
- Integrates with the devices' functionality
- Easy to use
- Interactive
- Live status or information updates

How can you release an effective app. or plan to release an effective app? Our job, most likely, is not to physically develop an app, but to plan a good app to solve our problems. We can get another company to do the actual development.

An effective app has to be built around a specific need. It has to have a clear utility value. So, I ask you, what is the value of your app? What is the value that the user of the app will get?

An effective app has to be integrated with the device functionality, to make it easy to use and interactive. Eventually, it can give you live status and information updates, so you can get the wind direction, the wind speed, how many calories you are burning, and so on.

App Development Process

The app development process should include the following steps:

1. Justify
Justify why you are developing an app. State the specific utility value. Define your goal for the customer and the business.

3. Submit
Be aware of the submission routine and approval timelinesfor relevant app stores.

5. Measure
Be aware that measurement happens through the apps store in terms of measurement and purchases but also in analytics in terms of mobile OS.

Justify | Build | Submit | Promote | Measure | Update

2. Build
Choose experienced Developers. How will this App integrate functionally? How will consumers interact? How often will you update data and functionality? Test before going live.

4. Promote
What type of marketing and promtion will be adopted for the app: Submit for Review, Social Media, Digital Marketing. Drive early and concentrated sales for postion in charts.

6. Update
Consider the frequency of data updates in real time. Also schedule functionality upgrades to maintain usage levels.

What is the process and steps for app development? First, you justify the reason why you need to build the app. Then you build it, then you submit it to the App Store, then you promote the app. Don't expect that just because your app is amazing that "I'm going to become a billionaire in one week!" Nobody knows about your app. Even if you really build a life-changing game, or an app that will revolutionise humankind, nobody knows. Once it is published to the App Store or to the Google Play Store, still nobody knows about it. Therefore, you need to promote your app, in the digital and the traditional world. Then you measure the results and you update the app.

Whenever you go to any company or agency to develop an app for you, make sure they give a one-year warranty, because even the best, perfectly working app today can develop some glitches in few months' time. If you have a one year warranty from the developer, whatever happens—for example, the new apple iPhone 6, 7, 8 comes out—they will need to check if it works, and if not, fix it. You cannot expect the app to work forever.

SMS Marketing

The oldest way to do mobile marketing was SMS marketing, but apparently, when I moved to Dubai, not one single company or freelancer was doing it. Only after several years did companies finally start to come back to SMS marketing again. Everyone was so focused on Social Media, the latest thing, that we forgot about the basics: the SMS marketing.

Now, more and more companies are doing SMS marketing daily. Unfortunately, they are doing it the wrong way: the bad way, nasty, annoying way!

Short Message Service (SMS)

"SMS Short Message Service is the common term for the sending of 'short' (160 characters or fewer, including spaces) text messages to mobile phones." Source: Digital Marketing Institute

Today, we are spoiled customers. A few years ago, if you got a flyer on your doorstep, you would say, "Oh, there's a flyer. Let's read it. Okay, this is going to be good for my wife!" But when you get a pile of piece of flyers every day, you don't bother reading them. If you get one SMS, you think, "Oh, so cool!" Now, when you get hundreds of SMS, you don't care about what they say. When they send you targeted advertising, it is okay, but you don't like when it is not targeted. When some advertisers are getting so much better at this, bad advertisers are going to look terrible, and SMS is an example of this.

*Opt-***In** *and Opt-***Out**

In the United Arabian Emirates, there is a law from the Telecommunications

Regulatory Authority (TRA) that says you need to allow customers to opt-in and opt-out.

Opt-in: Mobile marketing is opt-in marketing, or permission-based. Consumers must pre-qualify themselves and opt-in before they are approached via mobile marketing. Opt-in means you have to send a message after somebody requests to get messages from you. However, here, whenever a marketing manager leaves a company, they take the database. They go to a new company and the company says, "Oh great! We hire you!" However, in the new company, nobody has the permission to send messages to the contacts on the database.

Opt-out: Similarly, the consumer must be allowed to opt out the same way they "opted in." This could be by dialling or by SMS. Opt-out means that you need to explain to the user how to get out. For example, when I subscribe, I fill in this little questionnaire because I wanted to win a Ferrari, and, from then on, I get 25 SMS advertising. You need to have the option to opt-out and remove yourself from the list. I remember, many years ago, there was a law in Italy that you could opt-out from SMS, but to do it you had to read the instructions and send a letter to the headquarters. They said it took 15 days to activate the procedure in order to be removed. That is crazy!

Why use **SMS**?

- Targeted
- Relevant
- Timely
- Personalised
- 98% open rate (Your Region?)
- Possibility of integration
- Part of marketing mix

Why use SMS? SMS has 98% open rate. This is the main reason to use SMS. When you receive an SMS, most of the time, you open it within an hour. Nothing else has such a large opening rate. I go to home and I see a bunch of flyers, I take them and put them in the trash, even if maybe some of them may be offering a life changing opportunity. But with SMS, you open every one of them. You open and you read. Why is that? Because with SMS, when you see a number, your brain says, "Aren't you curious to know who sent you the SMS?"

Statistics *for SMS*

- Despite a 47% smartphone penetration rate, **91% of smartphone users still use basic text message**, 2.5 and 8 times higher than any mobile message application (Souktel)
- Thanks to mobile penetration, **Saudi Arabia has the largest telecom market in the GCC sized at USD 11.6 billion in 2010** (Delta Partners Group)
- Text messages are read within 4 minutes, compared to 48 hours for email (Zawya)

- Response rates via SMS are 8 times that of email (Souktel)
- There are twice as many active SMS users in the world than active users of email (Zawya)
- 55% of global SMS subscribers say they use the technology to communicate with clients, customers, and business partners (Zawya)
- **67% of mobile phone users worldwide subscribe to an SMS text messaging service**; 2.1 billion people actively text on a regular basis (Zawya)
- The Arab world saw a 23% annual growth rate in mobile subscriptions between 2006-2012, making it the second fastest-growing region in the world, surpassed only by Africa (Souktel)
- In South Africa, Google says 25% of its searches during the week are via mobile, rising to 65% on the weekends (CNN)

SMS Marketing **Goals**
What do you want to achieve with mobile marketing?

- **Business Goals**: lead generation, sales, cost reduction
- **Customer Service Goals**: satisfaction, referral, repeat business
- **Product Goals**: product research, design, enhancement
- **Communication Goals**: communicating brand personality, reputation management
- **Marketing Goals**: branding, awareness, engagement, response, lead generation, conversion

A well-crafted SMS marketing message is concise, high impact, targeted, relevant, and context sensitive.

Campaign considerations

- What is my campaign objective?
- Do I have a mobile contact database?
- Have the contacts given permission to be contacted?
- Will my campaign be measurable?
- Where will the analytics come from?
- Do I need a short code?
- Will I use a keyword?
- **A well-crafted SMS marketing message is concise, high impact, targeted, relevant, and context sensitive.**

Here, I am going to show you the best SMS I ever received:

SMS #1: *"Time is running out. Own the best waterfront hotel apartment in Burj Area Dubai. AED 864,000 only. Sale open 21 Sep. Phone number/Email address."*

Why is this great? First of all, it starts with, "Time is running out." This is something in NLP (Neuro-Linguistic Programming) and also in copywriting, which is called "scarcity." So, when you read, "Time is running out," you say, "Oh, what's going on?! I need to be ready for action." So, they don't start with a description, "blah, blah, blah . . ." First, they catch your attention. Then, they make you feel that you already "own." They don't ask you if you want to "buy," they tell you that you already own, so they make you feel that you are already an owner. What do you own? Not a normal apartment, but a "waterfront apartment," and also a "hotel apartment." You feel that you already own the best waterfront hotel apartment. You are the king of the universe! When they talk about the price, they write "only," so you think it is cheap! Lastly, you see that they open sales on 21 September. And you check: that is tomorrow! They don't send you this message two weeks before, they send it one day before the open sales. Otherwise, you would not remember it.

A concept in marketing states that you should never give the price. That way, people call you and they ask you, "What is the price?" and you can capture that person. But this campaign is for cash buyers, and it is sent to a large number of people. It is basically saying, "If you don't have 864,000 Dirham in your bank account, don't even bother me!"

SMS #2 (one day later): *"Own the best waterfront hotel apartment in Burj Area Dubai. From AED 1800/sq. Sales open today."*

They tell you the price for the apartment size, so you can understand how big these apartments are.

SMS #3 (one day later): *"Own the best waterfront hotel apartment in Burj Area Dubai. From AED 1800/sq. Visit Damac Office."*

That is, you are not too late, you can still visit the office.

SMS #4 (10 days later): *"Luxury Villas at Akoya by Damac. Booking starts from AED 653,000."*

This means they have started selling the cheaper ones. But this is also tricky, because it just mentions booking; this is not the cost of a villa, it is the booking amount. It is the amount you need to pay to book your villa. Then, when your villa is ready, you will pay the instalment, and many other costs.

SMS #5 (a few days later): *"Luxury apartments at Akoya by Damac overlooking Golf Course. Bookings start from AED 130,000 only."*

Now it is asking, "Do you have 130,000 Dirhams? Because we have apartments to sell as well." So, from the first SMS you started dreaming, and now you think, "Oh, even with only 130,000 Dirhams, I can still own a little bit of the dream!"

So, the entire SMS sequence was more than perfect! Even with an SMS campaign, you can get amazing results. Now you understand that planning an SMS campaign is very different from just sending a simple SMS. You need a strategy, a plan, and a budget, otherwise you will not get results. You could send 200,000 SMS and only get one inquiry.

SMS Campaign **Constraints**

- There is a strict requirement to be relevant
- There is a strict requirement to be to targeted
- There is a strict requirement to be specific
- Message is 160 characters, so choose words carefully
- Always have a call to action—link, short code, response
- Best practise is always to include an opt-out

- Be engaging with your message
- Anticipate what the response will be
- Is it a managed or self-service product?
- Is it accessible online as SAAS?
- Can I change the sender ID?
- Can I schedule texts?
- Do they support short codes?
- Do they support group lists?
- What are the upfront costs?
- What are the ongoing costs?

Legally, in theory, to send an SMS in the UAE, you need to apply, and you get a specific ID. It is a number given only to you. It costs 500 Dirhams for a one off. So, every time you send SMS in the future, you use the same ID. Why? Because if somebody wants to complain, they have your ID, and you can be tracked. You could go with the dodgy agencies, which send SMS from abroad, without ID, but it is not advisable.

Short codes and **Keywords**

- **Short code**: a short telephone number used in SMS marketing by service providers to address and run campaigns aimed at consumers
- **Keyword**: a word or name used to distinguish a targeted message within a Short Code Service

Example of SMS with short codes:

"If you want special deals on concerts and events from Circle City Tickets, text TICKETS to 71813."

Steps in running a **Successful** *SMS Marketing campaign*

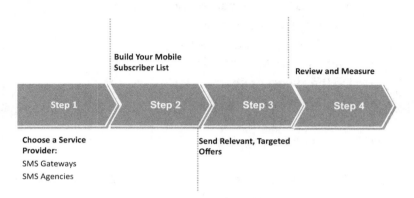

How can you run a good SMS campaign? First, you have to choose a Service Provider and then build your Subscribers List. You should not buy the list, and instead get the permission from your own people who already know your brand. Then, you send relevant and targeted offers, and review and measures the results.

SMS Campaign process steps:

1. Provider Selection
Justify why you are developing an app. State the specific utility value. Define your goal for the customer and the business.

2. Subscriber List
Choose experienced developers. How will this app integrate functionally? How will consumers interact? How often will you update data and functionality? Test before going live.

3. Landing Page

Be aware of the submission routine and approval timelines for relevant app stores.

4. Message Campaign

The type of marketing and promotion that will be adopted for the app: Submit for Review, Social Media, Digital Marketing, Drive early, and concentrated sales for position in charts.

5. Review and Measure

Be aware that measurement happens through the App Store in terms of measurement and purchases but also in Analytics in terms of mobile OS.

Why do I talk about landing page? Nowadays, all mobile phones have the internet. Even if they don't have internet 3G, everyone is on Wi-Fi. So, when there is an SMS and you put a short URL, a large amount of people click and see your website.

How can you track SMS? If you are smart enough, you create short codes connected to every mobile number that you are sending the message. So, I send a message to everyone, and for every person, there is a different code URL. When you open the SMS and you go to the URL, I will see in the tracking system that your specific mobile number clicked the URL, but the number of these persons did not click the URL. In this case, I know that I sent you a message, you read the message, but you did not click it. Either you do not have a smartphone, or you are not so interested, or it was not the right time for you. Other people clicked it, and they went to my website. So, the next day, I can run a telemarketing campaign. I call you, because I know that you went to my website, and that you are possibly interested. Then, I can convince you to buy the product, to register, or to do something else.

Regulations *regarding SMS communications*

The Rules and Regulations:

- Ensure all subscribers opt-in
- Maintain subscription proof
- Only send between 7:00 a.m. and 9:00 p.m.
- Do not ask customers to respond with SMS or premium calls
- Users must be able to opt-out
- Don't SPAM: Only send relevant adverts to your relevant database segment

Mobile Goals

What do you want to achieve with mobile advertising?

- **Business Goals**: lead generation and sales
- **Product Goals**: product downloads, interactions, upgrades
- **Communication Goals**: communicating brand personality
- **Marketing Goals**: branding, awareness, engagement

Mobile Formats

- *Standard*
- *Expandable*
- *Interstitial*
- *Rich elements*
  - » *Video*
  - » *HTML overlays*
  - » *Interactive elements*
- *Phone Functionality*

Media Platforms

How to publish Mobile Advertising:

- Search (PPC)
- InApp Adverts (Direct/Agency)
- Mobile Sites (Direct/Agency)
- Networks (Google/Agency)
- Wi-Fi advertising (Direct/Agency)
- SoMoLo (Social Mobile Local)

Mobile Search

1256 x 1440	1024 x 768	640 x 960
10 results	5-6 results	2-3 results
+ sidebar		

You can do many different things with mobile, but there is a particularly interesting fact about search. In search, with Pay per click (PPC), we see a big difference. On desktop, we search, and we see a little bit of advertising: only four. From a tablet, when you search, the majority of the first page is taken up by PPC. When you search on mobile, it is even more. Almost the entire visual screen is Pay per click advertising.

This means that even if you do SEO well and you are in position number 2 or 3, when people are searching from mobile, they don't see you. They only see advertising first.

When they scroll, they see you, but on the first screen, they see just the advertising. So think about it this way: when people are on the move, if you don't do Pay Per Click, you miss many mobile users.

Spend on Mobile advertising in 2012, for example, was still predominantly in mobile search (IAB UK):

- Up to 60% of smartphone owners use their mobile device to search the web on daily basis
- Search for products/services
- Where are you driving traffic to?
- Do you have a mobile optimised site/page?
- Is your phone number clickable?
- Use search to drive app downloads

In-App Advertising

In-App adverts present advertising that is relevant to what you are doing:

- Using a fitness app to track your activity
- Using an entertainment app to search for cinema listings
- Using a timetable app to track arrival times of trains
- Use a film advertisement to support its listing in the cinema app

When you do in-app advertising, be careful. Choose your apps one by one. If I am advertising a movie, I put my ad in every movie app. If I put my banner in every possible app, I will get some bad surprises.

I will tell you a story. When I launched a campaign in this way, I saw many clicks in the results, but a very low conversion rate. What happened? A lot of clicks came from banners placed into apps. So, why they did they not convert? Let us go deeper and see from which app they came. There was a single app that got 35 clicks. The advertising was about financial information, but the app was the torch, for using your smartphone as a light when you are into the darkness. This was the number one app for number of clicks. Why do people using the torch need financial information? Then I downloaded the app myself in order to see what was happening. When I opened the app, I saw that there was a banner advertising that slowly moved across the page.

I discovered that they are really clever, because the torch app owners make money every time that somebody clicks on the banners! This is why I realised it is bad to choose the option "every app." You need to select them one by one. Obviously, if you remove "all the apps," it costs you more, but you get conversions.

Response Mechanisms

Mobile Advertising support numerous response mechanisms that take advantage of the mobile device's functionality.

The goal with mobile advertising is to encourage the user to move beyond simply clicking an ad, and to use the immediately available functionality of the device:

- Tap to Expand
- Tap to Buy
- Tap to Visit
- Tap to Call
- Tap to Apps
- Tap to Video
- Tap to YouTube
- Tap to Tweet/Facebook/LinkedIn
- Tap to Maps
- Sync to Calendar
- Tap to Photo

Proximity Marketing and Geo Targeting

- Proximity marketing is the localised wireless distribution of advertising content associated with a particular place
- Transmissions can be received by individuals in that location who wish to receive them and have the necessary equipment to do so

Distribution is targeted to devices known to be in a particular area. The location of a device may be determined by:

- A cellular phone being in a particular cell
- A Bluetooth or Wi-Fi device being within range of a transmitter
- An internet enabled device with GPS enabling it to request localised content from internet servers
- An NFC enabled phone reading a RFID chip on a product or media to launch localised content from internet servers

The closer users are to a business, the more likely they are to click through a mobile banner ad for that business.

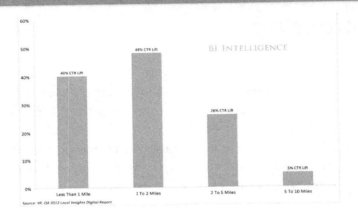

THE CLOSER USERS ARE TO A BUSINESS, THE MORE LIKELY THEY ARE TO CLICK THROUGH A MOBILE BANNER AD FOR THAT BUSINESS

Proximity marketing is a crazy concept. They discovered that people within 1 to 2 miles from a shop tend to take action more when they receive a message. If I send you a message, "Come to our amazing restaurant," but it would take a 2 hours' drive to go, you don't consider it. But if you are within 1-2 miles, you take action; more than if you are less than 1 mile! For some reason (and nobody knows why), if you are too close to a place, you don't take action as much as when you are 1 to 2 miles away.

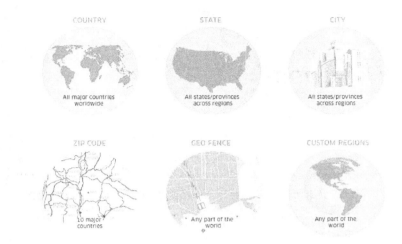

This is why some companies came out with the idea of Geo Fence and the Geo Targeting. This means targeting you when you are nearby a place. The Geo Fence is an area where, when you are coming in or out, I send you the SMS. For example, if you are getting closer to the Nike shop, when you are nearby, you receive the message, "50% discount on Adidas," so you go to Adidas. That is tricky, cheeky, clever.

QR Codes

- *A QR Code is a matrix barcode (or two-dimensional code), readable by QR scanners, mobile phones with a camera, and smartphones. The code consists of black modules arranged in a square pattern on white background. The information encoded can be text, URL or other data.* (Wikipedia)
- Advantages: Convenient, Cost Effective, Versatile, Measurable
- Used for: Linking to any web based content: Site, Video, Brochure, App, Contact, Feedback

How QR codes work:

- Create QR Code for free on web
- Publish QR Code on advert or poster
- User installs QR Code reader app on smart phone
- User scans QR Code
- User is redirected to Landing Page

QR Codes are good and bad. They are nothing new, having been invented in 1996; that is two decades ago. However, advertising companies only started using them in the last two or three years.

If you use the QR codes, don't expect many results because every mobile does not have a QR code reader installed, so you need to install the app first. When I went to Qatar, it seemed that everyone was going crazy for QR codes. Probably some agency was doing it, and they put them on the banners even on top of buildings. But if you are driving on the main street and you need to zoom the QR code with your smartphone, you crash your car! This really makes no sense. Use your brain first. You know what? I use the QR code on my business card, just to impress people. I don't expect people to use it.

I put it in the middle of my card and people ask me, "Does it really work?!" They try it and it works, and they are surprised!

I live in a country where there are many foreigners like me. People read my strange Italian name, and can rarely spell it right. Or maybe your phone number or your email is easy to write wrong. With the QR code, in one second, you can go to my website and see everything!

In advertising, the idea of using QR code was to connect with customers. I am driving my car on the main street. I see the banner, I scan the QR code, and I can continue following the company story without losing anything.

Practical Uses *of QR codes*
QR codes can be displayed on:

- The back of your business card
- Your brochures and other marketing materials

- The sides of trucks and trailers
- Product tags and packaging
- Convention and event nametags
- Restaurant menus
- Event ticket stubs
- Point-of-sale receipts

QR codes could link to:

- Installation instructions
- Sources for replacement parts and service
- Directions to your business
- The process for hiring your professional services
- Valuable coupons and special offers
- Recommendations for complementary products and services
- Free MP3 downloads
- Customer feedback forms

What is the practical use of QR codes? If you want to link to a map, for example, you can give away a flyer and you say, "Our location is here. Here's the link." But don't rely only on QR codes. Also, put the short URL. The QR code is a new experience, so the URL is for the more traditionalist users.

The cleverest QR code I have seen was in Tesco's virtual grocery store:

https://www.youtube.com/watch?v=nJVoYsBym88

As you can see in this video, this is at a metro station. It is not a supermarket, it is a printed billboard with one QR code for every product. So, while you are waiting for the metro, you scan with your phone the products you want: milk, sugar, orange juice, bananas, potatoes, etc. Then, you go into the metro, you check the things you want to buy, and you pay online from your smartphone. They know which station you are going to, and when you reach your station, there is a bag for you in a tiny little kiosk for delivery.

That is very clever. That is game-changing.

Mobile Trends

Identify key trends that illustrate the emerging use of mobile technologies in your region:

- Voice Activation: Siri from Apple or Google Voice search
- M-Commerce: E-Wallets, NFC Chips, Square
- Geo-Location: FourSquare, Groupon

Other trends:

- **Augmented Reality**: http://youtu.be/GBKy-hSedg8
- **Image Recognition - Google Goggles**: http://youtu.be/9apkpwDRl10
- **Gesture Based Technology**: http://youtu.be/LG7U_pNzM9U
- **Voice Recognition Advertising**: http://youtu.be/vu0g2i_uB6c
- **Google Glasses**: http://youtu.be/6BTCoT8ajbl
- **Samsung Flexible Screens**: http://youtu.be/CckFd79KDPg

The crazy clever **Shazam Advertising**

There are many crazy trends, but one that I consider very clever is Shazam advertising. Do you know what Shazam is? It is the app that, in 3 seconds, recognises any song being played around you. You can buy the song online, you can listen to it on YouTube, etc. This app has sometimes been used to do advertising. If you are watching TV, when you see advertising, sometimes there's the logo for Shazam. If you go to Shazam, it recognises the advertising and sends you to the link for the advertising. This is just a simple experience seeker game. It would be the same as putting the web URL on the screen. You go to your mobile and you write it in your browser. You get the same result.

Now you understand the difference between the experience seekers and the traditionalists. So, are you an experience seeker or a traditionalist? Why are you looking at me this way? Look at your face in the mirror. What are you thinking now? Write it down now. This will help you in your digital experience.

DIGITAL
PLANNING

Digital Marketing Plan Implications

What are the implications for marketing departments and their campaign planning?

> *"Understand what a Digital Marketing Plan is: a plan for implementing digital marketing within an organisation." (Digital Marketing Institute)*

What does it mean to do strategy and planning? It means to check and come back to our initial ideas, and go one by one, topic by topic, and put all of the topics together.

That looks simple. Yes, it looks simple, but it is not. How much of each ingredient should you put in? When is the time to put each ingredient into the mix? Now, I will ask you to write some things down.

There are three main things you must know:

1. *Which things am I already doing well? Make a list of these.*
2. *Which areas do I want to improve? Make a list of these.*
3. *What resources do I have? This can be people, tools, skills, companies, employees, colleagues, etc.*

Understand that I did not put what you "need" to improve but what you "want" to improve. Eventually, you will learn which topics are important and which ones are not. Therefore, it is up to you to decide.

I am already doing these things well:

_____

_____

_____

_____

I want to improve these areas:

_____

_____

_____

_____

I have these resources to help me:

_____

_____

———————————————————————————

———————————————————————————

Did you do this exercise? No? Do it now! It is really helpful for you.

Good! Now you have done it. That was the first step. Only when you understand where you are can you know where you want to go.

Strategy and Planning: Bringing It All Together

The questions we will answer in this chapter are:

- Where do I start?
- How can I put together a plan to reach my target audience?
- How do I select the right channels?
- How do I know if my campaign is successful?
- How do I improve my digital marketing over time?

Strategy and Planning Process

Strategy and Planning: bringing it all together:

- **Structure**: Start small and get bigger & better
- **Budget**: Start small and invest based on success
- **Calendar**: Organic with no end point
- **Personnel**: New work, so new skills required
- **Integrative**: We are all marketers now

The approach is simple. With the structure, we start small, and get bigger and better. With budget, we do exactly the same. We start small, and invest based on success (conversion). The calendar is organic without end points. Digital Marketing is a new job, so we need new skills and, eventually, new people. Also, it is integrative, meaning we are all marketers now.

As I said at the beginning, when you are working for a big organisation and you have received the approval from HR, if there are any important things to do, people need to act: every employee becomes a marketer.

3i *Principles*

3i principles are the foundation tenets of the Digital Marketing methodology:

- **Initiate**: Start with the customer and work towards your digital strategy
- **Iterate**: Continually learn from engagement and apply new knowledge on an ongoing basis
- **Integrate**: Integrate digital channels coherently, and in terms of traditional marketing activities

Strategy and Planning **Process Approach**

The Magic Wheel, with the pizza, is always the same: Effective Strategy & Planning is an iterative process.

1 APPROACH
- Framework
- Principles
- Structure

2 AUDIENCE
- Situation Analysis
- Information Gathering
- Audience Definition

4 ANALYSIS
- Measurement
- Analysis
- Iteration

3 ACTIVITIES
- Objectives
- Tools
- Action Plan
- Budget

We can see that the number of mobile phones is increasing rapidly and the number of mobile shoppers is also increasing rapidly. Every few quarters, there are more and more dollars spent through mobile devices. This means that people are purchasing from mobile devices more often.

Know Your Audience!

*"Start with the customer and work
backwards."*

Now, how do we gather information? We have to start with our customer and work backwards. What does that mean?

First, you understand what your market wants, then you give people what they want, and then you achieve your goals. How do you know what your market wants? There are several tools, and also websites, that give you that information. The first is your own Social Media. Second is the Social Media of your competitors. If you don't know who your competitors are, use socialbakers.com to identify them in any country. It shows you the big players in any industry. From that, you get a good idea of who the top players are.

Then, you see who gathered the most likes, you put them in Likealyzer.com, and you see which one is creating a good engagement rate. When you see that somebody is creating a good engagement rate, you understand who the winner is, and eventually you copy some of those tactics. Do not copy the posts, copy the tactics.

Market reality

Market reality is a better indicator of customers' needs than market research.

This is a very important chart. It shows you the difference between the traditional approach and the digital approach. In the traditional approach, you normally get a little bit of insight, you plan a big strategy, and then you create a focus group where you test with customers. Then you adjust, launch a big campaign, a big website, big adverting around the city, measure the results and then, again establish a new strategy with a new focus group.

This is how it has been done for decades. Companies have been doing this approach for a long time. But unconventional marketing and digital marketing starts with insights and then it starts with a little strategy. Then plan, design, launch and measure (the iterative cycle) your little strategy. Then you get more insights, you get your little strategy, adjust and again plan, design, launch, and measure another one. Then, again insight, little strategy, adjust, and things continue.

But the beauty of it is that even these little campaigns are ones that you can leave up and running. You do not need to think of digital as one big campaign; in fact, it is better to have a lot of small ones that can keep spinning.

I am talking about different products, different services, and different divisions of your business. You may have a wheel spinning for the training division, and another wheel spinning for the conference division, the new event launch, or whatever. They keep working independently, and you can easily and independently measure different products, different lines of business, and different services. Now, if something happens, you tweak only one of these. It is not part of a big master plan that nobody understands where you are going and you cannot even measure it.

It is so easy to have different wheels spinning! If some of them spin well, you put more budget into those. You make those ones bigger, though always within limitations.

Situation Analysis

Understand where you are now...

How do you measure up? Take this opportunity to assess your competitive position with respect to digital marketing in terms of your industry sector, peers, competitors, and customers.

Capabilities: Assess your internal capabilities, skills and knowledge with respect to digital marketing.

Activities: Assess the scope, depth, and effectiveness of your current digital marketing activities across the range of digital channels. It is important to have an honest and realistic baseline of your current activities in order to define a meaningful Digital Marketing Plan for the future.

What do you have to do?

- Audit your current online presence: website analytics, search engine visibility, inbound links
- Ask your customers how they use the internet
- Audit your competitors' online presence
- What does your market need? What is your market searching for online?
- Where are your customers online? Which sites/platforms are they using?

- Examine your industry sector in other markets. Examine related industries online

How do you **Measure Up**?

Measure your current digital activities in terms of your customer, sector, competitor and company.

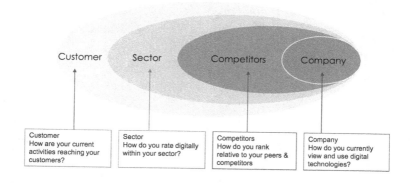

Customer	Sector	Competitors	Company
How are your current activities reaching your customers?	How do you rate digitally within your sector?	How do you rank relative to your peers & competitors	How do you currently view and use digital technologies?

How do we analyse? There are so many websites and so many ideas. We analyse based on ideas from our customer first, then we compare within our sector, then we compare among our competitors, and then we compare even within different divisions of our company.

For example, if we see one division of the company is going extremely well, let us try to find out why. Then, eventually, we can get the same result in other divisions and sections. Let us say you are in insurance: maybe the life insurance is going great, but the company insurance is not going well. Try to find out the difference between the two to get synergy.

Situation analysis: **Capabilities**

Where are you now? Rate your current capabilities from 1 to 5:

	Basic knowledge	Limited Experience	Practical Skills	Advanced Application	Expert Practitioner
Website					
SEO					
SEM					
Email					
Display					
Social Media					
Mobile					
Analytics					

This is the same scheme that you have seen at the beginning of this chapter. You need to be sure about what you place at the beginning. You need to make a clear decision. Right now, you have your marketing mix, and you write where you are going to put the big improvement.

Come back to the page once you have filled in the scheme and mark, by priority, where you are going to work on these topics. Sometimes, it depends on where you need improvements, and, sometimes, on where you see big potential. Come back to the first scheme and give a priority to whichever topic you want to work on from tomorrow. What it is going to be is your decision.

Describe your current activities under each of these headings, and rate your current activities on a scale of 1 to 5:

	Describe your current activities	Pre-Course Rating	Post Course Rating
Website			
SEO			
SEM			
Email			
Display			
Social Media			
Mobile			
Analytics			

We have already mentioned some of the activities you guys are doing. Possibly, in this more precise scheme, you can write the activities that you are actually doing right now, what was your knowledge before, and what your extra knowledge is now.

Hopefully, we have filled a big gap!

Information Gathering

There is a range of tools that can help you track mentions of your business and analyse your current situation. These include:

Social Tools:

- Socialmention.com
- Addictomatic.com
- Howsociable.com
- Twitalyzer.com
- Klout.com
- Likealyzer.com
- Socialbakers.com
- Local discussion forums

and Search Tools:

- Google Analytics
- Google Keyword Research Tool
- Google Media Planner
- Bing Ad Planner
- Google Alerts

Now, you have got all these possible tools you can use to gather information before launching your massive campaign.

Google Keyword Planner tool? Always use this. Never forget that, even if you are not doing a paper clip campaign, it still gives you an idea about the size of the market. If you are launching a new event—say we are launching a big event on dogs—is it going to be successful or not? I don't know. Let us check how many people search for stuff related to dogs. Then we will know how big the audience is in this country. Then we launch it, and we are more likely to allocate the right budget— less if we know that there are not so many people interested in dogs, and more if we know that a lot of people are interested in dogs. This is a big thing.

Who's Your Audience?

To get to know your audience better, you can do what is called the Online Persona. Sit down with your team, and brainstorm about who your typical customers are, and try to think like them. Who are your typical clients? Your perfect, ideal clients? Again, it is a human being. Even if you are a business to business (B2B) company, your client is still a human being. It is the purchasing manager of a company buying a product from you.

So, you plan and picture this person. Who is this person? What is their job? What is their family like? How many kids? What do they do for a living? How do they enjoy their spare time?

How old is the person? Which movies do they watch? What do they eat and drink? How do they dress? Which websites and Social Media do they use? Which devices do they use to connect online?

Once you do this, and you write it down exactly from A to Z, you are going to do every single action as though this Online Persona is in front of you. I am going to send an SMS. What is better to say? Is it better if I say, "Hello, it's a nice day," or "Dear customer, today is a beautiful, shiny day."

You have to think, "My customer is in front of me, what would they like the most?"

Then you know clearly, and not copy-paste a random campaign done by a random company. You know who your Online Persona is, where you want to reach, and you get there exactly.

Define your **Audience**

Clearly define the people who you will target through digital marketing. A clear understanding of your target audience(s) will impact all aspects of your Digital Marketing Strategy from marketing channels used, channel, message, layout and structure, content, down to the words and language you use to describe what you do.

It is crucial that you provide a detailed description of each of your target audiences. Build audience profiles or personas to better understand your customer in terms of:

- Age
- Gender
- Demographics

- Location
- Preferences
- Needs
- Understand their expectations and goals

"John lives in London. He is single. 25 years of age. Rents an Apartment. John enjoys sports and socialising, earns £35,000. He uses a smart phone, has broadband, and is an avid gamer."

In standard old-school marketing, we define the audience by age, gender, demographics, location, preferences, needs, etc. For example: the typical audience. This is one of the kinds of audience definitions. Now, when you know this, boom! You go after John, and all the people like John.

Audience **Ranking**

Having defined your target audiences, the next step is to rank them.

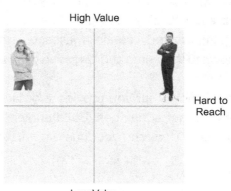

Samantha Social
B2C, 24-35 year old clinical assistant, single. Smartphone user on Facebook with disposable income. May be a high value prospect and readily accessible through digital channels

Brian Business
B2B, 40-55 year old purchasing manager, married with 2 kids. Limited digital skills, but is on LinkedIn. May be a high value prospect but reachable only through limited digital and traditional marketing channels.

High Value

Hard to Reach

Low Value

When you have more than one audience, you rank them based on value and how difficult it is to reach them. So, in this case, we have Samantha, a typical young, social, single clinical assistant with disposable income. She may be a high-value prospect, and readily accessible through digital channels.

Brian, a middle-aged B2B professional with limited digital skills may be a high-value prospect but reachable only through limited digital and traditional marketing channels.

Normally, managers and senior managers are rarely on Facebook, and if they are, they are not going to purchase your product or say, "Ah, now that I have been working all day, let me look again for more work-related things on Facebook." They don't. So, you use different channels.

The 3 important **Questions**

An action plan provides a coherent project structure including milestones, deliverables and resources.

WHY
Understand why your target audience uses digital channels:
- Product research
- Product comparison
- Product purchase
- Product support
- Feedback
- Community

Actions

HOW
Understand how your target audience likes to be communicated with. What tone works in what channel?

Timeframe

Resources

WHAT
Understand what kinds of digital channels they use:
- Search
- Social Media
- Mobile
- Email
- Digital Display

To understand your audience better, we answer on their behalf these three questions: why, how and what.

Why?

Understand why your target audience uses digital channels:

- Product research
- Product comparison
- Product purchase
- Product support
- Feedback
- Community

How?

Understand how your target audience likes to be communicated with. What tone works in what channel?

What?

Understand what kinds of digital channels they use:

- Search
- Social Media
- Mobile
- Email
- Digital Display

5Ps: customer search **Insights Model**

In any web search, the user reveals valuable information about themselves. Search Term: "Adventure Holiday in March Belize"

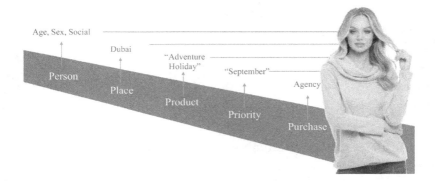

Always remember the search model—the 5Ps for search—because this is another way to classify and define our audience. These are the 5Ps: Person, Place, Product, Priority, and Purchase. Based on that, we define the audience, and accordingly define the keywords, your strategy, payment strategy, etc.

Always remember the iterating session. Nothing works amazingly the first time. You always need to iterate.

Digital Marketing Objectives

Where do you want to be?
Recognise how setting objectives within your digital marketing plan provides:

- Structure
- Stated targets
- Accountability for ROI
- Basis for measurement and analysis

Ask yourself, "Where do I want to be?" The moment that you have to plan your goals, which is before even starting, you are going to plan what your structure is going to be, the targets, accountability for ROI. Whatever you are doing, make sure you can measure it so that you can analyse, give recommendations, and increase the salary of the relevant people when you are successful.

Set clear **Objectives**
Understanding what to measure

Just because it can be measured does not also mean it is useful.

Always remember what I told you about goals. There are Digital Goals, which should help the organisation, but they come from Marketing Goals. And, the bottom line is, you need to bring cash. If you do not bring cash, you just make somebody a little bit happy in your organisation, but you are never going to go far.

What do you want to achieve with digital marketing?

- **Business**: lead generation, sales, cost reductions, profit
- **Audience**: satisfaction, referrals, feedback, repeat business
- **Product**: product research, design, enhancements
- **Brand**: communicating brand personality, reputation management
- **Marketing**: branding, awareness, engagement, response, conversions

Objectives can be around business, audience, product, brand, or marketing. We have already seen that many times. Still, it is important that you take this page, and you highlight your objectives. I recommend you do it now. Take a highlighter or a pen, and simply mark some of these things that you see on this page, because when you know where you want to go, you can plan properly accordingly.

I suggest you highlight or circle those about which you think, "These are mine. These are what I have to do, because my company measures me based on that, because my goals are based on that, and because I believe that if I focus on this, I am going to be successful and my company is going to be successful." So, circle those that really make sense to you.

Set your **SMART** objectives

- Specific (usually a number)
- Measurable (systems are in place to track results)
- Actionable (the required actions are within your power)
- Realistic (reasonable to achieve)
- Timed (calendar bound)

Example: There are 20,000 searches in the UAE/KSA per month, which are closely related to the services we provide. There is limited competition for most of the search terms. With aggressive search marketing and a very strong sales focused website, we estimate we will generate 35 qualified sales leads or more per month by December 2020.

These are my SMART objectives:

_____

_____

_____

_____

_____

Digital Marketing Tools

*What do you want to achieve with digital
marketing?*

- **SEO** provides for your digital marketing plan: positioning, engagement, conversions, and competitive advantage
- **PPC** provides: targeting, relevance, campaign management, and customization
- **Display Marketing** provides: reach, awareness, branding, and influence
- **Email Marketing** provides: relevance, personalisation, interaction, and traceability
- **Mobile Marketing** provides: immediacy, contextualised, location based, and scenario driven
- **Social Media Marketing** provides: engagement, interaction, advocacy, reach, and branding
- **Analytics** provides: measurement, visibility, capacity to iterate, insights, and empowerment

Which tools do we use? According to what you marked on the previous page, you know that.

Normally, when you need branding or awareness, you generally tend to do Digital Display Advertising, because it is picture, picture, picture, impression, impression, impression in the customer's face. Normally, when you need more conversion, you tend to do a little bit more Pay Per Click and SEO.

So, this is exactly what to look for to find out what you need to do based on what you want to achieve. It is a very important thing. because when you start launching a campaign, you say, "Okay, we have 200,000 dirhams. How do we allocate this? Let us put everything in Facebook because this is the only thing we know how to do!" Or, you know what you want to achieve and, based on this, you allocate a little bit in this channel, a little bit in this one and that.

In my opinion, this is **one of the most important infographics**. And yet, I don't like it. I have my own version of it that only the students in my class can see.

And obviously you, who is reading my book!

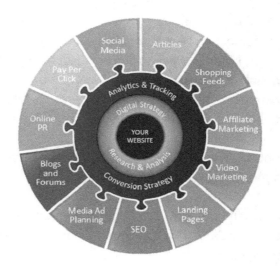

The Farioli Method

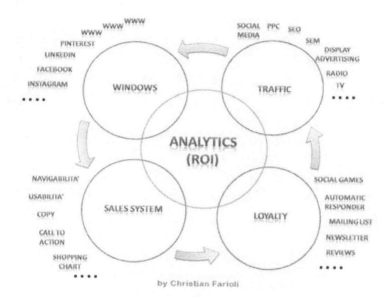

by Christian Farioli

I came up with this concept five or six years ago, or probably even more. And I am still using it today, even with all the additions, and all the new Digital Marketing tactics, tools, ideas, and craziness. This is still what I am using even today with every single client of mine. What I noticed was that every company will place their website at the centre of their digital marketing strategy. To me, that was the biggest mistake ever, because your website changes and evolves. Sometimes you redesign your website and it is down for a while. What is it like? It is like you switch off the electricity of your company. It does not look so nice, with the electricity off. You cannot rely on just websites. It was good in the 2000s—perhaps up to 2005—when there were only websites and nothing else. Now, there is more. Google, Facebook, Instagram, Pinterest . . . Plus, every few months, there are new things. Somebody comes along and says, "The future is Pinterest." A few months later, "The future is Snapchat." A few months later, "No, the future is whatever, whatever, whatever . . ." What do you do? Do you stop your company and change the strategy upside down? No.

That is why, I came out with my own Farioli model to find a way to make sure the strategy works not just for one or two years, but even if major changes occur in the digital world. Regardless, you should be able to continue your strategy. I can tell you this model is going to work even in ten years' time. It is a bold statement.

In my model, I have four main blocks. These are my four rings of a chain. When the rings are linked, the chain works. If one link is missing, the chain does not work.

1. Traffic

The first block is traffic. We have so many ways to get the traffic to a company. It is not important which one we use. It is important that there are traffic sources like Display, Pay Per Click, Social Media, SEO, SMS, Mobile, etc.

You see how many traffic sources you can find. What happens if two or three of these fail? Life goes on. What would happen if Mark Zuckerberg decided to close Facebook to give everything to charity? You survive. Life goes on.

2. Windows

Then what happens after traffic? We drive all this traffic to your windows. What does it mean, windows? It means that you have one window on your website, but it is not the only one. Just as you have a shop in every mall, you have different windows on your digital shop. One of them is your website, but what happens if your website is down? Do you need to close down the company? No. Why not? Because you also get people from other places, something like a Facebook page. Even if your website is down, I see your contact on your Facebook page, and I can call you directly. So, on Facebook, I do not force people to directly come to the website and fill out a boring form. They are not going to do it. From Facebook, I have a Call to Action. I mention "Call us" straight away. Thus, from Facebook, you get your traffic.

Is there only Facebook? Obviously not. There are many other places, like Twitter, YouTube, and Instagram. Instagram people, as you know, love pictures.

You can have an Instagram account even for your insurance. You can have nice pictures on it. Now don't expect that somebody who loves to scroll pictures is going to like to click and come to your website and fill out a long and boring form. They are not going to do it. Again, in the picture, write, "Call us. We'll solve your problem, blah, blah, blah." This is how you get the person to look at a different window in your shop and interact with you.

Websites are not the be all and end all. But actually, I can give you more. Eventually, you will have a second or third website. Who says that you need to have only one website? Every manager will tell you, "Yeah, but this is confusing . . . no, no, no, we only need one." How many shops do you have? 25, one across each city. So why do you only need one website?

I will give you an example. There is a company renting short-term apartments. They have seven websites. The apartments are exactly the same, taken from the same database, and appear on seven different websites. Why is that? One website is focused on British people. The website is .co.uk. The messages are for the British. The pictures are happy British families. When British families go to that website, they love it. They book an apartment.

Another one is for businesspeople. It shows a dark, slick businessperson in a suite, with a trolley. The message is, "All of our apartments are well-communicated, well-connected, have very fast internet access, and international TV channels in every room." The one for family says, "All of our apartments are in front of the beaches. There are shopping malls. We give you a voucher to go to the aqua park, and we have cartoon networks channels on the TV." The apartments are the same, but you see how different clients will love it.

Another one is in Arabic language, for Arabs. Imagine somebody from Saudi, when they go on holiday in Dubai and rent an apartment. The wife is checking where the apartment is, and she sees a picture of a Russian lady in a bikini sitting next to the beach. The wife may say, "Forget it, we will stay in Saudi this year. We won't go on holiday." And the opposite: Imagine a Russian lady, from a Russian family, who wants to go to the beach. They want to go to Dubai and check the website, and there are only Arabic guys in kandura and Arabic ladies in abaya. That Russian lady may chose the apartment from another website.

This is why you need different websites. Even if you have only one product, you may have more websites. If you have more than one product, it makes even more sense to have more than one website. It is not good to have everything under one roof. People believe, "Ah, because you are on my website, you will see that I have a lot of products for you and buy them all." Wrong. This is like going to a supermarket where you find bananas, fish, meat, biscuits, mobile phones, computers, etc. But if I really want to get good meat, I go to the butcher. If I want to get a good computer, I go to a computer shop. So, you split your line of business into different websites.

3. Sales system

What does this mean? From the moment that you enter into any one of these windows we saw before, you go through steps, you go through places, you enter IKEA, you go to a supermarket, you go through the corridors. This is the sale system. You need to plan in advance where people will go when they enter through any of your windows until they finally purchase the product.

What do I include in the sale system? The sale system includes web navigability, web usability, text, something so simple like the Call to Action. The CTA makes the difference between an average website and a top class website. Each product and service should have a perfectly crafted Call to Action. Then there is copywriting: you may pay some crazy copywriter to write crazy stuff that convinces you do things as soon as you read them.

All of these are part of the sale system, including the shopping cart (for e-commerce websites). If you get a complicated shopping cart, you convert less. Then, there are the payment processors, like PayPal, worldwide accepted, easy to understand, easy to pay, works reliably.

So, what happens if you do something wrong? Our visitors, who we spent a lot of money getting in, go through our windows, eventually leave and are lost. Time and money wasted. But if we do things right, what happens? Cash! Now, this is good. Then, after we convert a visitor into a client, what do we do? We can say, "Okay, now that you bought from us, go far away. I don't care about you anymore." Or what is smarter, we keep them, and we send them to the next step: the loyalty block.

4. Loyalty

The loyalty block acts as a way to get our customer, and send them back as another source of traffic. Thus, the circle continues.

It took us time, effort, money, strategy, and planning to convince somebody to come from the initial source, follow the entire way around, and finally to get converted. The best thing we can do is to keep that person, make them happy, and make them come back. We should not think that because they came to our supermarket once, "Ah, now they know us!" No. Every day, somebody is going to try to convince that person to buy the product somewhere else. "I'll give you better products than this guy. I'll give you discounts. I'll even give you free products." Everyone is trying to steal this customer from you. Do not think that because they bought once that your job is finished. You have to get them to come back. How?

Another channel for loyalty is email. I don't like it much because you are limited by the permission from the customer to send them emails. And, normally, if the customer does not know you, they will not give you permission.

Often, companies get the permission in a sneaky way, and on the backside is mentioned, "We are going to be spamming you every day." But, when somebody bought from you, they are happy, and then you can send them email in the form of news-letters, etc. because they know you. They bought from you, and you can speak in a different tone. You can say, "Hey, cus-tomers! New line of products! Now, what about these newslet-ter promotions? Would you like to know more about it?" You enter a different level.

Also, in the loyalty, you can use any Social Games. Here you can ask your customer, "Hey! Do you want to play a social game and possibly win these prizes? Simple Like our page. Simply click on this Facebook item. Simply comment on your Facebook, or do this or do that." Okay, if I know you, eventu-ally, I will play your stupid game. It takes me only 5-6 seconds. But if I don't know you and you send me a message, "Hey, why don't you play this amazing game and send us a picture and post and click and like and do this and do that so you can win an iPad?" Who cares about your iPad? But here is the moment you have been waiting for. When you do Social Games, magically, you get more people. They become loyal and they become a traffic source.

With loyalty, you can try to get advocates. More advocates bring you more customers. When they post on Facebook, when they are happy because you gave them two insurance deals for the price of one, they think, "That's cool stuff. Hey, pal, did you know that he gave me two insurance deals for the price of one? How cool!" To you, it costs twice as much. You get nothing. But if you make sure that if they get this reward, they will post it on Facebook, then their 3,000 other friends get the advertising, not only one or two friends. Thus, you expose yourself much more.

On top of that, I also put in the loyalty block something that nowadays is increasing in importance. That is reviews. Reviews are a huge factor. The first companies that started caring about reviews were hospitality, such as restaurants, and then hotels based on TripAdvisor. Customers make decisions based on TripAdvisor. Now, if you are not in hospitality, there are many other reviews. If you are in the healthcare industry, there are websites that review hospitals. That is important.

I even know day-care centres that get reviews of their teachers. This is a big thing. It is not easy, but people are going to review you, whether you want it or not, whether if you like it or not! If you do not allow me to comment on your website if I am unhappy, I will write it everywhere else and you will not be able touch it.

But when you get good reviews, you need to have a system in place to collect more reviews. Do not expect that people are going to leave reviews. Imagine how many people attend an exhibition: 10,000 or maybe more. How many of those have written reviews? Not even a single person. Why? Because we do not ask in the right way. Not a single person of the 10,000 people will ask when they leave, "May I write about you on Facebook?" Nobody is going to do that!

But when you send the follow up email saying nice things, and you know that the person was already happy because they already rated you 5/5, you have happy customer. Once you are sure they were very happy, you can ask them, "Do you mind leaving a review? Do you mind saying the same in a review?" Bingo! Then you get pam, pam-pam, pam-pam, five-stars, five-stars, five-stars!

So, when your customer is ultra-happy, you ask, "By the way, do you mind just saying the same in a simple review?" People are afraid to write a review. "I'm not a journalist. I'm not English native. If I make spelling mistakes, people are going to laugh at me. I'm going to look stupid." You can answer, "No, you need to say just simply say one line: I was happy. Or whatever you just said, say the same in the review."

And you mark in your notes: follow up with this customer in two or three days. Don't expect people to leave a review just because you asked. "Yeah, I'll leave the review! Okay! Okay!"

Two days later, nothing happens. Normal. Obvious. At the same time, send the link that they can click and write the review. Follow up after two or three days. "Hey, Mr. X. How are you? I called you because we finally sent you the invitation for our next event as promised. By the way, I have not received your review." Now, he feels so bad that he is going to write it, no matter what.

I never said that it is easy to get a review. But if you don't ask, you will never get it. If you don't ask properly, you will never get it. And one day, somebody is going to write a bad review about you. You cannot avoid a bad review, but if you get 150 good reviews and one bad, who cares? In Italy, we say even Jesus was doing good, and God crucified him. No matter how many good things you do, sometimes somebody will complain.

"Each good review will sell for you day and night."
(Christian Farioli)

Good reviews are bingo-bingo-bingo! You get trust, new customers, more traffic. You get everything.

5. Analytics (ROI)

One more thing, the chain is good, but we can make it even stronger. How? By placing another ring—strong, big, the most important of all them—that keeps all other rings together. What is this? It's not a pizza but Analytics.

Why Analytics? Because whatever we are doing in this world, this is the one that tells us what to do and why to do it. And it will tell it to us, our boss, our director, our shareholders, our board of directors. Because, if your ultimate goal is to become the CDO—Chief Digital Officer—this is your world. This is how you talk, based only on the numbers.

With this, we can see how many visitors we get out of each platform or tool, from Facebook, from SEO, from Social Media, from Pinterest, from whatever craziness in 10 years somebody will invent. We will know how many people will come in, and we will know how much we are spending for each one of these. But, in particular, we will know how many of these people are converted.

Conclusions

Now you know that, whatever you want to do, that is the way. And, with this scheme, I can tell you this:

> *If you are promoting any business in human history, the Farioli Method works in the same way.*
> *(Christian Farioli)*

I am using this for a non-profit company, for hospitality, for concerts, for events, for B2B, for B2C, for the most boring company to the cleverest company, to the most advanced to the most old-school. Everything works in the same way. Now, maybe from experience, you know that to promote some businesses, some traffic tools will work better than the others. But, even if you know everything: there is always a way to improve.

I HAVE A GIFT FOR YOU
GET YOUR E-BOOK FROM MY WEBSITE!

Matching Tools and Objectives

Choose the most relevant digital tools for your plan, based on the target audience and the objectives set.

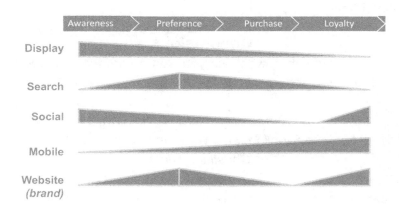

The digital consumer's experience should be different depending on your digital objectives!

This is my opinion on another extremely important scheme. It gives me, in one shot, the area where and when I should invest my budget. You can see the 5 main channels: Display, Search, Social, Mobile, and Website, and how much money you are investing, based on the marketing phase.

I have already told that, at the beginning, we are in the aware-ness phase, and you need to make sure that the people know your product. Once they know you, they can choose between you and your competitor. Then it is the purchase time, and finally, the loyalty time. Based on the phase, we know how much budget we should invest.

In website, at the beginning, we are just developing the web-site. When the website is under development, our social media is already powerful, up and running. We don't need to wait until the website is ready. We do Social Media first. In the meantime, the website is going to be ready. When the website is ready, good. Then you spend nothing because the website is already there. Our costs decrease. But if you have low loyalty, you need to play again with the website to make your increasing custom-ers who come back to your website happy. This is when you invest in your website.

Channel Suitability *B2C and B2B*

Select the channels on the Digital Marketing Framework in terms of how effective they will be for engaging with your tar-get audience.

Samantha Social

B2C, 24-35 year old clinical assistant, single. Smartphone user on Facebook with disposable income. May be a high value prospect and readily accessible through digital channels.

B2C normally works better with email, Social, and mobile. I say normally because every product is different. For B2B, normally, it is SEO, PPC, and, again, Social Media.

Brian Business

B2B, 40-55 year old purchasing manager, married with 2 kids. Limited digital skills, but is on LinkedIn. May be a high value prospect but reachable only through limited digital and traditional marketing channels.

Achieving your objectives

Some points to consider:

- Targeting: audience and segmentation
- Online conversion strategy: what are you selling, what tasks do you want your target audience to perform?
- Product and market position to be adopted?
- Brand identity to be conveyed online: value, price, quality, etc.
- The Digital Mix to be used?
- Your website strategy: single or multi-site, scale of site required?
- Your customer retention strategy: e-CRM, etc.
- Your plan for integrating online with offline marketing?

Which are the points to consider? Mainly the targeting and, even more importantly, the online conversion strategy. What you are going to measure as a conversion?

Integrate! **The Magic Pyramid**

There is a quality scale in the level of audience interaction with your organisation.

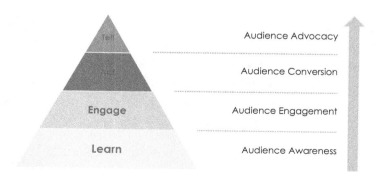

Remember this is the magic pyramid of the level of engagement. We start with awareness, then we go for engagement,
purchasing, and we try to get existing clients to become advocates. Imagine what will happen with your customer that you
call for a survey and make him ultra-happy. This is how you
build advocates. And what are advocates going to do? They
fight for you and get you more clients by sending you their
friends.

Which tool and objectives?
So many choices, so little time!

There are tasks you do in-house, tasks you hire people to do,
and tasks you outsource. At the last event I participated in, I
heard the founder of the Suq Al Bahar, the luxury market in
Dubai, talk about the big difference for her between traditional
advertising (Sheik Zayed Road style) and the digital advertising. She gave her personal experience because she has done
both. She said the best thing about traditional is that it is so
easy. You give the money to the agency and it is done. They
design the banner and have the banner running, finished. Your
job is done.

The difficult part is with the digital, because you have to plan
the campaign, the channel, the audience, plan the targeting, each step is crazy! But you cut the cost heavily, and you
increase the exposure heavily, but most importantly, you can
measure it. She tried both and said, "For me, the possibility to
measure what is going on is priceless."

You cannot survive with one campaign. You need to launch more. But every time you launch a campaign, you need to learn from the previous one. What can you learn from the campaign on Sheik Zayed Road? Or from a campaign on TV? Nothing. Yeah, your two or three friends will tell you that it was cool or bad, and that is all. Finished. What do you learn from it? Next year, you just give it a double budget and be done with it!

Budget

It's all about the money...

A digital marketing plan has budgetary constraints. A budget is typically a minimum budget to start; an open ended, upfront commitment, often small and agreed in response to campaign success.

Distinguish between various types of costs:

- Media Spend (ads)
- Digital Media (websites, content, creative)
- People Costs (internal or external)
- Systems (hosting, third-party systems, analytics)

Ad Budget Estimation:
Each of the advertising channels typically has budget estimation tools. These allow you to estimate your budget based on the mechanism for payment:

- Pay Per Click (Google Adwords, Facebook Advertising, some Banner Advertising)
- CPM (Digital Display, LinkedIn)
- Cost Per Engagement (Twitter Advertising)

In budgeting, we distinguish between these four. With each one of the traffic channels like SEO, PPC, Social Media, and whatever, you pay for four things: Media, Advertising, Content, and Social Media. Social Media is free, though, right? No, you have to pay people to do Social Media for you. These are three salaries: the graphic designer, the copywriter, and the Social Media Manager. So, you have to pay People and Systems, like a software, etc. Therefore, when you plan your costs, plan it properly because, for each strategy, you are going to get costs for four different things.

Action Plan

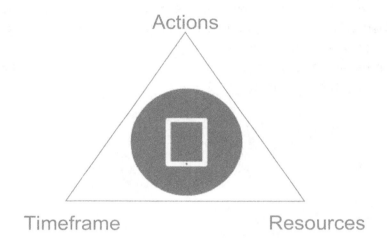

An action plan is always based on Actions, Resources, and Timeframe.

For SEO (Search Engine Optimisation), you pay for content and people, or outsourcing. For SEM, it is media, people, and the systems. For Email marketing, you pay content, people, and systems, etc. Let us explore this in detail.

Search **Optimisation**
Digital Marketing planning scheme for Search Engine Optimisation

Objectives:
Penetration, interaction, advocacy, conversion

Action Items and Frequency:

- Data collection and cleansing (ongoing)
- Segmentation (ongoing and per campaign)
- Newsletter creation (dependent on publication schedule)
- Tracking and monitoring (ongoing)

Measurement Tools and KPIs:

- Email Marketing System and Analytics (delivery rate, open rate, Click Through Rate, goals and conversions)

Spend:

Media	Content	People	Systems
	X	X	

Search *Marketing*
Digital Marketing planning scheme for Search Engine Marketing

Objectives:
Positioning, engagement, conversions, and competitive advantage

Action Items and Frequency:

- Keyword research (Quarterly)
- Targeting (Monthly)
- Scheduling (Weekly)
- Bidding and budgeting (Weekly/Monthly)
- Tracking and reporting (Daily/Weekly)

Measurement Tools and KPIs:

- Adwords and Analytics (Click Through Rate, conversion rate, cost-per-click)

Spend:

Media	Content	People	Systems
X		X	X

Email *Marketing*
Digital Marketing planning scheme for Email Marketing

Objectives:
Penetration, interaction, advocacy, conversion

Action Items and Frequency:

- Data collection and cleansing (ongoing)
- Segmentation (ongoing and per campaign)

- Newsletter creation (dependent on publication schedule)
- Tracking and monitoring (ongoing)

Measurement Tools and KPIs:

- Email Marketing System and Analytics (delivery rate, open rate, Click Through Rate, goals and conversions)

Spend:

Media	Content	People	Systems
	X	X	X

Social Media *Marketing*
Digital Marketing planning scheme for Social Media Marketing

Objectives:
Reach, interaction, advocacy, conversion

Action Items and Frequency:

- Posting (text, photos, videos, links, offers)
- Engaging (comments, questions, polls, surveys)
- Promoting (ads, apps, jobs, competitions, promotions, events)
- Community Building (conversation, comments, suggestion)

Measurement Tools and KPIs:

- Social Media Insights and Analytics (connections, likes, comments, Click Through Rate, goals, and conversions)

Spend:

Media	Content	People	Systems
X	X	X	X

Mobile *Marketing*
Digital Marketing planning scheme for Mobile Marketing

Objectives:
Reach, interaction, advocacy, conversion

Action Items and Frequency:

- Mobile Optimised Website (ongoing)
- Apps (ongoing)
- SMS Marketing (per campaign)
- Mobile Advertising (per campaign
- Proximity Marketing (per campaign)

Measurement Tools and KPIs:

- Advertising Networks and Analytics: Per campaign type analytics, for example, mobile display (no. of impressions, no. of clicks, Click Through Rate, conversions)

Spend:

Media	Content	People	Systems
X	X	X	X

Calendar

Know when to do what before it is too late...

A Digital Marketing calendar contains:

- order of the actions
- dependencies
- tart dates and end dates

ACTION PLAN: CALENDAR

Know when to do what before it's too late...

A Digital Marketing calendar contains:
* order of the actions
* dependencies
* start dates and end dates

What does a digital calendar looks like? You create an Excel file, and you put your action plan in day-by-day. This is the best way because then you can move things. But, as I always explain to my students, a digital calendar is always dynamic. It is always without an end, so you are ready to move things around.

Planning

Things to consider...

1. *Focus on building a plan around the customer, not around your products and tactics*
2. *Situations and plans change, especially online, so ensure plans are usable by having a clear vision for the year and keeping real detail to a shorter term 90-Day focus*
3. *Make your marketing plans fact-based and state any assumptions, so they are easy for others to buy into*
4. *Keeping the jargon light is best. It helps others to get on board with what you are saying*
5. *Keep plans up-to-date: monthly is more than enough*
6. *There is no such thing as a perfect planning template, the "need" changes according to each business!*

Focus on building a plan around the customer, not around your product and tactics. Your customers' needs are more important than your product. Normally, things change, so when you have a good action plan and you have a 90-day focus, you are okay because, in 90 days, you will adjust. You cannot plan from now for six months ahead.

So many things can change. You plan, write it down, and keep everything fact-based. There is no such a thing as the perfect planning template. This is something every organisation learns with time and with results.

Integrate!

The difference between paid, owned, and earned media.

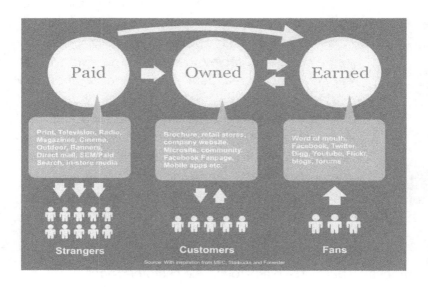

This is another interesting concept. Outdoor or traditionally is only Paid Media. However, the Owned Media, for example, is within your store, where you can advertise yourself. Within your digital page, you advertise yourself. Earned Media is when other people are talking about you, and they are spreading their voices on Facebook, Twitter, YouTube, etc. Then, you earn media space from others.

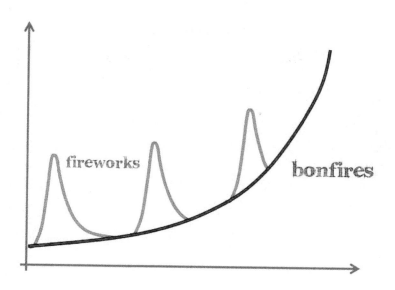

Short- *and* **Long**-*term activity*

What do I need? Short-term or long-term activity? You need both, and you have to combine them. Combining short-term and long-term activity is another crazy clever concept.

In Digital and in marketing, it helps to have both strategies. One is called fireworks and one is called bonfire. So, what happens? If you have 300 dirhams, you may decide to put 300 dirhams, every day 1 dirham. Little by little, 1 dirham a day. Nobody even notices that you exist. Or, one day, you may decide, "Let us put our 300 dirhams in one day!" Then you make an impact. People go, "You see what happened? You see what that company launched?" Rather than little bit, little bit, little bit, and nobody knows.

This is why there are both fireworks and bonfire tactics playing at the same time, the fireworks go off. Boom! Boom! Boom! And the bonfire is constant. If you do both, people will notice you and remember you. You launch two different tactics.

The fireworks are your big events, and the bonfires are your daily activities. Even in Social Media, you post daily, you advertise a little bit daily, and then, from time to time, you do a big shot of advertising, then you come back and boost again . . . boom!

So, the rhythm is this. Little bit, little bit, little bit, little bit . . . boom! Little bit, little bit, little bit, little bit . . . boom!

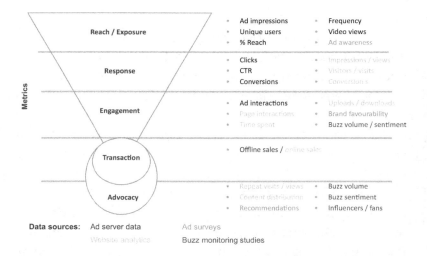

Measurement

You need to know what to measure according to what you want to get.

Reach/Exposure:

- Ad impressions
- Unique users
- % Reach
- Frequency video views
- Ad awareness

Response:

- Clicks
- CTR
- Conversions
- Impressions/views
- Visitors/visits
- Conversions

Engagement:

- Ad interactions
- Page interactions
- Time spent
- Uploads/downloads
- Brand favourability
- Buzz volume/sentiment

Transaction:

- Offline sales/Online sales

Advocacy:

- Repeat visit/views
- Content distribution
- Recommendations
- Buzz volume
- Buzz sentiment
- Influencers/fans

For example, engagement on a website means how much time people spend on your website. If you spend 26 minutes, that is a crazy engagement. Even if you don't write or comment, if simply you spend time on a page, you interact with a page.

For transactions, you measure online/offline sales, but how do you measure advocacy? How do you measure whether your customer loves you enough to promote and fight for you? You measure it with repeat visits/views and content distribution. When your customers and followers share content, recommendations, or reviews, this creates the buzz volume, which is what tells you the brand sentiments. It tells you if people are talking positively or negatively about you; good, then you have advocates. These are ways to measure what you want to get. You want to get advocates? Good. Start measuring it, so you know how many advocates you are getting. Are you growing or decreasing? If you are decreasing, you need to do something to increase it.

But you can measure it.

Integration, Storytelling, and Interaction

When you do advertising, you need integration between the different channels. When you do only one thing, that is okay. You can do only Pay Per Click, or you can have only one website; people may subscribe to the newsletter, that is all. That is okay.

But, if you plan a multichannel campaign, it makes an impact. You have banners advertising, and someone on Facebook, you can feel the same things going on across your platforms. You post and people comment about the same things. You use your YouTube channel to show the same things; all of the platforms are going to be the same. Or, for example, you put a QR code on your flyer that makes the people go online.

In terms of storytelling, I will mention a brand that I like called NKD Pizza. You know I like pizza, right? But, in this case, it is a brand that I like, not the pizza itself. Don't tell anyone that NKD Pizza make awesome pizzas that Christian likes. It is not true. I just love the brand.

I like the NKD Pizza brand because it is very smart and friendly. It makes you willing to interact with them because of the entire brand. They use storytelling a lot. People don't care about the promotion, they care about storytelling. They want to know the story. This is what the fashions artists have been doing all their lives. Look at the famous Italian and French brands like Armani, Dolce Gabbana, or Versace. They all have an amazing story, narrated with emotional, touching storytelling; stories about how the owner built the first Ferrari for competition and Mr. Lamborghini, and Mr. Maserati, and Mr. Bugatti, Storytelling increases your brand. It gets you more followers and advocates.

Now, I will tell you a story of a very clever interactive on-offline interactive app, made by McDonald's in Stockholm. You see: I also do storytelling! Here is the video I suggest you watch because it is really great:

https://www.youtube.com/watch?v=IGZ9r0GiIrk

Have you seen the video? No? Go now, otherwise you will not understand what I am going to explain here.

So, why do you think it was extremely clever? First, mobile phone: another concept of #SoMoLo (Social Mobile Local). You do not need to install an app when the mobile website is enough to click and move the things. It works, no trouble. Plus, there is something else. McDonald's already has big billboards in the streets. But when you go to a main street in a main city, you are not like, "Oh! Look at the beautiful shiny McDonald's billboard!" No, you look at the great square, like, in this case, in Stockholm, and you see that there is a McDonald's there. But this idea makes you look at the screen.

First of all, you play. You look at the screen for 30-40-50 seconds. Second, when somebody stares up and starts playing with it, other people do the same thing. They look in the same direction. They watch you playing. So, other customers look at the billboard. If you engage people in this way, you spread cheer. Then when you win, the digital billboard shows you where to go and get your gift: an ice-cream at the McDonald's located in the square.

You know what happens? When a lot of people are doing one thing, they follow the leader. When the leader goes somewhere, people will eventually follow. So, this is really genius to the next level. And you could tell me, "Oh, it looks so simple! It is not a million-dollar app!" You are right, it is not even an app. It is a simple mobile website, and you can still do really basic things like pressing up and down.

This is why this is a top genius idea!

Unique Digital Identity

You need to be unique in the digital future

How can you be unique in the digital future? I will give you the biggest tip I possibly can. If you are describing your company as *"The best market leader, number one, top, awesome, amazing, innovative,"* etc., you are just like everyone else! Everyone is saying exactly the same things.

You need to be different. You need to be remarkable.
You need to distinguish yourselves in a big way.

Then people will say, "Hey, but these guys are different."

As people often say, "Yeah, but Apple is different. Not because of the number of megabytes and gigabytes. Apple is different."

Why is it different? Who was the most remarkable person in its history? Our beloved Steve Jobs. He made the difference. He was a brand.

It is the same for the most famous Italian brands, as I mentioned earlier: Ferrari, Dolce & Gabbana, Lamborghini, Versace, Armani.

WHAT'S NEXT?

I have a gift for you: as I am finalizing this book, I am creating new systems, and I would like you to be the first to know the latest digital tools, tactics, and trends.

Scan this QR code

or go to

https://m.me/ChrisFarioli.
And in case you need me and my team to help you grow your company by drafting a strategy or implementing any digital marketing activity or participating in a tender, contact my company at

https://esd.me/.

From startups to Fortune 500, we've got you covered.

CPSIA information can be obtained
at www.ICGtesting.com
Printed in the USA
LVHW080745270120
644891LV00009B/177